RAILROAD
CONSOLIDATION

RAILROAD CONSOLIDATION

ITS ECONOMICS & CONTROLLING PRINCIPLES

BY JULIUS GRODINSKY

BeardBooks
Washington, D.C.

Copyright 1930 by D. Appleton and Company
Reprinted 1999 by Beard Books, Washington, D.C.
ISBN 1-893122-41-7

Printed in the United States of America

PREFACE

A decade has now passed since the passage of the law designed to encourage and promote railroad consolidations. During this period considerable progress has been made. Much has been said and written about the steps taken to realize the projects of some carriers, and even more about their hopes and ambitions. Most of the discussions, furthermore, relate to the regulatory aspects of the problem—the decisions of the Interstate Commerce Commission, the powers of this Commission over holding companies, the scope and context of prospective legislation, etc.

The moves made by the agencies of the federal government have been largely restrictive in character: that is, the government has disapproved most of the important projects created by railroad interests. Despite official political disapproval, these projects remain. What are the business—not the political—forces that underlie their creation? What are the primary factors that lead the railroads as business enterprises to press forward so persistently and urgently with their plans for consolidation?

This is the viewpoint from which this volume approaches the subject. From the strictly business standpoint an attempt is made to appraise the merits of the movement—what present defects in the railroad service it is intended to cure; what tangible results it aims to accomplish; and to what extent these expectations are likely to be realized in practice.

The author is deeply grateful to Dean Emory R. Johnson of the Wharton School of Finance and Commerce for his encouragement and helpfulness extended in the preparation of this work.

J. G.

CONTENTS

		PAGE
Preface		v
Introduction by Emory R. Johnson		xi

CHAPTER
I.	General Economic Factors	1
II.	Interchange	24
III.	Control of Traffic Movements	48
IV.	Long Haul and Short Haul	75
V.	Connections and Competitors	106
VI.	Direct and Indirect Routes	133
VII.	Closed and Open Routes	160
VIII.	Channels of Trade and Commerce	191
IX.	Traffic and Trackage Agreements	228
X.	Consolidation in Action	267
XI.	Legislative Principles	303
Index		329

MAPS

	PAGE
Five Line Pittsburgh–St. Louis Route	35
New England and New York Gateways	41
Chicago, Rock Island & Pacific–St. Louis Southwestern Routes	141
Routes *via* Buffalo, Rochester & Pittsburgh	149
Chicago–New York Routes: Baltimore & Ohio and New York Central	255
Natchez Route	261
Missouri-Pacific System Routes	283

INTRODUCTION

The relation of the railroad carriers to the public, to the government, and to each other is a subject of perennial interest and vital importance. The dependence of the public upon the railroads and other carriers—upon adequacy, dispatch and economy of service, instead of diminishing, becomes greater with the development and specialization of industry, the growth of population and its increasing concentration in cities, with changes in the processes of production and distribution and in the ways of living. Improvements in transportation services have enabled manufacturers to carry smaller quantities of materials and to accumulate limited stocks of manufactured goods; have made it possible for merchants and other middlemen to use less capital to do a given volume of business, and for home-keepers to secure from the shops and stores day by day whatever may be required to meet family needs. If railroad consolidation will be helpful to the carriers, it should be beneficial to the public.

The relation of the government to the railroads has changed fundamentally with the successful development of public regulation. Formerly government regulation of railroads was mainly concerned with the elimination of abuses; now the chief aim is adequate and efficient transportation at rates that are fair to the public and that will (to quote the Act of 1920) "adequately sustain all the carriers . . . which are indispensable to the communities to which they render the service of transportation." It was to aid in realizing this aim that Congress substituted for the prohibition of railroad consolidations legal provisions permitting such groupings with the approval and under the regulation of the Interstate Commerce Commission.

INTRODUCTION

The general purpose that the government had in mind in authorizing the voluntary consolidation of railroads was to bring about the grouping of the many roads into a limited number of large systems of relatively equal financial strength and stability, all capable of serving the public efficiently at like rates of charge. The language of the Act of 1920 was: "the several systems shall be so arranged that the cost of transportation as between competitive systems and as related to the values of the properties through which the service is rendered shall be the same, so far as practicable, so that these systems can employ uniform rates in the movement of competitive traffic and under efficient management earn substantially the same rate of return upon the value of their respective railway properties."

Without doubt the members of Congress who advocated the consolidation provisions of the Transportation Act of 1920 expected that railroad grouping would enable the railroads to be operated not only more efficiently but also more economically. It was represented, not so much by the carriers as by others, that large economies would result from consolidation. It was undoubtedly the hope of those who brought about the passage of the Act of 1920 that the operating economies resulting from the consolidation of railroads would be sufficient to enable the carriers to reduce their rates substantially. There is evidence that the results that could be obtained by railroad consolidation were overestimated and that hopes were entertained that could not be realized.

The motives or aims of the carriers were not necessarily the same as those entertained by the legislators who brought about the enactment of the consolidation provisions of the Act of 1920. The motives of the railroad officials and of those responsible for the financial management of the roads were mixed and in large part misunderstood.

It is quite clear, first of all, that financial gains could not and cannot be the carriers' primary motive in bringing about railroad consolidations. The law is so framed as to give the government control over the financing of railroad consolidations. Those effected by lease or purchase of the property of one railroad by another railroad company have to be approved by the Commission. The same is true of complete mergers, and in the case of mergers the securities issued may not exceed in par value the value of the properties brought together. The Interstate Commerce Commission has ample authority to regulate the financing of railroad consolidation.

In spite of the power of the Commission to regulate the financing of consolidation, large sums of money have been made by individuals in connection therewith or in carrying out plans looking to possible consolidations. The Van Sweringen brothers, in building up the Nickel Plate system and in allying other railroad companies with that system, are reputed to have made large sums of money. This has been accomplished both by building up the earning power of the properties over which they have acquired control and by associating those properties with each other at a time of rising values. Mr. L. F. Loree had the foresight to purchase large blocks of stock at an opportune time and to sell his holdings at a greatly appreciated value to the Pennsylvania Railroad interests, who made the purchase because of their desire to secure control of the Lehigh Valley and the Wabash systems at such time in the future as the consolidation of the eastern trunk lines may be effective. Many others have shared in the profits made possible by the railroad situation that has obtained during recent years. It should be noted, however, that while there have been many instances of profit in the acquisition of railroads during recent years and that the acquisitions have been made with reference to possible consolidations, similar financial transactions might have, and probably would have, taken place if the consolidation of railroads under the Transportation Act of 1920 were not in prospect.

While it has been claimed that much can be saved in the

operation of railroads as the result of consolidation, it is not incorrect to say that operating economies are not the major reason prompting carriers to seek to bring about railroad consolidations. It is true that in all applications to the Commission for approval of proposed consolidations, such as the applications made by the Nickel Plate, by the Baltimore & Ohio, by the Great Northern–Northern Pacific companies, substantial operating economies are claimed to be possible, and doubtless the claims are not exaggerated. Such economies refer to details rather than to the general problem of railroad operation.

It is extremely doubtful whether large railroad companies can be more economically operated than those of a moderate size. Indeed, it is often claimed that a railroad system with 2,000 to 5,000 miles of line can be more efficiently and consequently more economically operated than can a far-flung system of 20,000 miles of road. This is a debatable subject concerning which there is no unity of opinion, but the weight of evidence is in favor of higher operating efficiency for the smaller-size companies.

Another reason why the enlargement of our already large railroad systems, by carrying out the proposed plan by grouping or consolidation, may not reduce operating costs is that the consolidation of trunk lines and major systems has to be accompanied by the acquisition of the short line roads in the territory served by the systems being brought together into a consolidation. The services rendered by the short lines, and there are hundreds of them, are often inferior to the services performed by the large strong lines. The wages paid are frequently less, and operating expenses are kept to a minimum. When the branch or short line is made a part of a large consolidated system, the higher standard of service on the system as a whole will be maintained on the lines acquired. Often higher wages will be paid. Expenses will be increased.

The foregoing statements indicate that railroad consolida-

INTRODUCTION

tions do not give much promise of material reductions in rates and fares. Consolidations will make possible better and more adequate services, and the stronger companies that will result from consolidation may accelerate the technical development and improvement of railroads. It is because railroad consolidation may give us stronger railroad companies, more adequate and better services, and may assure to all parts of the country like high standards of railroad performance that the public may well be interested in the achievement of railroad consolidation. Dr. Grodinsky correctly states: "Consolidation of railroads is justified as a national policy by the erection of a limited number of properties of approximately equal financial strength and earning power capable of competing as equals in the rendition of a high standard of service at reasonable rates."

The primary motive that the carriers have in seeking to bring about railroad consolidations is set forth very clearly by Dr. Grodinsky in his book. The motive is said to be to obtain control of the routing of traffic, and a wealth of information is presented by the author in support of this thesis. In the first chapter of the book Dr. Grodinsky quotes with approval the statement that "the basic idea underlying the consolidation movement is a traffic problem; not financial; not operating; not one directly and necessarily calculated to preserve the so-called weak roads"; and in the same paragraph the author asserts that "consolidations are made in response to . . . those forces which enable the acquiring roads to capture the business of the acquired road, to force its movement over the line of the acquiring road and away from its competitors."

Dr. Grodinsky's thesis is of great significance. His volume presents railroad consolidation from a new viewpoint. In his argument consolidation becomes an economic, not a political, problem—it becomes a transportation question. Without ignoring the other aims that carriers may seek to achieve by

INTRODUCTION

means of consolidations—economies of administration and operation, fuller coördination of services, and simplification of interline and intersystem rate adjustments, the author brings out in high relief the major motive for the enlargement and rounding out of railroad systems. Railroads exist to move traffic. The channels through which traffic flows may be influenced by the establishment of realignment of carrier routes. Railroad consolidations are worked out for the purpose of creating traffic routes favorable to the carriers concerned.

Dr. Grodinsky has, thus, clearly set forth the chief reason why railroad companies are interested in consolidation. The aim that railroad companies seek to achieve is, moreover, one that under wise government regulation will be of advantage to the public, if it is achieved. Consolidation by promotion of economic routing of traffic will enable the carriers to perform their services more economically and efficiently and will make it possible for them to strengthen themselves financially. The shipper as well as the carrier is primarily interested in traffic movement and it may be assumed that the interests of the shipper as well as those of the carrier will be understood and be safeguarded by the Interstate Commerce Commission in performing its task of regulating the railroads.

The problem of government regulation of railroads, particularly the work of rate adjustment, will doubtless be simplified by reducing the number of railroad systems through the process of consolidation, but the importance of effective, wise, and constructive regulation will not be lessened. To harmonize the interests of carrier and shipper, to further the balanced and continuous economic welfare of the country as a whole by facilitating the development of an adequate transportation system, will always be the task of government regulation of railroads and other carriers. It is because railroad consolidation may enable the government to perform this service more completely and helpfully that the public as a

INTRODUCTION

whole may look with favor upon the accomplishment of the grouping of railroads as contemplated by the framers of the Transportation Act of 1920.

Two special features characterize Dr. Grodinsky's book. One feature is its new and illuminating presentation of the main motive that the carriers have in seeking to bring about railroad consolidations. The other feature of the volume is the wealth of information it contains regarding financial and traffic problems of American railroad companies. The reader of the volume may obtain a comprehensive knowledge of the financial and traffic affairs of a large number of individual railroad companies and of the interrelations of those companies with each other. All students of transportation will be grateful to Dr. Grodinsky for marshaling and clearly interpreting instructive information regarding American railroads and for applying that information to the illumination of the involved subject of railroad consolidation.

EMORY R. JOHNSON

RAILROAD CONSOLIDATION

CHAPTER I

GENERAL ECONOMIC FACTORS

Railroad consolidation has within the last few years become a subject of general interest. It has filled many columns of press news and has served as first page headliners. Aggressive personalities have added the touch of personal magnetism; and even a halo of romance has added color to the consideration of the problems involved.

It is not surprising that railroad consolidation has suffered the fate of all subjects receiving the attention of laymen and of their self-appointed representatives—the newspaper editor and the staff correspondent. The public is told of the insistent requirements of the Pennsylvania for a direct line to Buffalo, or for an east and west line along Lake Erie; and of the imperative need for the Central Railroad of New Jersey of both the New York Central and the Baltimore & Ohio. Shall there be four or five trunk lines in the east? Shall the Wheeling & Lake Erie be owned and operated by competing trunk lines? Or shall it be tied up with connecting carriers on both sides to form a new through line from the Mississippi River to the Atlantic seaboard? There are the topics headlined. And it is not surprising. These matters are tangible; and they lend themselves to journalistic glorification.

The respective interests of the rival lines may be important; and, in theory at least, the totality of their interests contribute substantially to the public interest. But in many, if not in most cases, their direct and immediate interests clash. Where, then, do the interests of the public lie? There is danger that, not only the general public, but even those in high authority may be victimized by this point of view. There is danger that the ultimate purposes designed to be realized by consolidation may be lost sight of.

More than nine years have passed since Congress enacted the law on this subject. It may be fair to inquire to what extent the purposes of the law have been fulfilled and to what extent the interests of the public have been promoted thereby.

The railroads of this country owe the public the duty of providing excellent and nondiscriminatory railroad service at reasonable rates; and the public in turn owes the railroads the opportunity to earn a fair return on invested capital. All government regulation aims to accomplish these ends; and consolidation, as a phase of regulation, is no exception to the rule. The framers of the Transportation Act decided that the wisest way to build up a strong railroad net lay in the provision of an earning power designed to enable the roads to earn a fair return on the fair value of their property. The regulatory Commission was enjoined to fix rates so that the carriers as a whole could earn this return. But the practical execution of this principle was complicated by the existence of competitive railroads, which, with uniform rates, earned varying returns. Some were well managed, some poorly managed; some were conservatively capitalized, and some were

GENERAL ECONOMIC FACTORS

not; some enjoyed the profits arising from the possession of lucrative traffic alliances, and others bewailed the losses arising from the lack of sufficient traffic obtained from their neighbors. But whatever the cause, uniform rates did not produce uniform revenues. Consolidation was the solution—the consolidation of what was euphoniously termed the weak and the strong. The establishment of a few large equally powerful systems would replace the many existing roads—some large, and some small. Uniform rates by a few roads equally well managed and well financed, with uniform capital costs, would, it was expected, produce approximately similar results.

What interests do the users of the railroad service have in this? Why should those who send freight over, and ride on the roads, concern themselves with these problems? Why should they insist upon service by a few consolidated systems instead of by the present corporations, providing the service is the same? This question answers itself: the service, so it is said, is not the same. The road which under present conditions does not make a fair return does not possess the ability to render good service. It possesses no funds, and no credit to obtain funds, with which to furnish the additions and betterments required to supply good service. A consolidated system, it is expected, will be able to earn the fair return stipulated by law. It will thus possess a good credit standing, and be able to obtain the capital needed to furnish a high-class service.

It is the financially weak road that represents the crux of the problem. It cannot render high-class service to the public, and in some cases is not sufficiently prosperous to insure its continued operation. Its possible abandonment becomes a problem of serious concern to those dependent upon it for communication with the outside world. Consolidation proposes to settle these difficulties. The financially strong roads are to absorb the financially weak. And various inducements are provided to justify the strong roads in assuming the burden.

This is the theory; these are the expectations. What actually has taken place since the passage of the law in 1920? To what extent has the administration of the law on railroad acquisitions and consolidations increased the standard of service and promoted the establishment of an equitable and reasonable rate structure through the absorption of weak by strong lines?

The past years have witnessed a rejuvenation of the financially weak roads of the country. In New England, the Boston & Maine, the New York, New Haven & Hartford and the Maine Central have recovered a good measure of their former earning power. Their extraordinary increase in operating efficiency aided by an increase in the division of through rates has placed them in the class of properties able to furnish a service adapted to meet all the reasonable needs of the community.

The most important weak line problems in trunk line territory have reached a fairly satisfactory solution. The Erie, aided by important traffic alliances and by unusually excellent operation under a new management, has attained a good credit standing and renders a satisfactory service to its shipping public. Both the Wabash and the New York, Chicago & St. Louis (the Nickel Plate), the other financial sore spots in trunk line territory, have been removed from the class of weak sisters. The automobile industry has played a great part in recovering the earning power of the Wabash, as well as that of the Pere

Marquette and the Ann Arbor. The ill-fated group of Gould roads involved in the proposed organization of a new through route to the eastern seaboard have fairly well established their earning power. The Pittsburgh & West Virginia—the successor to the old Terminals Company—is on a dividend paying basis; the Wheeling & Lake Erie and the Western Maryland, whose fuller recovery have been retarded by the depression in the union bituminous coal fields, have earned (with gradually widening margins) the interest on a heavy funded debt.

In the southeast, the improvement in the financial standing of the important properties has been characterized chiefly by the astonishing progress of the Southern Railway. Its credit now ranks among the best. On the other hand, the expansion program of the Seaboard Air Line, involving new constructions and acquisitions of existing properties—a program nurtured and fathered by the official approval of the federal regulatory body—has not been productive of good results. An earning power based on the Florida inflation was deflated—perhaps only temporarily but not the less surely and rapidly—with the deflation of the boom. Here, probably, there may be proof sufficient that the impartial, even-handed scales of regulatory expert judgment may be imperfect. And this is not the only mistake in the active *administration* (as contrasted with judicial regulation) of American railroads by the federal government.

The southwest has witnessed perhaps the most phenomenal recovery of railroad financial strength. Such roads as the St. Louis & San Francisco, the Chicago, Rock Island & Pacific, the New Orleans, Texas & Mexico, the Texas & Pacific have been lifted from the depths of bankruptcy to the heights of dividend resumption. Other roads in the hands of receivers such as the Missouri Pacific, and the Missouri-Kansas-Texas have also enjoyed extensive increases in earnings, though their common shares as yet pay no dividends. The increasing agricultural diversity combined with the Oklahoma and West Texas oil booms have played an important part in contributing to their increase in financial strength.

The ulcer in the northwest—the Chicago, Milwaukee & St. Paul—has been removed in part by a financial reorganization. A succession of excellent grain crops combined with the efficiencies produced by extensive capital investments is contributing to a fairly sustained increase in earnings.

Little of the financial recovery of these properties can be attributed to any effects arising from union with other properties. The two chief exceptions are the New York, Chicago & St. Louis and the Missouri Pacific system. The former union represents the only complete merger effected since 1920. It was carried out under the laws of the respective states in which the roads operated. The new company then successfully applied to the Interstate Commerce Commission for a certificate of convenience and necessity to operate the lines.[1] The latter union represents the result of two separate applications: the acquisition of the stock of the International Great Northern by the New Orleans, Texas & Mexico;[2] and of the majority share control of the latter by the Missouri Pacific.[3]

Both of these systems were approved by the Commission practically on the case made out by the interested parties. Only points of minor importance were raised by

[1] The notes will be found at the ends of chapters.

GENERAL ECONOMIC FACTORS

the Commission in its final decisions, none having any vital bearing on the outstanding results to be expected from consolidation. In the earlier case, the Commission deemed it desirable to defend the legality of a merger carried out under state laws; and in the Missouri Pacific decision it took exceptional pains to criticize the ethics of a banking house in exacting an unwarranted compensation for its services (alleged by the Commission to be unnecessary) in carrying through the sale of the shares of the New Orleans, Texas & Mexico to the Missouri Pacific. In neither case was any discussion given to the strengthening of the weak roads through absorption by the strong.

To these important decisions may be added the series of system leases effected by the Pennsylvania and the New York Central. Upon the basis of a showing of relatively minor economies, the former was permitted to lease properties it had theretofore controlled by stock ownership only: the Grand Rapids & Indiana, the Pittsburgh, Cincinnati, Chicago & St. Louis, and other less important properties.[4] And the latter, upon an equally barren showing, was allowed to acquire working control through lease of the properties of the Kanawha & Michigan, and the Toledo & Ohio Central.[5]

Again nothing was said about the public necessity of taking over the burdens of the weak carriers.

In a relatively unimportant case decided in 1925, the Commission hesitatingly declined to assert that under the terms of the Consolidation section of the Act of 1920 it had authority to condition the acquisition of one line upon the acquisition and maintenance of another—the latter being a financially weak short line. Should the former's acquisition tend to lead to the latter's "ultimate extinction," as alleged, as a common carrier (that is, if its operating revenues should at any time become insufficient to pay its operating expenses), then the connecting trunk line was to maintain adequate service over the weak line until such time as the Commission authorized its abandonment.[6]

Subject to this minor exception, it was not until the early months of 1926 that the Commission considered it necessary to discuss the weak line problem. In the Nickel Plate decision it finally took a firm stand on the subject. It issued a dictum throwing the responsibility for providing for all of the short lines in a particular territory upon the particular road asking for permission to acquire other properties.[7] Since then, no road has seen fit to apply these principles to its own program of consolidation.

The New York Central in the summer of 1926 laid its program for the unification by lease of its share controlled subsidiaries before the Interstate Commerce Commission. It did not propose to acquire any of its weak, short line connections. The Commission after two and one-half years of consideration refused to sanction the proposal of the New York Central except upon condition that it offer to acquire a number of intervening short lines upon the basis of their commercial value. The value was to be decided either by agreement between the parties or by arbitration.[8]

It presently came to be recognized, however, that the motives behind consolidation arising from the so-called public interest were widely divergent from the motives actuating railroad men. The blocking out of control of extensive railroad properties, particularly in the east and

GENERAL ECONOMIC FACTORS 9

the southwest, had stirred most of the other properties into activity. Consolidation plans were announced and executed that seemed to defy those principles that theoretically should have been respected in the public interest. In the east a localized and regionalized bituminous coal carrier, the Chesapeake & Ohio, obtained working control of an important trunk line;[9] and a small anthracite road in eastern Pennsylvania and New York, the Delaware & Hudson, reached across the state of Pennsylvania to lease the Buffalo, Rochester & Pittsburgh: a soft coal property separated from its proposed lessee by over two hundred miles.[10] Another anthracite carrier, the Philadelphia & Reading, moved to effect control of *the* two noncongested lines in the Delaware Valley which serve as a vital part in a through route from the south and west to New England.[11] And farther west in Ohio, three important trunk lines, the New York Central, the Baltimore & Ohio, and the New York, Chicago & St. Louis, secured working control of the Wheeling & Lake Erie, an important line with which the acquiring lines competed for available traffic at many points.[12]

In the southwest, the chairman of the board of directors of the St. Louis Southwestern publicly assured its shareholders that its true destiny lay with a carrier forming part of a transcontinental route. "In the disposition to the Chicago, Rock Island & Pacific Railway Company of substantial holdings of St. Louis Southwestern stock . . . I have, to that extent," he stated, "promoted what I conceive to be the true destiny of the St. Louis Southwestern property. The alliance with the Rock Island Railway Company commends itself upon geographical, traffic, and economic considerations as a mutually beneficial arrangement. It commends itself as a definite public advantage and as a logical development of the legislative policy which favors natural and voluntary selection as against arbitrary or compulsory grouping." [13] The authorities representative of the public interest promptly rejected this vital proposal,[14] and the new owner as promptly sold its control to the Kansas City Southern.[15] Representatives of the road whose ownership was thus bandied about spoke as vigorously in favor of the control by the first owner, as by the second. The report of an examiner recommending that the Interstate Commerce Commission deny the Chicago, Rock Island & Pacific permission to acquire control of the St. Louis Southwestern indicated, in the opinion of the latter's counsel, "that there is (was) not a line of testimony in the record which in any way indicates (d) that the public interests would be injured by the granting of this application, but on the contrary, that there is (was) overwhelming evidence that the control would be in the public interest." [16]

And many were the advantages outlined: competition would be preserved, service would be improved, economies would be secured, and traffic would be diversified.

Other proposals for consolidation, seemingly as inconsistent in some cases, were made, and not infrequently carried out. Be it noted that in all these (with one or two notable exceptions) no prosperous road proposed to acquire a financially weak road. None desired to assume any financial burdens. On the contrary, in the most ambitious unification program yet devised, the proposed system carefully excluded the lessee from assuming any responsibility to those parts of the leased trunk lines that were notably weak financially. In the original Nickel Plate

Unification proposal the curious division of the Erie into two sections (one to be operated directly by the new system and the other to be operated independently) was explained by their respective financial strength and weakness.[17]

These extensive plans resulted in the establishment of systems, which, for practical purposes, were equivalent in working control to those represented by existing trunk lines.

Some of these unions constituted complete consolidations of ownership and operation.[18] These were effected under state laws; and the Interstate Commerce Commission, by an interpretation explainable only by the exigencies of the situation, approved the acquisition and operation by the applicant corporation of lines formerly owned by the old one, and under the terms of a section of the law which appear to have no bearing on consolidation. Section 1, paragraph 18 of the Transportation Act, which gave the Commission power to regulate the construction of new and the abandonment of old lines, was stretched to embrace "the acquisition by the parent company of the physical property of a subsidiary operated as a part of its system." [19]

These consolidations were assumed by the law to be legally possible only in the light of an all-embracing plan to be worked out by the governmental regulating body. That body confessed its inability to prepare such an all-sufficient scheme. It vainly asked Congress to relieve it from this duty.[20] But the roads did not remain quiet. They did not await government initiative. They proceeded persistently in the formulation and execution of their plans for consolidation.

Their plans were not in any substantial way connected with consolidation for ownership and operation called for by the Transportation Act. Consolidation into a single system for complete ownership represented the ideal of the legislators. This ideal could not be realized until the Commission had announced its plan of consolidation. And this had not been done. The distinction, however, between consolidation based on complete fee ownership and unification based on share control or lease contract was not necessarily demanded by practical circumstances. Most of the strong railroad systems of the country have not been built up through conveyance of fee ownership. Some of the western lines—like the Chicago & North Western, and the Chicago, Milwaukee & St. Paul—which extended into virgin territory by continuous construction are perhaps exceptions. The majority of the roads developed their systems through the use of the various well-known media of finance. A lease, a traffic agreement, a trackage agreement, a majority share interest, a joint control and guarantee of outstanding or newly incurred debts were the tools employed on different occasions.

A system developed in this manner is not ideal. It represents the result of the workings of those trades and negotiations that characterize business life. But it serves its purpose well. The system functions as an organic unit. It is dominated by a unity of purpose and a unity of action. The Baltimore & Ohio traffic salesman is not seriously handicapped in soliciting for business from Chicago to New York because a large part of its system is not directly controlled in fee ownership. Its multiformity of ownership does not impair its service. Traffic is solicited as effectively and moved as efficiently over a system owned kaleidoscopically as over a system fully crystallized in ownership.

This is not to gainsay the evident advantages of a system in single ownership and operation. Fnancial institutions and wealthy investors have acquired a predilection for bonds secured by mortgages on property owned in fee. They are willing to pay a higher price, other conditions being equal, for bonds so secured than for bonds secured by leasehold contract, share collateral, or by mortgages bearing the slightest degree of inferiority in the mortgage hierarchy. Bonds of a system wholly unified in ownership sell at a higher price than bonds of one unified indirectly by lease contract or share control.

There is this further, and under particular circumstances, significant advantage: the road need not concern itself with the embarrassing problem of rights of minority shareholders. (It may be stated parenthetically that a lease disposes of minority shareholders equally well.) Minority shareholders have a claim proportionate to their ownership on the earning equity of the company. Anything done that should not be done, or not done that should be done, which impairs the company's earning power, impairs proportionately the property interests of the minority shareholder. If the majority shareholder be the controlling carrier in a system, similar action or inaction may not impair its vital vested interests. The road may control a route between common points, duplicate to or alternative with that controlled by the parent road. At times it may be most economical to send available traffic over the line of the parent company. This would decrease the earnings of the other company with resultant damage to the property rights of its minority shareholders.

What the parent system might lose in lower earnings on its controlled company, however, it might more than gain by a corresponding increase in its own earnings. The parallel routes of the old Lake Shore & Michigan Southern and the present Michigan Central between Chicago and Buffalo on opposite sides of Lake Erie is a case in point. Under a system wholly unified in ownership or wholly leased, the traffic may be routed in the best interests of the system as a unit, and incidentally in the best interests of the public.

These advantages are well known and thoroughly appreciated. But they are not essentially fundamental in rendering a decision upon the merits of consolidation. The Van Sweringens preferred to unify through lease the properties of the New York, Chicago & St. Louis, the Pere Marquette, the Chesapeake & Ohio, the Hocking Valley and the Erie. The Commission's rejection of this plan [21] led not to the dissolution of the system, but rather to a change in its corporate form. The controlling interests then proposed to unify the system through share control. Consolidation and unification both aim to control traffic movements, and both forces are well adapted for this purpose.

In preparing and presenting their plans the carriers eagerly accepted the opportunity of consummating acquisitions and unifications short of complete ownership. The law permitted the Commission to approve these plans upon a showing of public interest—whatever elusive meaning that term may connote. During 1925 and 1926 a large number of these plans were submitted to the Commission for its approval. The Commission's disapproval of the first major unification in eastern trunk line territory was

GENERAL ECONOMIC FACTORS 15

based on entirely extraneous circumstances—extraneous, that is, to consolidations from the viewpoint of the interests and motives of those who in law and in practice are the only parties who can initiate the plans. The Commission both in this case and in the major unification in southwestern territory (involving the association of the Kansas City Southern, Missouri-Kansas-Texas, and St. Louis Southwestern) approved the formation of both systems as engines of transportation service. But the one did not adequately protect connecting weak lines, and both were not properly financed in the opinion of the Commission. Its approval was therefore withheld.

What are the impelling motives which thus drive railroad men on without any government aid or encouragement—nay, in the face of regulatory rejection and disapproval? Is it the speculative profits that consolidation renders possible? There are just enough facts available to lend aid to those searching for evidence to support this viewpoint. The wholesale organization of paper holding companies, and the manufacture of collateral obligations to facilitate the acquisition of extensive properties with but a small cash commitment, is an accessory to the development of the largest unification thus far evolved.[22] This exception only serves to picture in bold relief the absence of any speculative profits on any extensive scale in the ordinary consolidation program.

Here and there may be found illustrations of consolidations based on operating or capital economies. The union of the Baltimore & Ohio and the Western Maryland might relieve the former from the necessity of constructing another track from Cumberland to Baltimore;[23] and the acquisition of the El Paso & Southwestern by the

Southern Pacific gave the latter a much-needed second track between Tucson and El Paso.[24] But it is fairly certain that expected economies do not represent the dynamic force behind consolidation. Some roads are acquired when there is no hope of any substantial economies. Such was the case in the lease of the Alabama & Vicksburg and the Vicksburg, Shreveport & Pacific by the Illinois Central. Chas. H. Markham, then President of the Illinois Central, being asked what economies would result from the proposed lease of the two lines to the road of which he was president, replied, "I am unable to answer it, your Honor."[25] Speaking of the situation in Jackson, Miss., he stated further: "I presume we will draw the agencies together there. The switching will be done under one yardmaster, the traffic of the town will be handled under one agency, and things of that sort will be obtained. Whether that will be possible at Vicksburg or not, I do not know, but there will be some economy there, but these questions have not been gone into yet, and we will not do so until after the question of our taking over the road is settled."[26]

In another situation involving the acquisition of stock control of the Ann Arbor by the Wabash, William H. Williams, Chairman of the Board, not only of the Wabash, but also of the Missouri Pacific system, expressed a substantially similar judgment. The presiding examiner queried:

Q. "Has any estimate been made of the operating economies that you expect to effect in dollars and cents?"

A. "No, sir. I think that is comparatively limited—only in this respect, that from the standpoint of hauling your freight in the direction of the prevailing movement,

GENERAL ECONOMIC FACTORS

your engine is not going to haul any more because of change of ownership." [27]

Characteristic of the savings that consolidation will give to the public is the statement of the Interstate Commerce Commission in its decision disapproving of the proposed acquisition of the Virginian by the Norfolk & Western: "Testimony for the Norfolk & Western is that any economies to be effected will not be reflected in reduced rates if the company can prevent it." [28] Many are the properties leased and controlled with alleged economies—both vague and unsubstantial. Economies in car supply that were supposed to flow from the lease of the Virginian to the Norfolk & Western [29] and from the lease of the Buffalo, Rochester & Pittsburgh to the Delaware & Hudson were dependent upon a synchronization of traffic movements that represents an ideal of every able and ambitious operating official.[30] The ideal, however, is not always realized.

There are, of course, savings that consolidation brings about. There are savings in accounting and financing. And on the other hand, consolidation will increase expenses in particular cases. On the evidence of no less an authority than Judge Lovett of the Union Pacific, the control of short lines by trunk lines almost always produces an increase in wages on the former. Many of the weak lines of the country pay substandard wages. Payment of the higher wage scale equivalent to that paid to the employees of the trunk lines results from absorption of the small by the large road. "As far as concerns small lines that are absorbed and are operated merely as branch lines," says this authority, "you could save the expense of their organization, the most of it. But on the other hand your scale of wages would at once become standard, and you would incur a great many expenses that the short line owner avoids to-day. I know that of my own experience on both the Union Pacific and the Southern Pacific, which extends over a great many years, I have often commented to our people, that I have never known an instance where we took up a short line when the expenses did not increase instead of decrease, very materially." [31]

The well-directed efforts of some short lines—and, be it noted, that the prosperity of the short line is not so uncommon as is usually supposed—to sell out to the trunk line connections has revealed many notable instances of the accuracy of Judge Lovett's opinions. The Atlanta, Birmingham & Atlantic, a road that remained in financial distress for almost the entire term of its corporate existence until its dissolution incident to its acquisition by the Atlantic Coast Line, paid a substandard wage scale. Low wages were made possible largely through the personal relations between the receiver and the workers.[32] The ambition of the New York Central lines to lease its stock-controlled subsidiaries produced valuable data on the point under consideration. The examiner's report in this proceeding referred to the inadvisability of official approval of the system leases pending further study of the allocation of intervening short lines. The New York Central thereupon prepared a careful study of all of its short line connections. The study revealed that practically all of the short line interveners asked the Commission to direct their absorption by the New York Central. Of these the Ulster & Delaware, the Delaware & Northern, the Southern New York Railway, and the Chicago, Attica & Southern do not pay standard wages. The Boyne City, Gaylord, &

GENERAL ECONOMIC FACTORS

Alpena pays only for actual hours worked; it does not pay overtime rates. The Federal Valley is not obliged to pay the overtime rates of the New York Central; nor does the latter enjoy the arrangement whereby the former succeeds in inducing the fireman and engineer to do running repair work when not engaged in running the train. The Casey & Kansas not only pays no standard wages; it also pays no salaries to its officials.[33]

And here is the climax. Another short line, the Fonda, Johnstown & Gloversville, an intervener paying substandard wages, urges that fact in support of the proposal for its absorption by the New York Central. . . . For "a step which will result in lower rates for shippers and higher wages for employees can hardly be said to be against the public interest." [34]

Railroads may, indeed, realize some economies from changes in corporate ownership of American railroads, and promoters may reap speculative profits. But these are not the impelling, the primary forces. The grand strategy of railroad consolidation does not revolve around these elements; nor are the great prizes valued in terms of superior savings or financial manipulation.

It is in another field of thought that the motivating factors lie. The law on consolidation lays down as the essential consideration, to which all others must be subordinated, the maintenance of competition and the preservation of channels of trade and commerce. The exact thought behind this provision of the law is not entirely clear.

It is apparently a shippers' provision designed to indicate their views that no consolidation should disturb existing trade centers, nor deprive them of access to markets. This concept, while satisfactory from the shipper's standpoint, is not entirely satisfactory from the more comprehensive viewpoint of the public interest. Consolidation necessarily need not, and in most cases, does not interfere with shippers' markets. The traffic merely moves over different combinations of lines, over different routes. The new routes may have better or poorer grades, be somewhat longer or somewhat shorter, be more or less congested, etc. They may, in short, furnish transportation service more or less economically. Both routes may afford the shipper equally good service; yet the public interest may demand the use of the more economical one. Indeed this possibility is frequently set forth as one of the major advantages of consolidation.

Routes between particular points are established by carriers in response to shippers' needs and upon the basis of well-settled business principles, discussed hereinafter in their proper relationship. Between important centers scores and even hundreds of routes may exist. The service over many alternative routes may not be vitally different, and yet some routes move little traffic, and some much more. By proper coöperation of connecting carriers, the business can be made to move over selected routes; proper coöperation between participating lines can create "traffic channels."

If two or more lines can be hooked up in such a way that traffic formerly moving over other routes can now be made to flow over the new combination, the essentials for a successful consolidation exist. Railroad men will unite such properties to increase the gross volume of business over the new combination.

By and large, with sufficient exceptions to establish the

truthfulness of the generality, consolidations are made in response to these traffic forces—the forces which enable the acquiring roads to capture the business of the acquired road, to force its movement over the line of the acquiring road and away from its competitor. A successful speculator may sense the latent possibilities of a number of lines if united. He may act to place the properties under one common control; and may thereby reap some large speculative profits. Certain economies may be possible as a result. In most cases they are small, in some cases, large. But the roads unite to capture the business primarily; the economies will take care of themselves. "The basic idea underlying the consolidation movement is, therefore, a traffic problem; not financial; not operating; not one, directly and necessarily, calculated to preserve the so-called weak roads." [35]

This inquiry into the dynamic—the traffic—factors that underlie the movement toward railroad consolidation is, it is believed, the first ever attempted. It is not expected that it will be free from errors. Its shortcomings are clearly evident to the author. If it should stimulate active work in this virgin and fertile school of economic thought, it will have served its purpose well.

NOTES TO CHAPTER I

1. Acquisition and Stock Issue by New York, Chicago & St. Louis Railroad, 79 I.C.C. 581.
2. Control of International-Great Northern Railroad, 90 I.C.C. 262.
3. Control of Gulf Coast Lines by Missouri Pacific Railroad, 94 I.C.C. 91. The Interstate Commerce Commission in passing upon the reorganization of the Texas & Pacific in 1924 approved the acquisition by the Missouri Pacific of almost all of its preferred stock. See 86 I.C.C. 808. The Missouri Pacific has also secured a large interest in the common stock of the Texas & Pacific without the approval of the Interstate Commerce Commission. A 50 per cent common stock interest in the Denver &

Rio Grande Western was approved by the Commission. See 90 I.C.C. 161.
4. Acquisition of control of New York, Philadelphia & Norfolk Railroad by Pennsylvania Railroad, 70 I.C.C. 299; acquisition of control of Cumberland Valley & Martinsburg Railroad, 70 I.C.C. 301; see also 70 I.C.C. 303, 306; 72 I.C.C. 128, 260, 674.
5. New York Central Leases, 72 I.C.C. 243.
6. Control of G. & S. I. R. R. Co., 99 I.C.C. 173.
7. Nickel Plate Unification, 105 I.C.C. 449.
8. New York Central Unification, 150 I.C.C. 322.
9. Nickel Plate Unification, 105 I.C.C. 425; also, Control of Erie Railroad, and Pere Marquette Railway, 138 I.C.C. 517.
10. Lease of Buffalo, Rochester & Pittsburgh, 131 I.C.C. 750.
11. Lease of Lehigh & New England, 124 I.C.C. 81.
12. Interlocking Directors of Wheeling & Lake Erie and Trunk Lines, 138 I.C.C. 643.
13. Statement of Edwin Gould, Chairman of Board of Directors of St. Louis Southwestern, as embodied in minutes of Board, March 11, 1925. For text see Brief of Chicago, Rock Island & Pacific Railway in Finance Docket 4809, p. 4.
14. Report of Examiner C. B. Burnside in Finance Docket 4809. Proposed acquisition by the Chicago, Rock Island & Pacific of the St. Louis Southwestern.
15. Unification of Southwestern Lines, 124 I.C.C. 405-406.
16. Brief for the St. Louis Southwestern in support of exceptions to the report of Examiner C. B. Burnside in Finance Docket 4809, p. 11.
17. Nickel Plate Unification, 105 I.C.C. 431. See also Brief for Interveners George Cole Scott, John Stewart Bryan, Lindsay Hopkins, George S. Kemp, and Berkeley Williams in Finance Docket 4671, pp. 228-229.
18. Acquisition by Pittsburgh & West Virginia Railway Company, 150 I.C.C. 84; further references cited.
19. *Supra.*
20. Annual Report of the Interstate Commerce Commission, 1925-1926.
21. Nickel Plate Unification, 105 I.C.C. 431.
22. *Supra.*
23. Construction by Pittsburgh & West Virginia Railway, Finance Docket 6229, Brief for Baltimore & Ohio Railroad, p. 109.
24. Control of El Paso & Southwestern Railroad, 90 I.C.C. 737.
25. Control of Alabama & Vicksburg Railway and Vicksburg, Shreveport & Pacific Railway, Finance Docket 4775. Brief for Interveners, R. E. Kennington, *et al*, p. 8.
26. *Supra,* tr. pp 138-139.
27. Control of Ann Arbor Railroad by Wabash Railway, Finance Docket 4942, tr. p. 35.
28. Control of Virginian Railway, 117 I.C.C. 84.
29. *Supra,* tr. p. 930.
30. Control of Buffalo, Rochester & Pittsburgh Railway, 131 I.C.C. 758.

GENERAL ECONOMIC FACTORS 23

31. Consolidation Proceedings, Docket 12964, Statement of Robert S. Lovett at the hearing in San Francisco, April 2, 1923, p. 50.
32. Reorganization of Atlanta, Birmingham & Atlantic Railway, Finance Docket 5454, Brief for Reorganization Committee in reply to Brief of Charles E. Cotterill, p. 15.
33. New York Central Unification, Finance Docket 5688, 5690. Abstract of evidence on further hearing for the applicant.
34. *Supra*, Supplemental Brief of Fonda, Johnstown & Gloversville, p. 7.
35. Julius Grodinsky, "How Consolidations Affect the Movement of Traffic," in *Railway Age*, June 30, 1928, p. 1503.

CHAPTER II

INTERCHANGE

American railroad traffic moves largely over two or more lines. There are few roads that connect many sources of production with many consuming markets. Those roads which originate cotton in Texas do not generally reach Chicago and those which penetrate the oil fields of Oklahoma do not generally reach the consuming markets north of the Missouri River. Again, the roads which receive the miscellaneous manufactures from the New England mills and factories have no tracks of their own beyond the Hudson River.

Yet the trade and commerce of the country require the continuous exchange of commodities between the agricultural south and west, and the industrial east. The citrus fruit of the Rio Grande Valley of Texas and of the Salt River Valley of Arizona must be brought to the breakfast table of the citizen in the Delaware River and Ohio River valleys. The farmer in the southwest requires the agricultural implements manufactured in the central west; and the mills of New England are helpless without the cotton from the south.

There are no roads, however, which connect areas of important raw material south of the Potomac and Ohio and west of the Mississippi rivers with consuming areas east of the Alleghenies. And there are but few lines joining the markets of the middle west with the great sources of mineral and agricultural wealth of the south and west. The Atchison, Topeka & Santa Fe does operate from San Francisco to Chicago via Kansas City; and the Chicago, Milwaukee, St. Paul & Pacific does control a through line from Chicago to Seattle. These are, however, the notable exceptions. The great southwestern carriers—the Missouri Pacific, the Missouri-Kansas-Texas, the St. Louis & San Francisco—stop short at the Mississippi River. The Union Pacific, with its loaded cars of grain, lumber, and fruit, comes to a halt at the Missouri River. The Southern Pacific cannot operate its own trains of fruit, oil and cotton beyond New Orleans in the southeast and northern Texas and Louisiana on the north. The major southeastern lines do not cross the Potomac; and so cannot carry the food and the raw materials of industry into the centers of large population and intense industrial activity. The New England lines are isolated entirely. They reach neither the mines which supply the coal required for the operation of their factories, nor the communities which furnish the outlet for the articles made by their industries.

A large proportion of the bulky raw materials are destined for points east of the Mississippi Valley. This is due to the disproportion between the area and the spread of our population. "In 11 per cent of the country's area are embraced 42 per cent of the total population in the Eastern and Northeastern Atlantic seaboard territory, and in that zone are produced to-day 70 per cent of the total of all manufactures. More than this, north of an air line drawn roughly from Toledo to Norfolk, excluding the states of Maine, New Hampshire and Vermont, are 5 per cent of the country's area and, in cities of 100,000 and over alone, more than one-fifth of the total population." [1]

Westward bound are the miscellaneous and manufactured articles produced in the industrial centers of the north, primarily north of the Ohio and Potomac valleys and east of the Mississippi. The raw material and foodstuffs eastbound bulk heavier than the miscellaneous and manufactured products westbound. This produces a preponderant eastbound trend of traffic and a large westbound movement of empties. The railroads of the country, as a whole, are laid out to correspond with this fact of commercial geography. However, few corporate entities control lines which connect the large areas which originate traffic and those to which it is destined.

Particularly fortunate indeed are those roads which operate over their own lines from important centers of production of traffic to important consuming centers. Properties like the Atchison, Topeka & Santa Fe; New York Central; Pennsylvania; Chicago, Burlington & Quincy; and the Illinois Central enjoy unusually long hauls on local traffic, traffic that is not interchanged with other roads. Local traffic in most instances is, however, short haul traffic. Short haul business is distinctly unremunerative. It is what is commonly designated in business circles as small-scale business. The overhead, i.e. the constant expenses, are relatively stationary. They do not appreciably increase for ten carloads over what they are for one carload. The overhead per unit of transportation service is high on short haul—mostly local business. The same phenomenon holds true of almost every manufacturing small-scale operation.

It is a problem not applicable alone to the railroad business. Its financial incidence is, however, different in railroad than in many industrial activities. Selling prices of industrial organizations reflect the higher costs of small-scale operations: it costs a publisher substantially more to print a book per copy in an edition of one thousand, than it costs in an edition of fifty thousand; and a votary of the antique fad pays more for a piece of rare —real or alleged—furniture, than an economical housewife pays for standard stock manufactured en masse on a large scale.

Railroad rates do not, and in large measure cannot, reflect this cost concept. Intensely complex considerations of business and regional competition make it impossible in part to charge every shipment with its duly proportionate part of overhead costs. Much traffic would not move if rates embodying the full extent of the overhead charge were assessed.

The financial aspects of short haul traffic have been greatly intensified by the new forms of competitive transportation service. The private passenger automobile and the motor truck, by diverting considerable short haul passenger and freight traffic, has sharply increased the overhead per unit of the remaining business. And here again another outstanding difference between the railroad and the industrial activities is emphasized. A manufacturer, finding his product so reduced in demand that the remaining production can be made only at a high cost per unit, liquidates his enterprise; voluntarily if possible, forcibly otherwise. Not so with a railroad. Many are the carriers who, under compulsion of the law, carry traffic financially unprofitable but otherwise necessary to the rendition of a proper standard of service to a community. Many phases of this economic phenomenon are well illustrated by the attempt of the Boston & Maine to abandon many of its branch lines. At that time (in 1925) approximately 42 per cent of the mileage handled but 3 per cent of the ton miles.[2]

The short haul business is thus becoming progressively unprofitable. It is the length of the haul that makes a train movement financially profitable. As the train leaves the terminal and moves over the main lines its revenue rapidly piles up. Every ton-mile brings with it increased revenue. Expenses per train-mile do not increase in the same proportion. Each additional train-mile means only a relatively small increase in the wages of the crew, and in the cost of fuel. The relative profitableness of long haul traffic is enhanced by the rate policy of the federal regulating body, as expressed in its efforts to achieve a uniformity in rates. Each class rate, it appears, must bear some reasonable proportion to some other class rate; and each rate must bear some reasonable proportion to distance traveled. This demand for scientific uniformity in rate-making may be justified by other considerations; but it assuredly operates to increase the profitableness of long haul traffic.

It is this insistent and persistent urge for the long haul that tends to explain many of the moves in the field of railroad consolidation. A surprisingly large amount of the business strategy is directed towards obtaining the long haul, and by long haul is meant not necessarily, although usually it is so, the haul longest in terms of miles. The long haul in practical railroad parlance is the haul that yields the greatest profit on a particular shipment.

With a goodly part of their overhead fixed regardless of the volume of business carried, all roads strive to get

INTERCHANGE

all possible hauls available. Part is secured from local business but an ever growing proportion is obtained in a keenly competitive struggle with other lines. And consolidation plans with other lines, properly conceived and executed with due regard to all relevant considerations, is an important factor in this struggle for additional business.

The corporate entities of American railroads being such that few carriers stretch from the major sources of production to the major markets of consumption, it becomes necessary to interchange traffic on a vast scale. There are no roads of any consequence that do not deliver to and receive traffic from another road or roads. The financial importance of this interchange traffic varies with different properties. Trunk lines reaching important traffic producing areas and important primary and secondary markets enjoy the possession of a comparatively large volume of profitable local traffic. Take the Chicago, Burlington & Quincy, for an illustration. Here is a road which originates large tonnages of wheat, corn and livestock that it delivers over its own lines to many important markets on the Mississippi and Missouri rivers. Its lines also penetrate to Chicago and the Twin Cities. It has lines down through Illinois gathering fuel for its own use. And even with such favoring conditions its interchange traffic represents more than half of its total tonnage.[3] It interchanges more than 10 per cent of its total tonnage with its two parent lines alone.[4]

Here is the Louisville & Nashville—one of the strong systems of the country with a stable and well-sustained earning power. Besides originating a lucrative coal tonnage in the non-union, low-cost coal fields, it has access to most of the important southeastern points west of the Alleghenies. It is a heavy producing carrier, originating more than 85 per cent of its tonnage in 1921. Of its total traffic, however, only one-third is free from the problems of interchange; the remaining two-thirds is either delivered to or received from connections.[5]

Observe the Chicago, Milwaukee, St. Paul & Pacific —a transcontinental carrier operating from the north Pacific coast at Seattle to Chicago over its own lines. It reaches many of the most important markets of the middle west; Milwaukee, the Twin Cities, Omaha and Kansas City. Many trainloads of lumber, wheat, and fruit are consumed in the large centers reached by the St. Paul's lines. Yet for 1924 only a little more than half of its traffic was local to its lines.[6]

It is these powerful trunk lines, originating large volumes of long haul traffic, that dominate the strategy of the interchange situation. In the west the Union Pacific brings its long trainloads of traffic to the Missouri River; the Southern Pacific to the north Texas gateways; the Atchison, Topeka & Santa Fe to Chicago. In the southeast the Louisville and Nashville, the Atlantic Coast Line, the Southern, and the Seaboard Air Line haul their traffic to Ohio and Potomac River gateways. At these points they trade traffic with connections. Many are the lines that want the traffic. But not all get it. Indeed, at many junctions, it would appear that the old Biblical principle that "For whosoever hath, to him shall be given, and he shall have more abundance: but whosoever hath not, from him shall be taken away even that which he hath," is still in operation. The originating carriers balance the comparative importance of many factors in deciding the road to which they deliver the traffic. They enjoy the whip hand in trading out traffic and they expect substantial advantages in return.

Interchange traffic is indeed important to the revenue of trunk line carriers. Even the strongest find their interchange indispensable to the maintenance of satisfactory service to the public and of stable earning power to the stockholders. Within limits they dominate the situation sufficiently to enable them to command a reasonable share of the interchange traffic available. They control the lanes of interchange traffic, and it is improbable that any rearrangement of the ownership of connecting lines on any reasonable scale is likely to exert a really serious effect upon their earnings.

The problems associated with interchange business develop more complex angles and present more serious effects on earnings on those roads usually described as terminal properties. These roads have this in common with the strong trunk lines: they both originate substantial volumes of traffic. But they do not enjoy the same strategic bargaining power with their connections. They serve, as a rule, highly industrialized traffic centers; and originate manufactured articles that frequently compete in common markets with those produced on the lines of the connections to whom they deliver and from whom they receive traffic. Most of the terminal lines perform an expensive gathering service and enjoy a short haul. Even their longest hauls are comparatively short. They are, therefore, burdened with high capital and operating costs; their overhead is high.

The terminal properties not only originate; they also terminate extensive tonnages of traffic. Located as they are in regions of active industrial activity, they serve large consuming markets. Traffic necessary to feed, clothe, shelter, and to indulge the luxuries of the population is received from many carriers for movement over their lines. So it is that the Philadelphia & Reading admits the New York Central, the Erie, the Western Maryland, and the Lehigh Valley into Philadelphia; the Central Railroad of New Jersey admits the Baltimore & Ohio and the roads with which it forms through routes from the south and west into New York City; the New York, New Haven & Hartford, and the Boston & Maine give most of the trunk lines access into New England. Most of the terminal lines, of course, perform both an originating and delivering service.

Through many years of experience and as a result of many factors to be considered subsequently, traffic has come to flow to and from particular lines. In some cases as a result of some unity of interest in financial, operating, or traffic matters, traffic has tended to be interchanged year after year unvaryingly with particular lines. This is the case with the Philadelphia & Reading and the Central Railroad of New Jersey. The former gives the latter entrance into Philadelphia; and the latter gives the former entrance into New York. Both in turn, as a unified terminal line, give the New York Central entrance to Philadelphia, and the Baltimore & Ohio entrance into New York.

In other instances the traffic shifts in interchange from one connection to another. Here the mutuality of interest is based on shallower foundations. The mutuality may indeed be temporary, and even forced to some extent. Witness the so-called Natchez route. (See map on page

INTERCHANGE

261.) Here was a patched-up through line from Shreveport, Louisiana, to Mobile, Alabama, formally approved by the Interstate Commerce Commission, and repeatedly declared by the body as an arrangement in the public interest. The integrity of that route was based on a one-year trackage agreement of that part of the line of the Gulf, Mobile & Northern Railroad extending from Beaumont, Mississippi, to Mobile, Alabama, which for purposes of this route can be considered as a terminal line; and upon a one-year lease of a branch line from that carrier. The refusal to renew the trackage agreement and the lease eliminated the through route.[7]

Terminating and originating lines may form routes that are keenly competitive with other routes. They must be particularly solicitous about making arrangements with connections calculated to produce such a flow of traffic as to produce the largest possible net revenue, for interchange business constitutes a substantial proportion of their traffic. Eighty-one per cent of the Central Railroad of New Jersey,[8] and 82 per cent of the Wheeling & Lake Erie tonnage in 1926 was interchanged with connections;[9] while 79 per cent of the revenue tons of the New York, New Haven & Hartford revenue tonnage in 1924 was so interchanged.[10]

Observe also how heavy is the interchange of these terminal lines with particular carriers. Over 70 per cent of the freight revenue of the Pittsburgh & West Virginia in one year was received from traffic interchanged with the Wheeling & Lake Erie traffic that flowed over a route, a goodly part of which was competitive with the one-line routes of the Baltimore & Ohio, the Pennsylvania and the New York Central.[11] And this route, so vital to the maintenance of the earning power of the Pittsburgh & West Virginia, depends for its success in turn upon three other roads without whose active coöperation the route could not exist. The traffic involved—mostly iron and steel—originates on the Pittsburgh & Lake Erie; from that road it moves over the Pittsburgh & West Virginia, the Wheeling & Lake Erie, the Northern Ohio, and the New York, Chicago & St. Louis to St. Louis. A failure of one hour in a schedule can destroy the usefulness of the route. The large volume of business which the route carries is due largely to a train service about thirteen hours quicker than its closest rival. It is obvious, therefore, that all five participating carriers must work harmoniously, or else they all lose the business. A delay in switching out a load at a small point in Ohio by the Wheeling & Lake Erie recently caused a delay of from seventeen to twenty-two hours on a Pittsburgh–St. Louis shipment. As a consequence of the switching trouble, connections with the Northern Ohio were missed; and the latter in turn, missing connections with the New York, Chicago & St. Louis, was obliged to hold its train over all night. (See map.)

This five-line route, over which a large volume of profitable traffic moves, can thus exist only if all the participating carriers work in close unison. If any consequential delay occurs, the route is impaired through the slowing up of train service. The traffic salesmen of the one-line route, which controls the shipment from origin to destination, will solicit the shippers, and point out the disadvantages of a five-line route, dependent for its efficiency upon a unity of harmony among five separate managements. They will contrast these conditions with the assurance of superior train service afforded by the one-

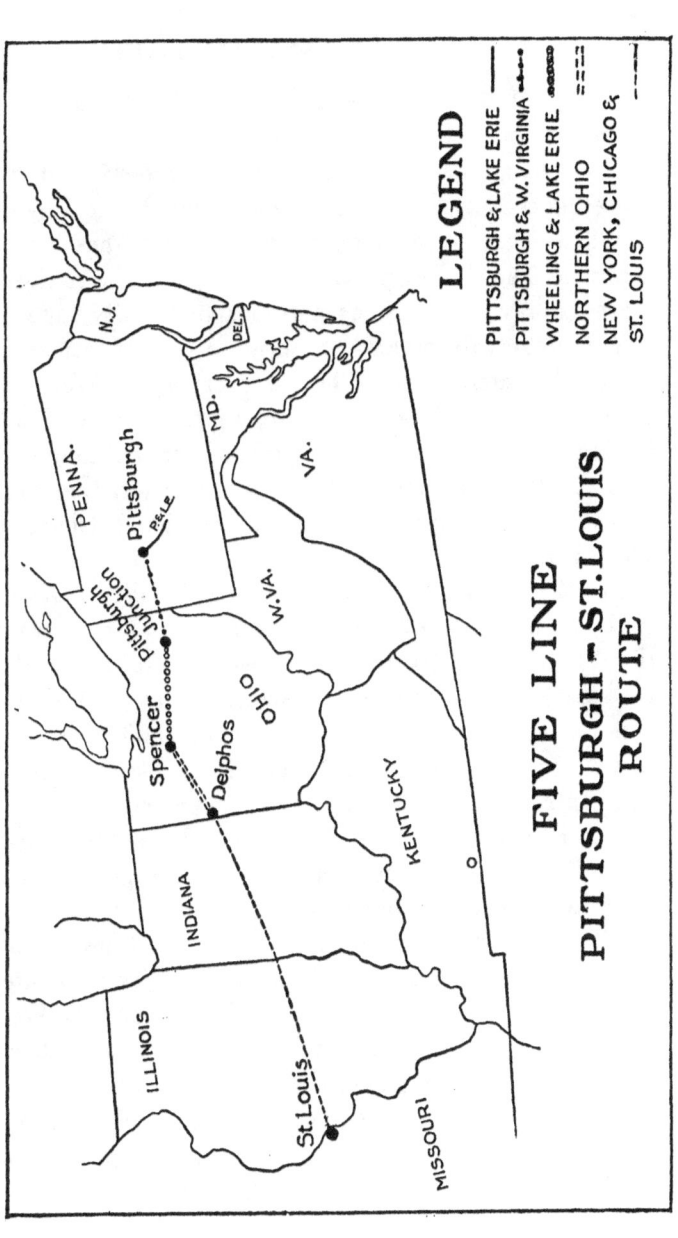

line route of the Baltimore & Ohio, or the Pennsylvania, as the case may be.

The triangular trunk line stock ownership of the Wheeling & Lake Erie having been declared illegal by the Interstate Commerce Commission, its control has become doubtful. The Allegheny Corporation holds the majority share interest. This is of questionable legality, and its title thereto will perhaps be decided in the courts. A substantial interest is held by the Pittsburgh & West Virginia. The dual stock ownership, representative of conflicting business interests, promises to exert an interesting effect on the interchange between the two terminal properties: the Wheeling & Lake Erie, and the Pittsburgh & West Virginia.

The Pittsburgh & West Virginia is vitally interested in the perpetuation of the existing through route of which the Wheeling & Lake Erie is an essential unit. Indeed, a good part of its increasing prosperity is due to the business made possible by its formation in 1923, and it believes that part of the interchange will be lost if the trunk line control of the Wheeling be consummated.

The Pittsburgh & West Virginia and the Wheeling & Lake Erie do not stand alone as terminal properties in their dependence on interchanged traffic with particular carriers. Observe the Central Railroad of New Jersey, which interchanges almost 50 per cent of its total interchange with the Philadelphia & Reading;[12] and the Western Maryland, which interchanges approximately 60 per cent of its total interchange with the Baltimore & Ohio.[13]

The maintenance of such heavy interchanges are clearly necessary to the stability of a road's earning capacity. Any disturbance of the inward or outward flow of traffic with

INTERCHANGE

connections might impair the volume of business done, and the ultimate financial status of such a carrier. A substantial proportion of its traffic, however, originates on its own lines. Not all, but a goodly part of it, can be moved over any connection to a greater or lesser extent. As long as the traffic-producing industries remain in operation, the business must move regardless of the corporate ownership of the connection with which the traffic is interchanged. To move the business, and move it efficiently, is the measure of the public service of a railroad.

Yet it is equally clear that extensive changes in proprietary control of connections might reduce some of the through business of a terminal carrier. In accordance with principles to be discussed in a subsequent chapter, a trunk line connection can oblige the originating line to deliver traffic at some point of interchange, short of that at which it could realize the longest haul and the largest revenue.

Interchange traffic is thus important even to the strong trunk lines and the prosperous terminal lines. This traffic contributes substantially to their earnings. But it is to a different class of carriers that the interchange traffic represents a major business problem. It is their life blood; and to them the prospect of consolidations with the inevitable disturbance of the flow of traffic between connections is either the harbinger of salvation from all business ills or the cause of probably serious adversity.

There are many important stretches of track in this country which form an essential part of through routes. They frequently operate through a country which creates no substantial volume of traffic. But they serve as bridges, connecting roads on either side which serve important areas of production and consumption. Here is the Southern Pacific carrying a trainload of fruit from the Salt River Valley of Arizona to a market in Illinois. It reaches north Texas; and there its lines terminate, but connect with the St. Louis Southwestern which carries the traffic to St. Louis.

Into the Delaware Valley come long trainloads of bituminous coal from West Virginia destined to New England. The New England carriers are some miles distant. Connecting up the road which carries the traffic with the one that receives it are two small lines: the Lehigh & New England, and the Lehigh & Hudson.

In the Missouri Valley, at Kansas City, is the Missouri Pacific transporting trainloads of high-class miscellaneous traffic to destinations in Texas. Its lines run south to southern Kansas and then sweep to the east to Little Rock, Arkansas, before turning west to Texas; a circuitous line reducing the competitive strength of the Missouri Pacific system on traffic from and to points in Missouri west of Jeffersonville, Missouri, from and to points in Texas. But here is the Kansas, Oklahoma & Gulf intersecting the Missouri Pacific just as it begins its wasteful eastward swing on Texas business, and by a north and south line making a direct connection with Missouri Pacific system lines at Denison, Texas. (See map on page 283.)

Many of these so-called bridge or overhead lines—specializing in the expeditious transportation of through traffic from one end of the line to the other—control direct and noncongested lines from and to important regions requiring heavy traffic movements. It would therefore appear to be in the public interest to subject them to intensive use. And it would also seem to the direct advantage of connecting carriers to utilize short lines capable of

INTERCHANGE

moving freight with considerable celerity. Excellent service could be accorded the shippers of the connecting lines; and traffic could be moved economically and efficiently. The financial stability of the bridge carriers would be assured.

These theoretical advantages are not fulfilled in practice. Many bridge lines with direct routes capable of transporting large volumes of traffic remain unused and the flow of traffic over alternative routes presents grave problems to the management of the bridge lines. Originating and terminating lines exercise a considerable control over the movement of traffic. They can within certain limits initiate policies calculated to force their flow over those connections productive of the largest possible revenue. They exert considerable effect upon the movement of interchange traffic. Bridge lines do not enjoy any substantial measure of control over their overhead business: business, that is, received from a connection at one junction on its line and delivered to a connection at another. The movement of the business is controlled by the originating or delivering lines. They decide largely the line over which the traffic will move after it leaves or before it reaches their lines. Only infrequently and to a limited extent can the bridge carriers reach out beyond their own lines into the territory of connections and induce the shippers to move their business over the lines of the soliciting bridge route.

Shippers as a rule do not designate the intermediate carrier in routing their traffic. Eliminating shipments from certain large industries with highly developed traffic departments, about 90 per cent of the shipments tendered (in the opinion of a veteran traffic official) do not show intermediate routes or junction points.[14] The Southern

Pacific can give an intermediate haul on an eastbound transcontinental shipment destined to a point beyond the Mississippi to the Chicago, Rock Island & Pacific; the Texas & Pacific; the Kansas City, Mexico & Orient; the Kansas, Oklahoma & Gulf; the St. Louis & San Francisco; the St. Louis Southwestern or even to the Illinois Central at New Orleans. The shipper in California looks to the Southern Pacific for good service and permits it to use its best judgment in taking the necessary steps, including the selection of intermediate carriers, to accomplish that purpose.

Considerations bearing on the rise and fall of interchange traffic are, therefore, of intense interest to bridge lines, for the possession of a strategically important line is no assurance of the movement of business. The Lehigh & New England is the direct line into New England from the Pennsylvania and Philadelphia & Reading territory in comparison with the circuitous route of its competitor, the Lehigh & Hudson.[15] Yet far more bridge traffic moves via the circuitous route of the Lehigh & Hudson, than over the direct route of the Lehigh & New England. The Pennsylvania Railroad makes no use whatsoever of the Lehigh & New England as a bridge route.[16] It moves its New Haven traffic over the Hell Gate Bridge and Harlem River routes, thus obtaining the long haul; and its Boston & Maine business over the Delaware & Hudson via Wilkes-Barre and Mechanicville.[17] In the event of a disturbance of the Harlem River route the Pennsylvania uses the Lehigh & Hudson,[18] with which it has traded trackage rights for the purpose of forming a through route.[19] (See map on page 41.)

The Philadelphia & Reading also refuses to make ex-

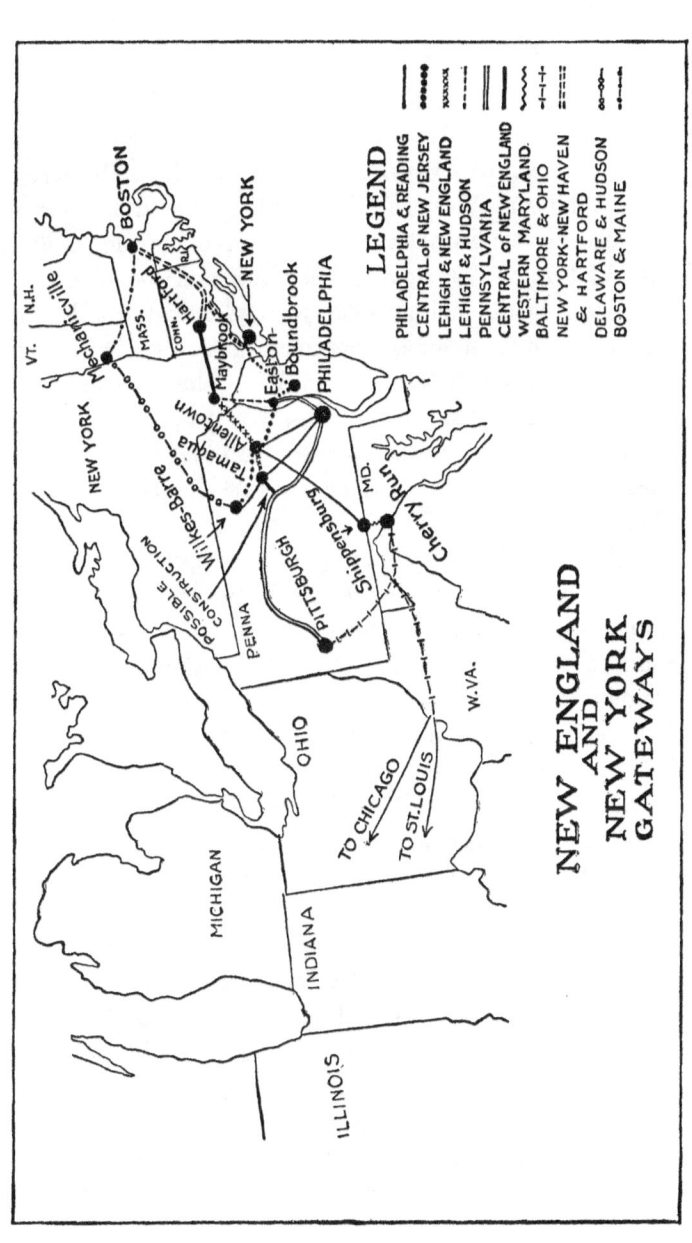

tensive use of the Lehigh & New England for New England bridge traffic. With two notable exceptions (the movement of bituminous coal received from the Baltimore & Ohio, and the Western Maryland by the Philadelphia & Reading at Shippensburg, delivered to the Central Railroad of New Jersey at Allentown and redelivered by the latter to the Lehigh & New England at Bethlehem; and the movement of cement from a limited local territory) the Lehigh & New England is a closed gateway for New England overhead business. Except for the two instances noted, the Philadelphia & Reading does not quote through rates via the Lehigh & New England on New England business.[20] The president of the Philadelphia & Reading has definitely stated that, "There has been almost no pass-over business on the Lehigh & New England into New England. Practically all of that business that comes from the south and west that has gone into New England over our line has gone in over the Lehigh & Hudson." [21] The Philadelphia & Reading (together with its stock controlled Central Railroad of New Jersey) interchanges its overhead New England traffic at Easton with the Lehigh & Hudson, rather than with the Lehigh & New England at Bethlehem, thereby getting an additional haul of eleven miles.

The circumstance that its connecting carriers happen to realize a somewhat longer haul via its line than via the line of the Lehigh & New England gives the Lehigh & Hudson a comparatively large tonnage. And it needs this business, too, for its originated traffic is very light, amounting in 1925 to less than 20 per cent of its total traffic.[22] It derives most of its overhead interchange from one line, the Central Railroad of New Jersey: this business amounting in 1923 to over 50 per cent;[23] and in 1924 to almost 70 per cent of its total tonnage.[24]

The continuance of this traffic movement is dependent upon the maintenance of present conditions respecting its connections—conditions over which it has no control. That these conditions will remain the same is by no means certain; on the contrary, it is probable that existing conditions may change to the detriment of the Lehigh & Hudson.

The attempted acquisition of the Lehigh & New England by the Philadelphia & Reading a few years ago promised to upset the flow of traffic towards the Lehigh & Hudson. The acquiring line announced its intention of moving its anthracite coal destined for New England via the Lehigh & New England, to the detriment of the latter's bridge competitor which now moves the traffic. It expressed its determination to open up through routes and establish joint rates on soft coal as well as on merchandise via the Lehigh & New England in connection with the Pennsylvania, the Baltimore & Ohio, the Western Maryland, the Norfolk & Western, and the Chesapeake & Ohio.[25] Not all, but most of the overhead interchange of the Lehigh & Hudson with the Central Railroad of New Jersey, which in 1924 amounted to 70 per cent of its tonnage, appeared likely to be diverted to the Lehigh & New England.

At about the same time the interchange of the Lehigh & Hudson appeared to be threatened from another direction. The reader may have reasonably well asked: if the Philadelphia & Reading–Central Railroad of New Jersey insisted upon moving traffic from Bethlehem to Easton to get its long haul via the Lehigh & Hudson, why should it not have insisted further upon moving the same traffic eastward to Jersey City for interchange with the New Haven via the Harlem River? The controller is here controlled. The New Haven, the terminating line, controls the originating line. The New Haven, for business reasons sufficiently sound unto itself, refuses to accept any business originating west of Hagerstown for movement via the Harlem River; that is, it refuses to do so on the basis of through rates—the only rates on which this business will move. This traffic, therefore, can only move over the inland routes—over the two valley lines. It is immaterial to the New Haven over which of these two lines the traffic moves. Its revenue is the same, for it receives the traffic at the same junction point.

This policy of the New Haven has never been approved of by the Central Railroad of New Jersey. It has not appreciated the equity of an arrangement obliging it to terminate its haul at Easton when it might just as well haul the traffic seventy-three miles farther east to Jersey City, and thereby increase its gross revenue (in 1923) about $1,700,000.[26] It therefore asked the Interstate Commerce Commission to compel the New York, New Haven & Hartford to establish through rates with the Central Railroad of New Jersey via New York Harbor. The effect of the establishment of these rates, had they been established as requested, upon the revenues of the Lehigh & Hudson, would have been serious indeed.

These complex considerations and their constant action and reaction cannot be controlled by the bridge carriers. Yet their operation may easily deprive them of the revenue indispensable to their financial integrity. Witness the St. Louis Southwestern, a fairly consistent earner, the prosperity of which is dependent largely upon bridge

INTERCHANGE

traffic received from and delivered to connections. Seventy per cent of its traffic neither originates on nor is destined to any part of its line.[27] From 30 per cent to 40 per cent of its net revenue was derived from traffic interchange with the Southern Pacific in 1925.[28]

One of the important problems confronting the management of this property is the maintenance of the present flow of interchange traffic along present channels. Recent railroad unifications in its territory have reduced its interchange business. The acquisition of the Vicksburg route (consisting of the Vicksburg, Shreveport & Pacific, and the Alabama & Vicksburg) by the Illinois Central has cost the St. Louis Southwestern the haul from Memphis to Shreveport. The Illinois Central, prior to this acquisition, had no line to Shreveport; and it delivered at Memphis to the St. Louis Southwestern a part of its traffic bound for Shreveport and beyond. With access to Shreveport through acquisition of the Vicksburg route, it carries its traffic to Shreveport over its own line—circuitous as this may be in contrast with the direct route of the St. Louis Southwestern.[29]

The acquisition of the Texas & Pacific, and the International Great Northern by the Missouri Pacific promises to reduce the traffic interchanged between the first two carriers and the St. Louis Southwestern. The traffic manager of the latter has stated "that if the consolidation (referring to the Missouri Pacific System) is as strong as it has been, and we expect it will be, they will succeed in turning at least 50 per cent of the traffic we now receive to their direct connection." [30]

The prospective union of corporate interests based upon existing interlocking directorates of the Chicago, Rock

Island & Pacific, and the St. Louis & San Francisco threatens the St. Louis Southwestern traffic interchange at another point. The Rock Island in recent years has delivered considerable traffic to the St. Louis Southwestern at Brinkley and Fordyce, Arkansas. The northbound movement of this traffic is controlled by the Rock Island, and it is within its power to divert it to the lines of the St. Louis & San Francisco at Memphis. These traffic diversions represent the logical consequences of railroad consolidation. Their effect upon the earnings of a carrier like the St. Louis Southwestern might be serious. If it were to depend for its prosperity upon the carriage of traffic it originates on its own lines, it could not exist. It must bend every effort to obtain a fair share of traffic from other lines. Under such circumstances, consolidation with other lines controlling the movement of a large volume of traffic seems to be the only solution. As will be shown later on, however, this by no means follows.

NOTES TO CHAPTER II

1. Consolidation Proceedings, Docket 12964, Brief for St. Louis Chamber of Commerce, p. 32.
2. Abandonment of branches by Boston & Maine, 105 I.C.C. 13; 68; 111 I.C.C. 500, 524; 117 I.C.C. 680. See also Applications for abandonments, Finance Docket 4475, etc., Applicant's Brief, p. 7.
3. Consolidation Proceedings, Docket 12964, Brief for Great Northern in support of consolidation of Chicago, Burlington & Quincy, Great Northern and Northern Pacific and subsidiaries, p. 53.
4. *Supra*, testimony of Hale Holden given at hearings, November 17 and 18, 1922; January 23, 1923, and March 1 and 2, 1923, p. 28.
5. *Supra*, exhibit no. 60, section no. 7.
6. Freight revenue traffic, separated as to source for the calendar year 1924, Office of Freight Auditor, Chicago, No. 6, 1925.
7. Acquisition of line by B. & H. S. R. R., 90 I.C.C. 448.
8. Consolidation Proceedings, Docket 12964, Brief for Port of New York Authority, p. 339.
9. Interlocking Directors of Wheeling & Lake Erie and Trunk Lines, Finance Docket 3584, exhibit no. 7.

INTERCHANGE 47

10. Communication from New York, New Haven & Hartford, dated October 28, 1925.
11. Interlocking Directors of Wheeling & Lake Erie and Trunk Lines, Finance Docket 3584, Brief for Daniel Willard et al, p. 43; see also testimony of W. H. Nehtken, Vice President and General Manager, Pittsburgh & West Virginia, *supra*, tr. pp. 758-759.
12. Consolidation Proceedings, Docket 12964, Brief for Reading Company, p. 103.
13. Interlocking Directors of Wheeling & Lake Erie and Trunk Lines, Finance Docket 3584, Brief for Daniel Willard et al, p. 7.
14. Central Railroad vs. New York, New Haven & Hartford, Docket 16721. Statement of C. L. Ewing, General Freight Agent, Central Railroad of New Jersey, tr. pp. 82-83.
15. Lease of Lehigh & New England, Finance Docket 5639, exhibit no. 9.
16. *Supra*, Brief for Reading Company, p. 34.
17. *Supra*, p. 68.
18. Central Railroad vs. New York, New Haven & Hartford, Finance Docket 16721, Brief for Central Railroad of New Jersey, p. 100.
19. Lease of Lehigh & New England, Finance Docket 5639, Brief for Reading Company, pp. 33-34.
20. *Supra*, p. 31.
21. *Supra*, Brief for Pennsylvania Railroad, p. 13.
22. *Supra*, exhibit no. 40.
23. Central Railroad vs. New York, New Haven & Hartford, 122 I.C.C. 661.
24. Central Railroad vs. New York, New Haven & Hartford, Docket 16721, Brief for Respondents, pp. 10-11.
25. Lease of Lehigh & New England, Finance Docket 5639, Brief for Reading Company, pp. 42-43.
26. Central Railroad vs. New York, New Haven & Hartford, Docket 16721, exhibit no. 26.
27. Proposed acquisition of St. Louis Southwestern, Finance Docket 4809, Brief for St. Louis Southwestern in support of Exceptions filed in opposition to report of C. B. Burnside, Examiner, p. 14.
28. Statement of W. E. Meyer in *Wall Street Journal*, September 28, 1928.
29. Southwestern Unification case, Finance Docket 5679, tr. p. 1229.
30. *Supra*, tr. pp. 1231-1232.

CHAPTER III

CONTROL OF TRAFFIC MOVEMENTS

Every road enjoys the possession of a monopoly on some volume of traffic. Shippers at stations local to one road have no preference; they are compelled perforce to hand over business to the single transportation property that serves them exclusively. But to think of the railroad business in any but competitive terms is an economic illusion. Few are the properties the local traffic of which is in sufficient volume to yield an adequate return on invested capital. Every important line needs a certain volume of through traffic in order to utilize its property most effectively. And every road is ready and able to carry its share of the through business. Only under most extraordinary conditions is a property operated to capacity to an extent obliging it to refuse to accept additional traffic. On the contrary, every road needs additional business—a need emphasized by the inroads of the gas engine, the steamship, and the airplane.

This struggle for additional traffic is never ceasing. And every road participates therein. Short lines with circuitous and unattractive routes send salesmen into far-off territory to fight for a bit of traffic. Agents of western roads in eastern cities, and agents of eastern roads in western cities represent the interests of their respective principals. The Chicago Great Western, controlling a line between the Missouri River and Chicago, solicits traffic in trans-Mis-

CONTROL OF TRAFFIC MOVEMENTS 49

souri territory. It requests shippers located on the Union Pacific to instruct that line to deliver their eastbound shipments to the Chicago Great Western at Omaha for carriage to Chicago. And the agents of the Union Pacific endeavor to persuade them to commit their interests to its protection. It delivers traffic safely and expeditiously. It has done so in the past, and will continue to do so in the future.

Many roads thus compete for the opportunity to carry the same traffic. And they all appeal to the shipper with their respective contentions. The shipper, it would appear, is the august dispensing agency, directing the movements of his traffic over this, that, or the other line. And the law of the land appears to support the shipper in the exercise of this power.

The shippers may enjoy the theoretical substance of power. In practice, however, the substance insensibly tends to fade into a shadow. With sufficient exceptions necessary to establish the validity of the rule, it will be found that the initial carrier is able to control the routing of the traffic.

Assuming that rates are the same over all routes, a shipper will route traffic over the line that affords him the best service (aside, of course, from considerations of personal favoritism). Excellent service comprehends such factors as time required for delivery, safety of goods in transit, promptness in settling claims and tracing shipments, and frequency and reliability in train service. If a shipper is satisfied along these lines, he cares little over what particular routes his shipment moves. James H. Hustis, former president of the Boston & Maine Railroad, has well stated that "so long as the quality of service is maintained, the question of routing should not be of material interest to the shipper." [1]

This is the crux of the situation. Every road endeavors to furnish the best type of service it can. It employs a staff of salesmen to solicit the shipper's business and to explain the advantages of shipping over its road. One road makes prompter delivery between selected points; another affords superior transit privileges; and yet another performs free switching services. These armies of salesmen are backed up by well-conceived traffic policies that are worked out by the executive traffic officials.

In this competitive struggle the home road is ordinarily successful in capturing the business. It succeeds because it can supply the best service; primarily because it is the home road; and there are many things a road can do, to use the language of the veteran traffic official of the Seaboard Air Line, "that make it almost necessary for the patrons of a line to use routes which are favored by the railroad upon which they are dependent for local facilities." [2] The immense power enjoyed by the initial carrier in obtaining a shipment for its long haul is but little understood. Its resultant ability to divert large volumes of traffic from one connection to another, thus changing established trade routes and channels of commerce, cannot be ascribed to artificial factors. It is the result of the working of sound business principles.

The primary advantage of the originating carrier is due to its proximity to the shipper. Its representatives are constantly accessible to him; and they are usually thoroughly known to him, as well. It furnishes him with his industrial sidings; it delivers his carloads on its team tracks, and it stores his less-than-carload shipments in its

CONTROL OF TRAFFIC MOVEMENTS 51

transfer houses. If the shipper wants any cars he calls on the initial line; and if he wants spotting privileges, this line must perform the work. In industries long established on the road, the physical layout of the plant is frequently adjusted to the physical plant of the carrier.

The size of financial strength of the home lines from this viewpoint is not important. As home lines, they have it in their power (assuming reasonably good management) to afford a superior grade of service. The strategic position occupied by large shippers at important industrial and commercial centers may obscure the vital underlying situation. They may seem to hold the whip hand, and they are not influenced by powerful dominant trunk lines, than whom in many cases they are financially stronger.

So complete is this control over traffic routing by large shippers, that they frequently allocate their tonnage between various railroads. The larger the shipper, the more likely is this practice to be followed, assuming that the service afforded by all roads is substantially the same. The process of consolidation, however, disturbs this very equilibrium of equality in service.

The acquisition of one road by another results in the establishment of a superior standard of service over the route formed by and with the acquiring road; and of an inferior grade of service, to a greater or lesser degree, by and with the route formed with the road which competes with the acquiring road. The discrimination in service does not always develop immediately. The traffic policies initiated by the new management do, however, tend to concentrate the flow of traffic over the line of the proprietary road. Even the most powerful shippers cannot retard the evolution of these forces; and when convinced of the superiority of service over the new route, divert their business accordingly.

Outwardly, the traffic relations of the acquired road with its connections appear to remain unchanged. The rates are the same; the through rates are the same; the divisions remain unchanged. Apparently, the shipper's legal right to route his traffic remains undisturbed. He can, if he so chooses, send his traffic over any one of the numerous connections available. But sooner or later, the individual shipper will find it to his advantage to route over the road, which has acquired the property to which he delivers his freight, and from which he receives it; the road upon which he must call for extra cars in time of emergency; the road which spots his car just at that particular point on his private siding which best facilitates his loading and unloading; the road to which he must appeal for a new transit privilege to aid him in competing in far-off markets. The right to designate the routing, as the Interstate Commerce Commission stated recently, is exercised by the shipper only in exceptional cases, the matter of routes being subordinate to service.[3]

The power of the originating road, in brief, to afford better service over its route and connections, than that afforded over any other, lies at the heart of these traffic diversions.

Aside from personal favoritism, railroad competition nowadays is almost entirely service competition. Now that the regulatory commission controls both minimum and maximum rates, it is improbable that any serious rate competition could ever develop. The constituent elements of service competition have been well stated in the following summary:

CONTROL OF TRAFFIC MOVEMENTS 53

(a) despatch, or time required for getting goods to destination; (b) safety of goods in transit; (c) promptness in settlement of claims, when lost or damaged, and absence of narrow technicalities in the process of adjusting claims; (d) frequency and reliability of the train service; (e) carrier's special equipment for handling such commodities as livestock and perishable articles; (f) carrier's special attention to certain types of traffic; (g) carrier's willingness to trace shipments or keep shipper informed of the movement of important shipments; (h) carrier's willingness to support shipper's desire for change in rates, rules, or classification; (i) situation of the carrier's line, to avoid congested districts, or to constitute an alternative route in times of traffic embargoes. Shippers also aim to favor with a long haul the carrier which does their intraplant switching.[4]

Perhaps the most important aspect of railroad service is the time required to move a shipment from point of origin to point of destination. This is particularly so under modern conditions of distribution. Few merchants to-day buy in anticipation of future demand. They buy in close accordance with their needs. They rush their orders from manufacturers. Expedited and efficient transportation service is imperative in such a scheme of distribution.

The organization required to produce the required highclass train service is complex. It requires a superior degree of coördination between the lines that form the through route; between the originating road and the shipper; and between the delivering road and the consignee. The various details (particularly on preference service): the time of departure, the time of arrival, the exact hour of interchange with connections, the adjustment of switching service to train schedules, the nice observance of reconsignment instructions, etc., can be perfected only through long and continuous experience and practice.

Expeditious movement of trains thus constitutes one important element of railroad service. Adequate terminal facilities are equally as important. The proper disposition of terminals is one of the knotty problems of consolidation. The subject is of extensive scope and import; and deserves, in fact requires, more elaborate consideration than it has received and which it can receive here.

That proprietary interest in terminal lines leads to preferential routing is well known in the railroad field. An extensive discussion of this subject would lead too far afield. A recent illustration will perhaps suffice. The Indiana Harbor Belt is a terminal line serving many important shippers in Chicago. Through stock ownership, it is controlled by the New York Central, Michigan Central, Chicago & North Western, and the Chicago, Milwaukee, St. Paul & Pacific. The road connects physically with New York Central lines, as well as with others, including among the latter, the Chicago, Indianapolis & Louisville. This property competes with the New York Central and they serve many points in common in Indiana and Kentucky. Both compete for the line haul on traffic originating on the Harbor Belt. A shipper located thereon enjoys the legal privilege to route his business over any trunk line. In 1921, a shipper forwarded a car from East Chicago to Ashland, Ky., via the Indiana Harbor Belt–Chicago, Indianapolis & Louisville. The delivery was made three days after loading by the shipper in East Chicago. The New York Central, however, was guaranteeing prompter delivery. This it could safely promise because it removed its cars from the shipper's industry tracks the same day the cars were loaded—provided the shipment was routed over its long haul. But if it were routed via its competitor, the cars were not moved so promptly. The delayed delivery on the Ashland shipment over the Chicago, Indianapolis & Louisville was called to the shipper's attention by a New York Central man.[5] Would any shipper continue to route his freight over a line which thus affords markedly inferior service?

Terminal lines like the Indiana Harbor Belt, Central Railroad of New Jersey, New York, New Haven & Hartford, of which there are many throughout the country, not only originate large volumes of freight. They also deliver freight originating on other roads. In that capacity they serve as extensive reservoirs through which this freight passes to destination. Such terminal lines bear the same intimate relation to consignees that the initial lines bear to the shipper. The same roads serve the same shippers in a twofold capacity. They expedite the outbound movement, and insure prompt delivery on the inbound movement. If the terminal line enjoys financial or traffic affiliation with one of its trunk line connections, it possesses the power (as does an initial carrier) of inducing a routing preferential to its friendly connection. Again there is no question of rates: uniformity of rates is assured by federal law. Only the service varies. Allow the friendly road better service than the other, and, in the absence of other factors, that road will secure the long inbound haul.

The flow of traffic over the New York City–Harlem River route between trunk line territory and New England may serve to clarify the point under discussion. The Central Railroad of New Jersey, Lehigh Valley, and

Pennsylvania interchange New England-bound tonnage with the New York, New Haven & Hartford. (See map on page 41.) The Pennsylvania has invested heavily in the stock of the latter; and both have a joint financial interest in the New York Connecting Railroad, which, in itself, helps in providing an expedited service to and from New England. It is natural that the two carriers should co-operate closely and go to great lengths in providing a service superior to that afforded to any other route. The superior service given the Pennsylvania by the New York, New Haven & Hartford may be told in the language of an official of the Central Railroad of New Jersey—the line, be it remembered, that interchanges the least traffic:

Daily three fast freight trains are operated, it is stated, from Oak Point to Boston without stopping at Cedar Hill. These trains contain P.R.R. merchandise freight, but no C.R.R. or L.V. freight. . . .

Each day there are 9 regular trains operated from Harlem River and 17 from Oak Point. The freight of the C.R.R. and L.V. is handled only in trains from Oak Point. In the effort, however, to give P.R.R. traffic special treatment some of its freight are rushed from Oak Point to be placed in fast trains handling pier freight from Harlem River, and on the other hand, some pier freight is daily hurried over to Oak Point to be made up into fast trains with P.R.R. traffic. By this manœuvering in and around Oak Point it is possible to start P.R.R. freight in fast trains from both Oak Point and Harlem River. Of course, Oak Point Yard was never designed for any such operation and the result apparently is that while P.R.R. traffic is expedited, C.R.R. and L.V. traffic are slowed up.[6]

The standard of train service, in short, is an important consideration in determining the shipper's choice of

CONTROL OF TRAFFIC MOVEMENTS 57

routes. And the originating carrier, ordinarily, enjoys the power (and in the absence of any more powerful balancing considerations usually exercises it) of affording superior train service to those who route their shipments via those lines and connections which yield it the best revenue.

Speed in the movement of trains does not spell the whole story of efficient railroad service. Elaborate terminal facilities must be provided to collect, distribute, and warehouse freight. Team tracks, private tracks, and sidetracks; car floats and lighters; coal and iron ore docks; warehouses and elevators are only some of the many that may be mentioned. These are in almost all cases furnished by the originating carrier; and it usually invests large amounts of fixed capital in their provision. It is, therefore, not unreasonable to anticipate that it will exploit their use in the solicitation of traffic for movement over those routes which afford it the best revenue.

The advantages of the originating road are ordinarily thoroughly exploited. In many cases the use of specialized terminal facilities are denied to competing roads and their shippers. The iron ore docks at Huron, Ohio, owned by the Wheeling & Lake Erie, are closed to the New York Central.[7] Only an insignificant tonnage is delivered by the Wheeling to the New York Central at Huron, amounting to seventeen tons in 1926.[8] The docks at Lorain, Ohio, owned by the Baltimore & Ohio, are, on the other hand, closed to the Wheeling & Lake Erie, so that little, if any, ore traffic is interchanged between these carriers at that point.[9] At Canton, Ohio, the storage warehouse owned by the Wheeling & Lake Erie is closed to the Baltimore & Ohio.[10] The traffic interchange of the Wheeling &

Lake Erie at that point is largely with the Pennsylvania, to the competitive disadvantage of the Baltimore & Ohio.[11]

This absence of business reciprocity between the lines seems to be carried out with a fair degree of consistency. A shipper served exclusively by the team track of one road cannot route freight over the other. The traffic is controlled by the road furnishing the team track. A shipper in Cleveland located on the team track of the New York Central cannot route Toledo-bound freight over the Wheeling & Lake Erie; and conversely, one located on the latter's team tracks in the same city, cannot route a Toledo-bound shipment over the New York Central.[12] Of the tonnage hauled by the New York, Chicago & St. Louis at Cleveland during a typical month in 1926—a tonnage amounting to 10.6 per cent of its total tonnage for the month—over 20 per cent was "loaded or unloaded on the team tracks or through its freight houses . . . and these facilities cannot be reached by the Wheeling & Lake Erie or by any other line." [13]

In the southwest at Kansas City the Missouri-Kansas-Texas cannot obtain access to many industries located on the terminal tracks of the Kansas City Southern.[14] In the northwest at a typical city like Seattle, Washington, recent studies reveal the extraordinary extent to which exclusive control of access to industries is reflected in the capture of competitive long haul tonnage. The Great Northern and the Northern Pacific on the lines of which approximately 75 per cent of the industries of the community are exclusively located, handle 71 per cent of the competitive tonnage originating at that point. And "at practically all other points in the Northwest," continues

CONTROL OF TRAFFIC MOVEMENTS 59

this study, "the same situation exists, although in varying degree." [15]

At Seattle, the Chicago, Milwaukee, St. Paul & Pacific is a comparatively new line. It does not connect with as many industries as do its northern competitors. It therefore obtains only about 12 per cent of the available business. In Milwaukee, Wisconsin, on the other hand, it is an old and well-established line. About 65 per cent of the industries of that city are situated on its own exclusive tracks; and it accordingly handles from 65 per cent to 70 per cent of the business of the city.[16]

The ownership of industrial tracks gives a carrier the preferential opportunity to command the routing of the business moving thereover. The road that has the rails gets the business.

Such a business situation does not prevail on all lines and in all parts of the country. For competitive reasons a road which controls track facilities may permit free routing over other lines. But again, it is important to observe that the originating road can, if commercially desirable, initiate policies which eventually will enable it to divert the line haul over such roads and connections which will yield it the most satisfactory profit.

An excellent illustration of routing control due to ownership of terminal facilities is afforded by the situation in Houston, Texas. Both the Missouri-Kansas-Texas and the Southern Pacific serve that city. A majority of the fruit and produce houses are located on the latter's tracks. A profitable volume of freight moves from the northwest to Houston. Most of it moves via the Fort Worth & Denver City as an immediate carrier. The Missouri-Kansas-Texas has endeavored to obtain a haul on that business but has found itself handicapped on account of its lack of terminal facilities in Houston. A good percentage of this traffic can move over participating lines to Council Grove, Kansas, thence over the Missouri-Kansas-Texas, thence to a connection with the Southern Pacific at a north Texas gateway. The Missouri-Kansas-Texas offered to establish concurrences via this gateway. Such a movement would have given the Missouri-Kansas-Texas a part of the haul, and a division of the rate. But the Southern Pacific refused to accept the offer. It apparently believed that once its competitor obtained the traffic it would move it all the way to Houston. Not even the offer by the Missouri-Kansas-Texas, that in such an event it would give the Southern Pacific the same division of the rate as if the shipment had moved over the Southern Pacific, would induce the latter to change its mind.[17]

Its industrial track layout in Houston thus enables the Southern Pacific to control the channel of traffic over which this business moves. This condition prevails in many of the principal cities in Texas. The Southern Pacific is "well entrenched, in an industrial way, at all of the principal cities in Texas and many of the towns and cities have been built up around them through the course of the last forty or fifty years, and they are in a position, by reason of their relation to the various industries, warehouses, and wholesale jobbing and distributing houses, to command a volume of traffic which could not be readily diverted from them." [18] The line enjoys the power to arrange its varied and complicated services, so as to make it good business for shippers to route over those lines and connections which bespeak good business for the Southern Pacific.

CONTROL OF TRAFFIC MOVEMENTS 61

The terminal situation at Kansas City is another illustration in point. The St. Louis & San Francisco operates a circuitous route from St. Louis to Kansas City. From St. Louis its line runs directly southwest to Springfield, before turning north to Kansas City. The lines of the Missouri Pacific, and Missouri-Kansas-Texas, its chief competitors, enjoy the use of a comparatively direct water-grade line. Yet "it is undoubtedly a fact," states the president of the St. Louis & San Franciso, "that the location of a manufacuring plant on the tracks of one line does tend to give that line an advantage in the solicitation of traffic which it ships or receives. This advantage has enabled the Frisco to control a great deal of traffic moving from St. Louis and points east to Kansas City for its long line through Springfield, Mo., a distance of 427 miles." [19]

Witness the terminal situation in Baltimore. Important piers at that point in Baltimore are owned by the Baltimore & Ohio. They are not available for use by the Western Maryland. (At least, this was the situation prior to the stock control of the latter by the former.) Freight arriving by the Western Maryland in Baltimore is delivered to ships at Baltimore & Ohio piers by lightering to the off-side of the ship. This entails unloading of the car on the pier and transfer from the pier to the lighter, the towing of the lighter about a mile to the ship side and the placing of the freight within reach of the ship's tackle. The cars of the Baltimore & Ohio, on the other hand, are delivered directly from car to ship and from ship to car (the piers being equipped with tracks).[20]

The advantages of its shipping facilities which include also the "most modern grain elevator along the Atlantic Coast and the most expeditious coal handling machinery anywhere" are brought to the attention of shippers by moving pictures displayed before shippers' organizations. "We rely on our facilities for attracting business as against our competitors," [21] properly says a Baltimore & Ohio official. Such business could not be as successfully attracted if the use of those facilities were open for use by its competitors.

Another group of valuable water-front terminal properties located in the New York terminal district represents a prize for which several powerful trunk line carriers have keenly contended. Next to the battle waged by the Chicago, Burlington & Quincy against the chopping up of the system of which it forms a part, the most vigorous battle perhaps engendered by the tentative consolidation plan of the Interstate Commerce Commission was that involving the control of the Central Railroad of New Jersey. Both the New York Central and the Baltimore & Ohio, represented by their respective presidents, debated its control before the federal regulatory body. This comparatively small road gives the New York Central an alternative entrance into New York City directly from the west; and gives to the Baltimore & Ohio its only entrance into the same city from the south. In addition it controls extensive piers, and (it is said) the largest area of undeveloped water-front properties in the New York terminal district. The prospect of the control of the Central Railroad of New Jersey by the New York Central led an executive of the Port Authority to declare that the New York Central in that event would "control the entire situation, that is, practically all of the water front and the facilities supporting the water front from a point just south of Edgewater all the way to Perth Amboy. Of course, having control of all

CONTROL OF TRAFFIC MOVEMENTS 63

the facilities, the New York Central would be able to control the routing of the traffic to a large extent." [22]

Beyond the exploitation of fixed plant facilities to control the movement of traffic over those routes which yield it the best return, the initial line has resort to many ingenious tariff devices grouped generically as transit restrictions. Efficient large-scale production under modern industrial conditions require a considerable degree of centralization. Low costs are essential to compete successfully and low costs require an assembly of raw materials, specialized machinery and skilled labor available only at selected points. Factories and mills are usually located many miles from the source of raw material on one hand, and the markets of consumption on the other. Wheat moves from the winter wheat fields of Kansas to mills along the Missouri Valley. It is there made into flour and then shipped to consuming markets. And grain from the spring wheat states of Minnesota, Montana and the Dakotas is forwarded to mills at Minneapolis or Buffalo for conversion into flour. To facilitate the carriage of grain from the fields, its conversion into flour at the mill and its delivery in the form of bread to the table of the consumer, many roads provide milling in transit arrangements. The entire movement from point of origin of the wheat to the point of destination of the milled flour is carried on one through rate.

Lumber from the stands of the northwest are carried to treating plants at intermediate points; there made into telegraph poles or railroad ties and shipped out to a destination on a through rate. A transit arrangement makes this possible.

Devices of this kind—transit arrangements, reconsignment provisions, concentration privileges, etc.—provide the initial carrier with further ammunition to capture the control of the routing of traffic. If shippers route over those lines affording the initial carrier the most satisfactory revenue, they are likely to secure the most desirable transit privileges; and conversely, should they insist upon routing their business against the revenue interests of the initial carrier, they are likely not to secure the benefits of the most favored tariff clause.

Examine this consistent demonstration of the point at issue in transcontinental strategy. The Great Northern and Northern Pacific both operate over their own lines from the Twin Cities to Seattle, Washington. They both reach Portland, Oregon, through the Spokane, Portland & Seattle, which they control through equal share ownership. If a shipment moves directly to Seattle over the direct line of the Great Northern or the Northern Pacific either property receives the full rate to destination. But if business bound for Seattle moves via Portland, it is transferred to the Spokane, Portland & Seattle at Spokane. The originating line loses a part of the haul and divides a part of the rate with another line. On corn, barley, and oats moving from Minneapolis and Sioux City to Seattle via Portland, the Great Northern and Northern Pacific grant no transit service. But if a shipment destined for Portland moves via Seattle, then the transit service is granted. For in the latter case, the lines of origin enjoy the long haul and full revenue.[23]

The Union Pacific pursues a policy reverse to that of the Great Northern and the Northern Pacific. It is located farther south, and its lines reach Portland directly from the south. It realizes a long haul on a Portland shipment

CONTROL OF TRAFFIC MOVEMENTS

and therefore grants transit service on such business. A shipper from Kansas City or Omaha can ship coarse grains to Seattle, Washington, and enjoy transit arrangements at Portland. But if a shipper at these points directs the Union Pacific to move Portland-bound traffic via Seattle, the initial carrier not only grants no transit, it also refuses to quote a through rate.

Another recent case before the Interstate Commerce Commission revealed that many eastern carriers—the Erie, New York Central, Lehigh Valley, Central Railroad of New Jersey, Delaware, Lackawanna & Western—grant milling in transit privileges only if flour moves out to destinations over specific connections via specific junctions. From Bangor, Pennsylvania, the Lehigh & New England runs south to a connection with the Central Railroad of New Jersey via Catasauqua; while the Delaware, Lackawanna & Western runs north and west to Taylor, Pennsylvania, to a junction with the Central Railroad of New Jersey. Flour from Bangor mills can move to southeastern Pennsylvania and New Jersey either via the Lehigh & New England or the Delaware, Lackawanna & Western. If the flour milled at Bangor with inbound grain from the south and west is sent out via Taylor, transit is afforded. If the flour is forwarded via Catasauqua, thus depriving the Delaware, Lackawanna & Western of an outbound haul, only combination rates apply.[24]

Reconsignment privileges have also become vitally important to commerce and trade. Distributing outlets for many staple commodities are nation-wide; the fruit of Florida, southeastern Texas, and southern California find common markets in Chicago and along the Atlantic coast. Markets for bituminous coal have within recent years overstepped the boundaries usually set by distance factors. Low volatile coal from West Virginia that found its major market in eastern points before 1920, now moves west in large volume and competes in the Ohio Valley with coal produced close at home in Illinois and Indiana. Of the three important carriers penetrating the southern West Virginia coal fields, only two—the Norfolk & Western and the Chesapeake & Ohio—control satisfactory lines to the west; and only they had given their coal operators the opportunity to solicit trade in the markets beyond the Ohio. The increase, for example, in the westbound coal traffic of the Chesapeake & Ohio has been remarkable, increasing from less than 17,000 tons in 1920 to more than 38,000,000 in 1925. The eastbound traffic during this period showed an increase from 11,700,000 tons to approximately 13,000,000.

The operators in Virginian territory—the third line—insisted upon an equality of opportunity. They wanted to compete in the Ohio and Mississippi valleys. But the Virginian was adamant. It refused to establish through westbound rates with connections. The road had been built chiefly to bring coal to tidewater at Hampton Roads; and it refused to participate in a westbound short-haul movement that would bring it no profit and possibly some loss.

The dispute was submitted to the Interstate Commerce Commission. The Virginian was ordered to establish joint westbound rates via the Chesapeake & Ohio.[25] That order the road resisted. It fought vainly to reopen the case. It then asked for an injunction to restrain the Commission. That was denied. It appealed to the United States Supreme Court; and the request for an injunction was again denied.[26] Joint rates via the Chesapeake & Ohio to

CONTROL OF TRAFFIC MOVEMENTS 67

the west were duly established; and it would seem that the Virginian, the initial line for the movement, would be obliged to take severe losses; since according to its president, the road lost money on every ton of coal that moved via the new route.[27]

The Virginian, however, had not shot its last bolt. It joins physically with the Norfolk & Western as well as with the Chesapeake & Ohio. The Norfolk & Western, with the Virginian, forms a route more circuitous than that of the Chesapeake & Ohio; and it compels the scaling of a number of divides. It does possess one great advantage, however, for it yields the line of origin a higher remuneration. On the authority of its president, the Virginian "breaks even" on every ton moving over this route, while on the other route established by the Commission order it loses money. So the Virginian established joint rates via the Norfolk & Western.[28] These rates under the law were equal to those established via the Chesapeake & Ohio. Virginian coal operators could now ship westbound via the Chesapeake & Ohio or via the Norfolk & Western. The shipper held the whip hand over the initial carrier; i.e., until the initial carrier again acted. It announced in its tariffs that coal moving west over the Norfolk & Western could be reconsigned en route under through rates to points west of Chicago and the Mississippi River. But, on coal moving west over the Chesapeake & Ohio, final shipping instructions must be given at the mine at the time of shipment; and the coal must move to the consignee that has actually bought the coal.[29]

The reconsignment privilege won the day for the Virginian. In 1924 no Virginian westbound coal moved via the Norfolk & Western Junction (Matoaka).[30] In subsequent years a large tonnage moved over this route,[31] while the movement over the Chesapeake & Ohio route showed only a passable increase.

Somewhat different in form and detail from the reconsignment privilege, but substantially similar in its practical significance, is the concentration privilege in the cotton business. Raw cotton from many local points is forwarded to a common concentration point. It is there compressed into bales, and thence marketed and reshipped. The initial carrier grants its shipper the opportunity to move the cotton from the cotton field, through the concentration point and then to destination on a through rate. This is known as a concentration privilege. Generally the original line adjusts its tariff to limit the privilege to those shipments which move over its lines and its favored connections.

The movement of cotton in the state of Texas affords a revelation of the scope of the business and economic importance of these privileges. All but two of the important carriers of the state control lines to Houston: the Kansas City Southern runs to Port Arthur and the St. Louis Southwestern has access to no port. It terminates at Waco. Each Houston carrier grants the privilege on shipments to that point but refuses to do so on shipments to Port Arthur. In that way it secures the longest haul and the largest revenue on the movement. The St. Louis Southwestern obtaining its long haul indifferently via Waco and the Southern Pacific to Houston and via Shreveport and the Kansas City Southern to Port Arthur extends the privileges to the shipments to both ports and via both lines. Partly for this reason Port Arthur has never developed an important export cotton trade. The Interstate Com-

CONTROL OF TRAFFIC MOVEMENTS 69

merce Commission has stated officially that one reason for the failure of the Kansas City Southern to move cotton to Port Arthur is the lack of concentration privileges, it "being unable to arrange divisions that would permit this with roads that originate cotton." [32] Meanwhile export of cotton through Houston increases steadily.

Many other tariff adjustments, having no bearing on rates, be it observed, may be resorted to for the purpose of advancing the traffic interests of the home road. This would involve an analysis of technical rate and tariff matters far beyond the scope of the present work. It may be pertinent at this point to observe that originating roads do not universally insert routing restrictions in their tariffs. From a business standpoint, they may lose more in other directions than they can possibly gain in this one. Neither do railroad acquisitions and consolidations necessarily lead to the adoption of a policy of restriction with a view to capturing immediately all the traffic of the originating lines. The power to direct the business these lines possess; that it is in their interest to do so must be established. This requires an examination of other considerations, which will serve as the content of succeeding chapters.

Even when fundamental geographical conditions operate against the initiating road in the struggle for competitive traffic, it can conceive a careful line of strategy in its struggle to capture the business. The sudden and rapid exploitation of the Smackover oil field in southern Arkansas in 1925 and 1926 furnished a background for the display of unusual tactics. The oil traffic requires expedited service and it is therefore routed over those lines which provide the most rapid haul from the point of origin to destination. The originating lines in the

Smackover, Arkansas, district—the Missouri Pacific, and the Rock Island—are the roundabout routes to consuming territory north of the Ohio River. The Illinois Central controls the short line, and in consequence most of the traffic is routed over that line. The originating lines thus perform one of the most unenviable services in the railroad field. They collect the traffic, perform the expensive terminal services and obtain only a short line haul. One of those lines delivered the traffic to its connection at one or two available junctions. The greater part was delivered at one junction, and the connecting road had massed its motive power there. Without any warning the originating line began to deliver traffic at the other junction. It endeavored to bring about a congestion, with the hope that the inevitable delay, even if temporary, would so impair the service over the connecting line that the shipper would be led to route his traffic over the road and connections of the originating carrier.[33]

An indication of the substantial driving power behind an innocent-looking transit restriction in the competitive struggle to secure more business is afforded by the tactics of a member of the Missouri Pacific family. The Missouri Pacific system represents the first extensive union of railroad properties approved by the Interstate Commerce Commission under the consolidation provisions of the Transportation Act. The so-called Gulf Coast Lines are a constituent unit in the system. It serves important rice fields in Louisiana. Part of this business formerly moved over the Gulf Coast Lines into Crowley, Louisiana, to a connection with the Kansas City Southern. The latter enjoyed a long haul to points north and west. By the expedient of inserting a tariff notice that milling in transit rates

CONTROL OF TRAFFIC MOVEMENTS 71

would be granted only if the rice moved over the Missouri Pacific System lines for the haul beyond Crowley the latter succeeded in diverting the traffic away from the Kansas City Southern.[34] The initial carrier wanted the business to move over a new (a system) connection; and the transit device was the means of execution.

There are exceptions here and there to the rule of control of traffic movements by the originating carrier. These are, however, surprisingly few. The almost defiant confidence of experienced railroad men in their ability to control the movement of traffic represents, perhaps, the best index to the truth. In the famous Van Sweringen unification cases—the most important of all those presented before the Commission not only in the aggregate property interests involved but also in the extensive publicity engendered—one of the most important contentions made by the Chesapeake & Ohio revolved around its ability to shift the movement of traffic from its own line to the other lines. Its president stated in the lingo of the business that traffic could be "thrown" to the Erie;[35] and to the Pere Marquette.[36] Its traffic vice president in referring to the projected new through route to the southeast via the Louisville & Nashville–Carolina, Clinchfield & Ohio–Atlantic Coast Line route, discussed the importance to the Chesapeake & Ohio of its ability "to strongly compete for and *control the routing of traffic* via the Chesapeake & Ohio—Clinchfield route."[37] The climax of the confidence in the ability to switch traffic is displayed by the following language of the traffic vice president of the St. Louis & San Francisco. He is referring not to the acquisition of any corporation interest in the Chicago, Rock Island & Pacific, to say nothing of a complete consolidation of ownership, management and operation. He refers to the results to ensue from permission by the Commission to the St. Louis & San Francisco to hold directorates on the Rock Island Board. Referring to merchandise traffic from the southeast:

"The Frisco has always been able to control a large volume of this traffic, which could be thrown to the Rock Island at Memphis." [38]

And further:

"There is a large movement of grain and grain products from western Oklahoma, also cotton and cotton seed products from southern Oklahoma, moving to the southeast and the Carolinas through the Memphis gateway, which could be thrown and would be thrown to these routes." [39]

Yet, again:

"The Rock Island production is distributed among various lines reaching the Mississippi River gateways and the Central Freight and Eastern Trunk line territories. A large proportion of this traffic could undoubtedly be controlled by the Frisco from Memphis to Thebes and East St. Louis." [40]

At another point, referring to wheat from western Oklahoma moving to Minneapolis, he declared "it would be possible, undoubtedly, to control the bulk of this grain to the Rock Island lines from Kansas City to Minneapolis, where it is now open, that is at Kansas City, to solicitation by any of the lines north of Kansas City, thus adding traffic to the Rock Island lines which traffic these lines do not now enjoy." [41]

Perhaps some other line (the Chicago Great Western, for instance) may need this traffic more than does the Rock Island. That may be. Nevertheless, in the free play

CONTROL OF TRAFFIC MOVEMENTS

of business strategy, the St. Louis & San Francisco will be able to give the Chicago, Rock Island & Pacific more traffic, and the Chicago Great Western less.

NOTES TO CHAPTER III

1. Consolidation Proceedings, Docket 12964, Statement of James H. Hustis before Interstate Commerce Commission, May, 1923, p. 19.
2. Control of Columbia, Newberry and Laurens, Finance Docket 5424, Statement of Charles R. Capps, tr. p. 52.
3. Control of Central California Traction Co., 131 I.C.C. 135.
4. *American Economic Review*, volume 14, Supplement p. 104.
5. Chicago Junction Case, Finance Docket 1165, Brief for Intervening carriers, p. 81.
6. Central Railroad *vs.* New York, New Haven & Hartford *et al*, Docket 16721, Brief for Central Railroad of New Jersey, pp. 106-107.
7. Interlocking Directors of Wheeling & Lake Erie, and Trunk Lines, Finance Docket 3584, tr. p. 38.
8. *Supra*, exhibit no. 5.
9. *Supra*, tr. pp. 419-420.
10. *Supra*, tr. pp. 419-420.
11. *Supra*, exhibit no. 5.
12. *Supra*, tr. pp. 614-615.
13. *Supra*, Brief for Daniel Willard, George M. Shriver, and Newton D. Baker, p. 31.
14. Unification of Southwestern Lines, Finance Docket 5679, 5680, Brief for Applicants, Vol. II, p. 53.
15. Great Northern–Northern Pacific Unification, Finance Docket 6409, 6410. Brief for Chicago, Milwaukee, St. Paul & Pacific, p. 40.
16. *Supra*, Brief for Applicants, Vol. II, p. 273.
17. Unification of Southwestern Lines, Finance Docket 5679, 5680, Brief for Applicants, Vol. II, pp. 67-68.
18. *Supra*, p. 65.
19. Interlocking Directors of Chicago, Rock Island & Pacific and St. Louis & San Francisco, Finance Docket 1618, tr. p. 69.
20. Proposed Construction by Pittsburgh & West Virginia, Finance Docket 6229, tr. pp. 2127-2128.
21. *Supra*, pp. 2128-2129.
22. Consolidation Proceedings, Docket 12964, Brief for Port of New York Authority, p. 76.
23. Portland Flouring Mills Co. *vs.* S. P. & S. *et al*, 88 I.C.C. 99. The difference in transit service referred to in the text was ordered removed by the Interstate Commerce Commission in this case.
24. Flory Milling Co. *vs.* C. N. E. *et al*, 93 I.C.C. 129.

RAILROAD CONSOLIDATION

25. Wyoming Coal Co. *vs.* Virginian Railway, 96 I.C.C. 359.
26. Virginian Railway *vs.* United States, 272 U. S. 658.
27. Construction by Virginian & Western, Finance Docket 6067, tr. p. 627.
28. Control of Virginian, Finance Docket 4943, tr. p. 24.
29. Construction of Virginian & Western, Finance Docket 6067, tr. pp. 132-134.
30. Control of Virginian, Finance Docket 4943, exhibit no. 43.
31. *Supra*, see also Proposed Construction by Guyandot & Tug River, Finance Docket 5161, Brief for Applicant, p. 56.
32. Construction by W. B. T. & S., 124 I.C.C. 790.
33. Sharp Competition Aroused by Oil Traffic, *Railway Age*, March 20, 1926, p. 859.
34. Unification of Southwestern Trunk Lines, Finance Docket 5679, 5680, Brief for Applicants, pp. 25-26.
35. Control of Erie and Pere Marquette, Finance Docket 6113, 6114, Brief for Chesapeake & Ohio, Vol. I, p. 64.
36. *Supra*, p. 65.
37. *Supra*, Vol. II, p. 41.
38. Interlocking Directors of Chicago, Rock Island & Pacific and St. Louis & San Francisco, Finance Docket 1618, pp. 50-51.
39. *Supra*, p. 51.
40. *Supra*, p. 81.
41. *Supra*, p. 88.

CHAPTER IV

LONG HAUL AND SHORT HAUL

For reasons already discussed, railroads desire a long haul on business moved. A long haul in the light of the economics of rate-making is a profitable haul. Ordinarily it is that haul which gives a road the longest mileage on a particular shipment. Sometimes the longest haul in terms of distance is not the most profitable. For most practical purposes, however, it is sufficiently accurate to consider a long haul in terms of mileage.

Because a long haul is most profitable every road endeavors to control its traffic for routing via those junctions and those connections which will give it the longest possible haul. To induce the available traffic to move in this way becomes the bounden duty of every traffic official. For it is thus that the invested capital is employed most intensively and the largest return realized. "Strong and profitable systems," says the former chief traffic official of the Southern Pacific, "have been those which have been able to obtain long haul traffic and our weak systems have been those which have been limited to short haul traffic." [1]

The almost universal desire of railroad men to long-haul their traffic seems to be blocked by provisions of the law carefully designed to protect the routing rights of the shipper. But, as has already been noted, the rights of the shipper to dictate the combination of lines over which his traffic should move are more nominal than real.

In the previous chapter the intimate relationships between an originating carrier and the shippers served were considered. The situation is such that the originating carrier commands the ability to route the traffic in its own business interests; and these are usually associated with its long haul. In insisting upon its line haul the carrier is aided by an important provision of the law—the so-called short haul provision. The Commission in establishing through rates is severely limited by the law from obliging the carrier to short-haul itself. In establishing a through route, the Commission, according to the law, cannot require any road "to embrace in such route substantially less than the entire length of its railroad . . . , which lies between the terminus of such proposed through route, unless such inclusion of lines would make the through route unreasonably long as compared with another practicable through route which could otherwise be established."

A long line of decisions has established the practical utility of this law to American railroads. Initial carriers which have found it necessary or advisable to cancel through rates that precluded them from realizing their long haul have, within extended and flexible limits, enjoyed a wide liberty of action.[2] The views of the Interstate Commission are indicated by the following statements, which are frequently repeated in many other cases: an originating road is entitled to the long haul, "unless the public interest would suffer thereby";[3] " . . . the spirit of section 15 (4) that if a carrier has unrouted traffic in its possession it should be allowed to handle it by its own line as far as it can unless the public interest will suffer thereby, cannot be disregarded."[4]

Controlling the routing of originated traffic because of

LONG HAUL AND SHORT HAUL

its control over service and supported by the law of the land, the initial carriers are able to obtain the long haul on a large proportion of the traffic carried. The gateways of heavy interchange are located at those points which give the initial carriers the long haul. These are the points of railroad freight transfers. Here many millions of dollars are invested in terminal and interchange facilities: the classification yards, the gravity yards, the switching arrangements, the cross-over tracks, etc., etc.

It is astonishing to observe the extent to which traffic tends to flow along the channels of the long haul and via the corresponding junction points. And yet on second thought, it seems obvious that this should be so. Railroads invest heavily in terminal and gathering facilities to collect freight. The overhead is high, excessively so, in these days of high land costs in important urban traffic areas. Railroads look to the long haul to recoup their terminal overhead and earn a profit. They have also provided necessary tracks and equipment to carry the existing traffic to distant markets. Some markets are located at local points; particularly on such roads as the Atchison, Topeka & Santa Fe in the southwest, the Chicago, Burlington & Quincy in the middle west, the Chicago, Milwaukee, St. Paul & Pacific in the northwest, and the Pennsylvania in the east, which own lines that extend from important sources of production to important centers of consumption. But the preponderating volume of traffic moves to markets located on roads other than those on the lines of which the traffic originates. Every principle of ordinary business management would seem to be violated by a compliance of the carriers with any arrangement whereby they would be prevented from using those tracks and equipment which they have acquired for the movement of traffic for which these facilities were supplied.

The roads of the country do no such thing. They are vitally alive to their business opportunities. In New England, the Boston & Maine interchanges most of its trunk line business at Mechanicville; very little is given to the New Haven for interchange at the Harlem River. In the case of a New England shipment destined to a point located on the Pennsylvania Railroad via the Harlem River interchange, the New Haven gets a haul; so does the Pennsylvania, since its lines do not extend further east or north. The Boston & Maine, however, is short-hauled by such a routing. Being the initial carrier, it controls the routing; and it secures its long haul and maximum revenue by hauling its trains to Mechanicville on the Hudson for delivery to the Delaware & Hudson. That road transports the freight to Wilkes-Barre for delivery to the Pennsylvania. By this movement the Pennsylvania loses the haul from New York to Wilkes-Barre; but the Boston & Maine, the originating line, realizes its profitable haul. It is not surprising, therefore, to find that over a period of years approximately 60 per cent of the traffic interchanged with the west by the Boston & Maine has been with the Delaware & Hudson.[5]

The New York, New Haven & Hartford, located in southern New England, reaches the Harlem River with its own lines. It obtains the long haul by interchanging at that point. The Pennsylvania's lines terminate at that junction from the south, and so get the long haul by a similar interchange. A mutual interest thus exists, and a large volume of traffic (equivalent to about 37 per cent of the total interchange with western lines in 1922) is

LONG HAUL AND SHORT HAUL 79

passed between these two properties. The acquisition of an important proprietary interest in the New Haven by the Pennsylvania is not at all surprising: the heavy volume of business between the two properties is thus protected. Practically all of the New Haven's interchange with its western connections is at its long haul junctions—either at the Harlem River in New York harbor, or at Maybrook via Poughkeepsie and the Central of New England. And of the total, by far its largest interchange with any connection is with the Pennsylvania.[6] (See map on page 41.)

In eastern trunk line territory the heavier traffic is eastbound. The bulky raw materials—the ore, coal, lumber—for manufacturing processes of the East and the food required for the nourishment of the masses of the population exceed in tonnage the manufactured and finished products that move west. The most northerly of the trunk lines, the New York Central, is the only road having direct rail entry into the borough of Manhattan—the heart of the country's metropolis. Its lines extend through trunk line territory to its confines in Chicago and St. Louis. Its heavy volume of eastbound freight is carried on system lines; and its density increases as the traffic flows eastward. Fed at Cleveland with business received from the Cleveland, Cincinnati, Chicago & St. Louis, the eastbound density shows a decided jump. And east of Buffalo the system lines—plentifully nurtured by Michigan Central interchange, by Lake Shore & Michigan Southern tonnage (a goodly part of which moved east via New York Central competitors prior to the system merger in 1914) and by heavy local traffic—attain their highest density. The New York Central retains its long haul and delivers but little of its traffic to its competitors for movement which can travel over system lines.

The rapidly growing southeastern section of the country powerfully illustrates the pull of the long haul towards the corresponding interchange gateways. The Louisville & Nashville operates in the western part of the region. It is predominantly a coal carrier, moving traffic largely northbound to markets north of the Ohio Valley; and its lines which, by and large, correspond to this traffic layout, terminate at the Ohio River points of Louisville, Cincinnati and Evansville, with a line to East St. Louis. To these four junctions, the Louisville & Nashville in 1921 delivered 71 per cent of the total tonnage delivered to all connecting lines.[7] Its system lines extend to Mobile, Alabama, on the Gulf of Mexico, passing through such important communities as Montgomery and Birmingham, Alabama, and Memphis and Chattanooga, Tennessee, etc., all requiring important deliveries to connections for local and regional traffic. Yet the main artery of traffic leads northward beyond the Ohio; and the Louisville & Nashville successfully bends its energy to the transportation of every possible ton of business for its longest haul.

Just as the Ohio River gateway interchanges yield the long haul and good earnings for the Louisville & Nashville west of the Alleghenies, so do the central and eastern Virginia gateways provide equal prosperity for the Seaboard Air Line and the Atlantic Coast Line east of the Alleghenies. Both of the latter have extensive gathering lines in Florida—representing in case of the former more than one-third of its system mileage—and both are urgently in need of the profitable haul to their northern termini. On trunk line business they enjoy fairly direct routes, and

LONG HAUL AND SHORT HAUL 81

compete successfully with their chief competitor, the Southern Railway. On northwestern business destined to points beyond the Ohio River, their competitive position is not so secure. Their route to the middle west via the Chesapeake & Ohio and the Norfolk & Western through the Virginia junctions is circuitous. The Southern controls the short route—particularly from the western Carolinas. A short route to the west does exist, however. The Carolina, Clinchfield & Ohio has built a line through the very heart of the rugged Piedmont region connecting the Seaboard Air Line and the Atlantic Coast Line system on the south and the east with the Chesapeake & Ohio and the Norfolk & Western on the north and west over a short interior route. But neither of the Clinchfield connections cares to use its line for through business. They have their own lines via junctions farther east; and here they secure their best haul and most satisfactory revenue. And, therefore, as officially stated by the Interstate Commerce Commission, . . . "very little use is made of the line as a link in through routes." [8]

The same situation holds true in southwestern territory in the region bounded by the Missouri River between St. Louis and Kansas City on the north, the Mississippi River on the east, the Gulf of Mexico on the south, and the eastern Colorado–New Mexico boundary line on the west. The indigenous carriers haul traffic, mainly cotton, to Gulf ports for export. The main carriers—the Missouri Pacific, the Missouri-Kansas-Texas, the Southern Pacific–Texas lines and the Chicago, Rock Island & Pacific run to Houston. Eleven roads have lines to that point. The great exception is the Kansas City Southern which serves Port Arthur. The carriers serving Houston haul the originating cotton to Houston and not to Port Arthur. The Kansas City Southern originates little cotton, and so the export traffic—mainly cotton—of Port Arthur languishes. The Kansas City Southern officials, it is stated, do everything possible to attract cotton to Port Arthur. But all to no avail. The other carriers get their best revenue by carriage to Houston; and why should they perform a non-compensatory haul from Houston to Beaumont, to give the Kansas City Southern a haul from that point to Port Arthur?

Equally well on the northbound traffic the southwestern lines obtain long hauls. They carry the traffic up to the primary regional gateways for interchange at St. Louis and Kansas City. The Kansas City Southern serves Kansas City with a direct line from the Gulf. It is a line of heavy traffic density, particularly on northbound traffic. It carries northbound a heavy volume of lumber and petroleum from points in Texas and Louisiana to St. Louis and points beyond. Interchange of this business via Shreveport and the St. Louis Southwestern would save a haul of approximately two hundred and eighty miles, and via Eve, Missouri and the Missouri-Kansas-Texas a haul of about one hundred miles as compared with the route of the Kansas City Southern via Kansas City.[9] Such possible savings are not controlling in the establishment of channels of trade and commerce. The revenue-producing possibilities of the long haul attract this business to the Kansas City gateway. That roughly one-third of the traffic delivered at all junctions by the Kansas City Southern should be delivered at Kansas City is therefore not at all surprising.

The Atchison, Topeka & Santa Fe, with extensive feeders in Texas, Oklahoma and Kansas, extends to and through

Kansas City, but does not reach St. Louis. The Chicago, Rock Island & Pacific controls a line to both gateways; but its line to St. Louis from the southwest is unduly circuitous and is not adapted for the movement of much southwestern business. The St. Louis Southwestern, on the other hand, extends to St. Louis but not to Kansas City; and the Missouri-Kansas-Texas, and the St. Louis & San Francisco, with comparatively light northbound traffic from the southwest, reach both gateways.

The Missouri Pacific runs to both St. Louis and Kansas City; its line to Kansas City, however, for considerable long haul traffic is indirect; and its traffic destiny beckons it to St. Louis.

The heavy southwestern outbound traffic of the Atchison, Topeka & Santa Fe, Kansas City Southern, and the Chicago, Rock Island & Pacific exceed in volume that of the carriers whose destiny is wrapped up with the long haul to St. Louis. If the principle of the long haul is operating, one should expect a heavier outbound movement through Kansas City than through St. Louis. And this is the case. A study made by L. F. Loree, projector of the Southwestern merger (the consummation of which has been delayed by extraneous considerations of personal and corporate ethics) based upon average figures for 1922, 1923, and in part, for 1924, reveals that the total annual northbound southwestern traffic moving through Kansas City and St. Louis amounts respectively to 12,370,000 tons and 9,310,000 tons.[10] So, in general, the southwestern properties move traffic in accordance with their business interests, the shippers adjusting their routing to the needs of the carriers.

The creation of traffic channels on southwestern business through the magnetic influences of the long haul can be illustrated by a consideration of the Chicago routes. Traffic from Chicago can reach the southwest via St. Louis or Kansas City. With the exception of the Chicago & Eastern Illinois, which reaches St. Louis but not Kansas City, all of the major southwestern roads operating from Chicago lead either to Kansas City exclusively, or serve both St. Louis and Kansas City. The former lines—Atchison, Topeka & Santa Fe; Chicago Great Western; Chicago, Milwaukee, St. Paul & Pacific—obviously interchange all southwestern traffic at Kansas City. But lines like the Chicago, Burlington & Quincy; Chicago, Rock Island & Pacific; Chicago & Alton; and Wabash enjoy the alternative of interchanging at one or the other of the two gateways. Witness the facts: the latter four lines in 1921 delivered to the Missouri-Kansas-Texas at its St. Louis gateway 1,547 cars, and at its Kansas City gateway 6,607 cars. The same four lines in the same year delivered to the Missouri Pacific's comparatively direct southwestern line from St. Louis a total of 8,528 cars, and to its comparatively indirect line from Kansas City a total of 10,609 cars; they also delivered in 1921 a total of 301,095 tons to the Kansas City Southern at Kansas City.[11] The Chicago, Rock Island & Pacific with lines to both gateways delivered, in 1925, to the St. Louis & San Francisco at St. Louis a total of 778.4 tons, and at Kansas City a total of 29,072.8 tons.[12]

Accurate interchange data are usually not available; and in this particular case it is by no means certain that all of the traffic delivered to the southwestern lines was destined to southwestern points. The Missouri Pacific might have carried some tonnage from Kansas City to

Omaha; and the St. Louis & San Francisco might have carried some from St. Louis to Memphis or Birmingham. The adequacy of the data presented above, relating to the ability of the Chicago lines to long-haul their business and increase their revenue, may be judged in the light of the statement of the president of the St. Louis Southwestern (a road with no line to Kansas City), "The traffic that does move out of the Chicago territory to the Southwest comes of course largely through Kansas City." [13]

That powerful middle transcontinental line, the Union Pacific, enjoys its long haul on the important eastbound fresh fruit, wheat, and lumber traffic by delivery at Council Bluffs. Its seven eastern connections, fighting for every pound of traffic, give it an enviable strategic position. It would indeed be a sad piece of business folly, were the Union Pacific to surrender this position of dominance; and to permit its shippers at will to oblige it to hand over its lumber traffic to the Chicago, Milwaukee, St. Paul & Pacific at Plummer, Idaho, or Marengo, Washington; or its fresh fruit traffic to the Chicago, Burlington & Quincy at Denver. Pursuing a policy of interchange at the Missouri River based squarely on its own interests, its decision exerts an important effect on the financial destiny of its eastern connections. It gives more traffic to the Chicago & North Western than to the Chicago Great Western, because the former gives it more westbound traffic than does the latter. And the Chicago Great Western sorely needing this eastbound business dispatches traffic solicitors out to Union Pacific territory to induce some shippers to oblige the Union Pacific to deliver their freight to the Chicago Great Western at the Missouri River.

Farther to the south, the Southern Pacific pursues the

same policy as the Union Pacific. Stopping short of St. Louis and Chicago, its lines terminate at the North Texas gateways. It can exercise ample opportunity in delivering its eastbound business to many junctions. Whereas the carriers struggling for Union Pacific interchange operate from one, or at most two, common junctions at the Missouri River; the possible beneficiaries of Southern Pacific policy are scattered over many gateways. It can deliver its eastbound business, among others, to the Texas Pacific at El Paso; to the Chicago, Rock Island & Pacific at Tucumcari; to the Kansas City, Mexico & Orient at Alpine; to the Kansas, Oklahoma & Gulf at Denison; to the St. Louis & San Francisco at Denison; and to the St. Louis Southwestern at various Texas points. The Southern Pacific distributes its bounty to all for reasons sufficiently satisfactory to the dispensing agency, but the greater volume of traffic is delivered to the St. Louis Southwestern; thus giving the Southern Pacific its long haul.

The extraordinary extent to which the transcontinental carriers in Southern California control the movement of traffic for the long haul is revealed by the data becoming available as the result of the competitive struggle of the Western Pacific to obtain a share of the lucrative traffic hitherto divided between the Atchison, Topeka & Santa Fe and the Southern Pacific. The Western Pacific has applied to the Interstate Commerce Commission for permission to build new lines and to acquire existing properties in California producing territory. Extensive testimony and elaborate exhibits are unfolding to the non-railroading layman some interesting facts and tendencies. On the authority of a traffic official of the Santa Fe, that road succeeded in hauling eastbound, over its own lines, all of

LONG HAUL AND SHORT HAUL 87

its 20,000 cars of deciduous fruit moved in 1924, except 81 delivered to the Southern Pacific; and 9 to the Western Pacific. And of the "much more" than 20,000 cars of the same business originated by the Southern Pacific in 1924 only 148 went east via the Santa Fe and 6 via the Western Pacific.[14] These figures are unusually useful in reflecting on the significance of a statement made by an executive official of the Southern Pacific System, that from 96 to 98 per cent of the transcontinental traffic is routed by the shipper.[15] The haul on this traffic is particularly long; and the net profit particularly good. Very little of the movement is lost by the originating line.

The desire, aye the urgent necessity to realize a return on every dollar of investment, prompts every carrier to fight for its long haul. The long haul is the gospel of the railroad man; by it shall ye know him: an efficient railroad man, sincerely solicitous and successfully so, for his employer's interest. It is the principle that underlies the traffic movements of the country. It is largely in response to this vital force that there are established "the existing routes and channels of trade and commerce," the preservation of which "as fully as possible and wherever practicable" is demanded by the law.

In the face of this, considerable short-hauling in many sections of the country seems to create an apparent paradox. It is another illustration of those seemingly irrational contradictions that characterize business life. Strange indeed seems the willingness of a carrier to surrender the right to do business on its own premises, and readily to agree to permit another property to perform that service and realize that revenue which its own property can perform and its own treasury realize.

88   RAILROAD CONSOLIDATION

Powerful carriers will execute trackage and traffic agreements calculated to deprive themselves of their long haul. The New York Central's main line which runs across northern Ohio is amply able to carry additional traffic. It, in fact, solicits actively for further business to be carried over it. Yet it will initiate a shipment from Chicago destined to Buffalo; haul it east to Toledo, deliver it there to the Wheeling & Lake Erie, and take it back from that line at Cleveland, and then carry it to destination over its own lines.[16] It will pick up a shipment at Rochester, New York, deliver it to the Wheeling & Lake Erie at Norwalk, Ohio, and take it back from that road at Toledo for carriage to destination.[17] A shipment starting on the New York Central lines south and west of Zanesville may be handed to the Wheeling & Lake Erie at Zanesville for movement by that road to Cleveland; there the New York Central will again receive the shipment and carry it to destination.[18] Some of these arrangements, on the authority of the traffic manager of the Wheeling & Lake Erie "might cover a very substantial part of the traffic which is considered as competitive with the New York Central." [19]

The New York Central System has lines between Cleveland and Toledo; between Zanesville and Cleveland; and between Norwalk and Toledo; and it can carry the business with profit to itself. But on "a very substantial part of the traffic" it does not do so. Not only that. It apparently encourages the competition of the Wheeling, since it increases the latter's competitive position by a grant of trackage between Cleveland and Wellington. The line of the Wheeling between Cleveland and Toledo is "roundabout and unsatisfactory"; [20] and the trackage via

LONG HAUL AND SHORT HAUL 89

Wellington gives it a fairly direct route, making the Wheeling between these two important points more effective for competitive purposes.

The Baltimore & Ohio for many years pursued an opposite course from that of the New York Central. Both trunk lines compete with the Wheeling & Lake Erie. But the Baltimore & Ohio refused to accept traffic at a junction point which short-hauled it. It took three years of active negotiations to change that policy. The Baltimore & Ohio made a bad error over a decade ago in surrendering its control of the Pere Marquette. It thereby lost access to Detroit and lost the opportunity of sharing in its lucrative automobile traffic. The Wheeling & Lake Erie possesses some soliciting strength in Detroit, and apparently can induce shippers to route traffic over its line. Both the New York Central, and the New York, Chicago & St. Louis possess their own lines to Detroit and will not short-haul themselves in order to give a haul to the Wheeling. The Baltimore & Ohio owns no line to Detroit. It would, therefore, lose nothing by allowing the Wheeling a long haul over its entire line from Toledo to Terminal Junction on such traffic that the Wheeling could solicit in Detroit. Partly for this reason and partly for others, the Baltimore & Ohio and the Wheeling & Lake Erie negotiated an agreement early in 1927 whereby on the basis of satisfactory divisions, the latter can move freight for its longest possible haul from Toledo to Terminal Junction.[21] Part of this traffic may originate in territory west of Toledo served by the Baltimore & Ohio. It may be traffic that it could have carried all the way to a destination beyond the eastern terminus of the Wheeling & Lake Erie. Yet it agrees to permit the latter to carry the business for a considerable portion of the haul—a service which the Baltimore & Ohio could have easily performed. This applies to originating business as well as that received from connections.

Statesmanship in the railroad business here works its beneficial results. When a road realizes it cannot secure the entire haul, it fights to get a part. Many a carrier, though not eminently a first-class trunk line, may possess a strong soliciting organization. It may have good traffic salesmen, and personal impressions alone attracts business in this field as it does in so many others. The Wheeling in important traffic centers, such as Chicago and Detroit, can solicit freight for movement over its line via many trunk lines. Why should the New York Central surrender the opportunity to haul business from Chicago to Toledo, and from Cleveland to Buffalo, because—and only because —it cannot haul the same business from Toledo to Cleveland? Should it insist upon the Toledo–Cleveland haul, the Wheeling might be disposed to route the shipment over the New York, Chicago & St. Louis, or the Baltimore & Ohio. So the New York Central wisely bows to business necessity, and takes three-quarters of a cake rather than lose even that because of its insistence upon having all or none.

The hard-headed and sound business strategy behind the apparent willingness of well-managed carriers to lose the long haul is illustrated in an interesting fashion by a traffic agreement concluded between two strong competitors in trunk line territory. The Pittsburgh & West Virginia, a tiny railroad that has made itself somewhat of a stormy petrel in the eastern consolidation strategy, operates a line between the Pittsburgh district on the east and a small town in eastern Ohio on the west. It is part and parcel of the effort of the Goulds to provide a new through line to the Atlantic. The road was built at a terrific cost; and subsequently crashed into bankruptcy. The proposed new through route to the East is *physically* available. The Wabash, Wheeling & Lake Erie, and the Pittsburgh & West Virginia form (or at least prior to the eastern consolidation farrago did form) a coöperating triumvirate from Chicago to Pittsburgh willing to carry freight to the seaboard. But there a hiatus occurred. From Connellsville to the east extends the Western Maryland; and beyond was the Philadelphia & Reading, and the Central Railroad of New Jersey ready to carry business to New York and New England. The Pittsburgh & Lake Erie formed an excellent connection between the Pittsburgh & West Virginia on the west, and the Western Maryland on the east. That road is a part of the New York Central system, however, and the Pittsburgh & West Virginia has never been able to convince the New York Central that the short haul of the controlled Pittsburgh & Lake Erie in transporting traffic between two small lines in western Pennsylvania was worth more to it than the long system haul from Chicago to New York. For the Wabash–Wheeling & Lake Erie–Pittsburgh & West Virginia–Pittsburgh & Lake Erie–Western Maryland–Philadelphia & Reading–Central Railroad of New Jersey route on Chicago–New York business was directly competitive with the New York Central route.

The effort to get a full haul through the Pittsburgh & Lake Erie promising to meet with a conclusive failure, the Pittsburgh & West Virginia followed the principles of wise business strategy by essaying to capture a part of it. The road connects with the Baltimore & Ohio at Bruceton, Pennsylvania—a point short of its eastern terminus. It successfully negotiated a traffic agreement with that trunk line system providing for through rates and divisions on business moving eastward over the Baltimore & Ohio system, and originating in Wheeling & Lake Erie territory. On any hauls moving through Bruceton and received from the Pittsburgh & West Virginia, the Baltimore & Ohio clearly short-hauls itself. Its lines can carry most of this business from point of origin to point of destination. The traffic manager of the Baltimore & Ohio commenting on this situation frankly stated that his road would be "glad to get additional business through the Pittsburgh & West Virginia, who opened up soliciting offices, or who said they would, and we would rather get a half loaf on their tonnage than none at all."

Q. "That is, while you expected to lose something from that route, you expected to gain more than you lost?"

A. "Yes, sir, precisely." [22]

The Baltimore & Ohio is willing to accept a haul from the Pittsburgh & West Virginia. But the latter must go out and create the business by active solicitation. True, indeed, it may solicit business away from the Baltimore & Ohio at some points of origin. The Baltimore & Ohio, in turn, depends upon its own soliciting forces to hold their own at those points. The Baltimore & Ohio cannot be expected to harbor any ardent wish for the movement of traffic over this route; and the practical traffic results since the establishment of the route indicate that it does not vigorously promote the diversion of business from its own line. Upon the basis of a detailed analysis of interchanged traffic for July and August, 1927, the traffic manager of the Pittsburgh & West Virginia declared that the Baltimore & Ohio supports neither its Terminal Junction route with the Wheeling & Lake Erie, nor its Bruceton route with the Pittsburgh & West Virginia. But the Wheeling & Lake Erie, on account of larger divisions, supports the Terminal Junction as against the Bruceton route. The Pittsburgh & West Virginia thus gets little business over its new Bruceton route, "except for such traffic as the Pittsburgh & West Virginia itself routes via Bruceton, practically closing the Bruceton route to competitive traffic." [23]

The impelling purpose behind short-hauling to capture a share of competitive traffic not otherwise obtainable is thrown into bolder relief by approach from a slightly different angle. Consideration has been given only to short-hauling to obtain business capable of solicitation by another line, but originating in the territory of, and in communities served by, the short-hauled carrier. The New York Central serves Chicago and Buffalo from and to which it carries business by participation with the Wheeling & Lake Erie which enjoys the Cleveland–Toledo haul. And the Baltimore & Ohio directly serves points in Ohio from and to which it accepts traffic for transportation to some eastern points on which the Wheeling & Lake Erie gets a haul. Both the New York Central and the Baltimore & Ohio have ample facilities to take care of the business which they now share with the Wheeling & Lake Erie.

Short-hauling on a national scale is more usually practiced to enable carriers to compete for traffic originating *on another road,* which is not reached by the lines of the road short-hauled. A road may surrender its right to the long haul on the business it originates, if thereby it can obtain a larger volume of traffic which originates on another line. In trans-Missouri territory the Union Pacific and the Chicago, Burlington & Quincy are keen competitors. The lines of the former extend west to the Pacific coast. On shipments bound for the Pacific coast, the Chicago, Burlington & Quincy realizes its long haul by interchanging with the Denver & Rio Grande Western at Denver. The Union Pacific is particularly desirous to obtain a larger share of this westbound traffic because its traffic is preponderantly eastbound. It therefore has a large percentage of westbound empties. On the other hand, the Union Pacific controls a large volume of eastbound business, a substantial part of which is exchanged with the Chicago & North Western at Omaha. Here is an opportunity for a mutually profitable trade. The Chicago, Burlington & Quincy delivers some of its westbound traffic to the Union Pacific at Omaha, thus short-hauling itself; and the latter in turn delivers a part of its eastbound traffic at Omaha to the Chicago, Burlington & Quincy.

A consolidated system conceived on sound transportation lines may even find it conducive to its best business interests to promote substantial system short-hauling.

The new Loree southwestern system, consisting of the Kansas City Southern, Missouri-Kansas-Texas and the St. Louis Southwestern was proposed in part for the purpose of increasing the length of the haul on intra-system traffic. Yet the system has formally agreed to short-haul itself for a considerable volume of traffic moving to southern Texas and beyond. Of the corporate entities of the system one is a competitive connection and the other a friendly one of the Southern Pacific. The Missouri-

LONG HAUL AND SHORT HAUL

Kansas-Texas competes actively with the Southern Pacific in southwestern Texas. They both serve Houston, Galveston, San Antonio, and many minor points; and there is therefore little interchange between them. The Southern Pacific delivers little of its heavy volume of eastbound transcontinental business to the Missouri-Kansas-Texas; and of its smaller tonnage of westbound transcontinental business the latter road delivers but little to the former.

The St. Louis Southwestern, however, is complementary to the Southern Pacific lines. The interests of these two roads do not conflict. Their lines connect in north Texas; those of the former beginning, and those of the latter terminating, their north- and eastbound movement to St. Louis. Both, therefore, realize their long haul through interchange at north Texas gateways, and for over a decade they have interchanged an ever growing volume of business. The St. Louis & Southwestern serves as an important bridge line, on a substantial volume of traffic received by it from the Southern Pacific; and it, in turn, delivers traffic to the Southern Pacific at the north Texas gateways.

This basis of exchange so profitable to the participating carriers, and so conducive to the interests of the shipping public, appeared to be threatened by the creation of a common business interest between the Missouri-Kansas-Texas and the St. Louis Southwestern. With the former in control of the latter the resultant system could facilitate the movement of traffic from and to such points as Houston and San Antonio over the St. Louis Southwestern–Missouri-Kansas-Texas rather than over the St. Louis Southwestern–Southern Pacific. The St. Louis Southwestern could adapt its soliciting strength to the movement of its originated traffic via the Missouri-Kansas-Texas and to the extent of this traffic, its efforts may have succeeded. But—and this is vital—it happens that the majority of the business involved neither originates nor terminates on the line of the St. Louis Southwestern. The greater part comes from connections at St. Louis for delivery to the Southern Pacific, and from the Southern Pacific for delivery to connections at St. Louis. This is overhead traffic to the St. Louis and Southwestern. It is business controlled by the Southern Pacific; that line can induce shippers to route their business in the way requested by its salesmen. About 80 per cent of the interchange between the two lines can be diverted from the St. Louis Southwestern to other connections by the Southern Pacific.[24]

The loss to the St. Louis Southwestern, should it have endeavored to interchange preferentially with the Missouri-Kansas-Texas was clear and certain. What, on the other hand, would have been its gain? or the gain to the Missouri-Kansas-Texas? The latter might have gained a little; it might have obtained the haul on westbound business received from the St. Louis Southwestern and destined to such points as Houston and San Antonio. This traffic is considerable, especially cotton destined for export via Gulf ports. But it is small as compared with the volume of Southern Pacific business that might have been lost to the St. Louis Southwestern. Probably of all the traffic now delivered to the Southern Pacific, the St. Louis Southwestern could have succeeded in diverting 35,000 tons to the Missouri-Kansas-Texas. The Loree system by insisting on its long haul for its south Texas and Gulf business would have lost more than it possibly could have gained.

LONG HAUL AND SHORT HAUL 97

The new southwestern system, appreciating these factors, gracefully conceded the necessity of short-hauling itself. Its management decided to continue the close traffic relations between the St. Louis Southwestern and the Southern Pacific. It negotiated an arrangement by which the St. Louis Southwestern agreed to solicit preferentially in favor of the Southern Pacific, and by which the latter agreed not to discriminate in its solicitation against the former.[25] The St. Louis Southwestern agreed to do all it could to move traffic over the Southern Pacific—a competitor of its own parent property, the Missouri-Kansas-Texas.

The same Southwestern system is faced with another fundamental traffic situation which will lead it for sufficiently sound business reasons to refuse to short-haul itself. Complex as the external manifestations may be, the underlying principle is clear enough: a carrier is interested in the realization of the largest net profit; and that is usually achieved through the long haul. But if not; if the largest gain is obtained through the short haul, then a road gladly short-hauls itself. The Loree system accepts the short haul on some business in order to capture a larger volume of business in return.

Observe, now, a situation that would produce a net loss if it accepted the short haul. So it declines to do so. The main trend of traffic in the southwest is south. The heavy southbound movement of cotton and wheat together with the miscellaneous manufactured products of the east exceed in tonnage and revenue the northbound movements of lumber, rice, sugar, sulphur, fruits and vegetables, petroleum and other products. Northbound move long trains of empty cars. This characterizes the region as a whole, with the exception of the Kansas City Southern, which hauls northward the refined oil and other finished manufactures from the Port Arthur industrial district. The other roads have comparatively little northbound business.

Here is a typical opportunity for profitable short-hauling. Roads with heavy southbound traffic may short-haul themselves to obtain some northbound traffic; and heavy northbound carriers may accept a short haul on some northbound traffic to obtain some southbound traffic. The points at which a net gain is resolved from the balancing of the comparative losses and gains is difficult to determine. Expert traffic and operating officials must supply the necessary data. The former determine the divisions on the long- and on the short-hauled traffic; they know the ton miles to be gained and lost by any contemplated traffic policy. The latter present the operating costs of the traffic gained and the traffic lost. Such considerations and many others must be examined before reaching a decision.

An opportunity for profitable short-hauling in this region presented itself in 1923. In that year a new railroad enterprise was projected: its success was largely based on the possible diversion of part of the northbound traffic of the Kansas City Southern for movement over its line. A new route to Port Arthur was to be built by a short line known as the Waco, Beaumont, Trinity & Sabine River Railway. After the completion of its proposed extension, the latter was to reach Waco, there to connect with the Missouri-Kansas-Texas and the St. Louis Southwestern. It also was to make connections with the Gulf Coast Lines at Beaumont. It already had physical con-

LONG HAUL AND SHORT HAUL 99

nections with the International Great Northern. Neither of the four roads mentioned had its own line to Port Arthur; and both the International Great Northern and the Missouri-Kansas-Texas had no lines to Beaumont. They both terminated at Houston and Galveston.

It was particularly to the latter two that the opportunity for short-hauling presented itself. Both dragged northbound many empty cars; and both enjoyed a fairly heavy volume of traffic southbound. Would it not be profitable for them to deliver some of their southbound traffic to the new line at a short-hauled junction in order to receive some northbound traffic in return: traffic expected to be diverted by the new extension away from the Kansas City Southern? Conditions appeared to be favorable. The Missouri-Kansas-Texas would lose a haul from Waco to Galveston; and the International Great Northern a haul from Trinity Junction to Houston. They would gain in return a long haul from those junctions to points many miles northward. Based on the experience of the Kansas City Southern, the northbound movements promised to be particularly attractive and lucrative. The hauls on the added northbound traffic appeared to be substantially larger than the haul on the lost southbound traffic.

When the project of constructing the extension from Waco to Port Arthur by an existing short line was originally broached, both the International Great Northern and the Missouri-Kansas-Texas expressed a willingness to establish joint routes and through rates on business interchanged with the short line. It may be asked why the Kansas City Southern had not similarly established such concurrences with the same lines. But the Kansas City Southern does not connect with these lines at such convenient junctions. The Missouri-Kansas-Texas connects with the Kansas City Southern many miles north of Waco —its junction with the proposed extension—at Eve, Missouri. And it makes no physical connection whatsoever with the International Great Northern. Interchange would be effected through a third party. Both would be obliged to lose a comparatively long southbound haul in return for a smaller northbound haul. This was an unprofitable arrangement, and they declined to participate in any interchange with the Kansas City Southern on such a basis.

Two extensive unifications affecting the lines under consideration completely modified the underlying traffic conditions. The acquisition of the International Great Northern by the Gulf Coast Lines gave the former a system line to Beaumont—an important city in the Port Arthur industrial district, and only a few miles from Port Arthur itself. The formation of the Kansas City Southern–St. Louis Southwestern–Missouri-Kansas-Texas system gave the latter a system line directly to Port Arthur. Interchange at Eve was now not so objectionable to the Missouri-Kansas-Texas. What it might lose on the Houston haul, the Kansas City Southern might gain on the Port Arthur haul. The system as an entity would not suffer. And, further, one could not expect the Kansas City Southern to permit a member of its official family to encourage another line to divert profitable traffic from system lines.

Both the International Great Northern and the Missouri-Kansas-Texas in response to their new property interests reversed their former positions. The latter opposed the construction of an extension calculated to take away business from a corporate system constituent. It made it clear that it probably would not establish through routes and rates with the new line through the Waco gateway. The traffic fundamentals had now changed. The new system of which the Missouri-Kansas-Texas was a part was now carrying all that northbound traffic for which, or rather for any part of which, it was willing formerly to short-haul itself on southbound traffic. Any northbound business the Missouri-Kansas-Texas received from the new extension would be diverted from the Kansas City Southern—its associate in the new railroad system.

The Loree system will therefore short-haul itself on southbound business moving over the Southern Pacific; but will insist on its long haul on business that might conceivably move via the new extension from Waco to Port Arthur, i.e., the Waco, Beaumont, Trinity & Sabine River Railway Company. In both instances the policy is dictated by the sound business principle of the highest return on a given investment. In the former case the system gains by surrendering a part of its controlled traffic in return for a larger and more profitable volume of traffic originating on, or controlled by, the Southern Pacific. In the other instance the system can gain little new business by surrendering a part of its long haul; it therefore insists upon its entire haul.

Short-hauling is not always voluntary, representing the free meeting of minds. The short-hauled carrier frequently loses part of its haul under conditions clearly adverse to its own business interests. The other carrier controls the situation, however, and can force the other to accept an arrangement suitable to its own needs. An important channel of trade and commerce, the preservation of which is required by law, may be formed in this manner.

The heart of the industrial region of the country creates the setting for such a channel of traffic. A large tonnage of coal moves from the mines of the Baltimore & Ohio and the Western Maryland over the Philadelphia & Reading to Allentown and thence via the Central Railroad of New Jersey and the Delaware Valley bridge lines to New England. On this business, as well as on a substantial volume originating in its own territory, the Central Railroad of New Jersey realizes only a short haul to Easton, Pennsylvania. It there surrenders its tonnage for carriage to New England over the Lehigh & Hudson. Why does it not carry this large tonnage to New York for direct transfer with the New York, New Haven & Hartford and thus realize its longest possible haul? (See map on page 41.)

The key to the solution is found by consulting the interests of the New York, New Haven & Hartford rather than those of the Central Railroad of New Jersey. The former controls a direct line to the Harlem River, making interchange with connections, other than the Pennsylvania, through floats. This is the short line to most points on the New Haven from territory west of the Harlem River. Its traffic density is somewhat high, particularly on the passenger business. Through its acquisition of the Central of New England in 1904, it opened up a new channel for the movement of traffic between New England and trunk line territory. The New Haven moved traffic west over its line to Hartford, Connecticut, southwest over the Central of New England via the Poughkeepsie gateway over the Hudson River, and thence in the same direction to Maybrook, New York, and over the Lehigh & New England or the Lehigh & Hudson for interchange with the Philadelphia & Reading and the Central Railroad of New Jersey. This route is somewhat circuitous; but it is non-congested, and its grades are satisfactory.

What is more important, however, is the investment of the New Haven in the Central of New England and in the provision of facilities for interchange at Maybrook. The Central of New England originates little traffic, less than 5 per cent of its total. To make the New Haven's investment profitable, it was necessary for the Central of New England to obtain business from connecting lines. After some slight hesitation the New Haven decided to go the limit allowed under the law for the purpose of encouraging the movement of business via its newly acquired line. It cancelled through rates via the Harlem River with all connections except the Pennsylvania and the Lehigh Valley. It established a rate level through the medium of a combination of local rates via the Harlem River materially higher than that prevailing via the Hudson River for its other connections. Bituminous coal from Baltimore & Ohio and Western Maryland territory destined to New England moving over the interior Philadelphia & Reading–Central Railroad of New Jersey route could not travel through the Harlem River gateway. The rates were too high. Reasonable rates for this business prevailed only via the Delaware Valley bridge lines and the Central of New England. And the business under consideration moved and still moves that way.

Definite channels of traffic are thus established. The Pennsylvania and the Lehigh Valley secure their long haul by interchange at the Harlem River. The Central Railroad of New Jersey loses a haul of 73 miles by interchange at Easton; the Erie a haul of 53 by interchange at

Greycourt, New York; and the Delaware, Lackawanna & Western a haul of 56 miles by interchange at Andover, New Jersey. Primarily, as a result of the new traffic route created by the cancellation of through rates via the Harlem River, the Central of New England tonnage increased over 700 per cent in the two decades following its acquisition by the New Haven in 1900.

The long haul is thus the first and cardinal principle underlying the establishment and maintenance of traffic routes. The long haul is the haul that realizes the largest net return on the invested capital. Viewed from this angle the short haul under some conditions is the long haul: it is that haul which, through its fertilization of the line with traffic obtained from other lines in an amount greater than that lost through the short haul, realizes the largest net.

NOTES TO CHAPTER IV

1. Consolidation Proceedings, Docket 12964, Statement of Lewis J. Spence, February 26, 1923, p. 27.
2. Ogden Gateway Case, 35 I.C.C. 139 and cases cited therein.
3. Western Maryland Routing, 66 I.C.C. 108.
4. Chicago, Milwaukee & St. Paul Ry. Co. *vs.* Union Pacific R. R. Co., 88 I.C.C. 318.
5. Consolidation Proceedings, Docket 12964, Statement by L. F. Loree, p. 13.
6. Report of Joint New England Railroad Committee, 1923, p. 153.
7. Consolidation Proceedings, Docket 12964, exhibit no. 60 A.
8. Clinchfield Railway Lease, 90 I.C.C. 127.
9. Unification of Southwestern Lines, Finance Docket 5679, 5680, Brief for Applicants, Vol. II, pp. 91, 100.
10. *Supra*, pp. 8-9.
11. Consolidation Proceedings, Docket 12964, Basic Data, Missouri Pacific, Missouri-Kansas-Texas.
12. Interlocking Directors, Chicago, Rock Island & Pacific and St. Louis-San Francisco, Finance Docket 1618, exhibit no. 21.
13. Consolidation Proceedings, Docket 12964, tr. p. 2830.
14. Control of Central California Traction Company, Finance Docket 5008 tr. p. 140; exhibit no. 40.
15. Consolidation Proceedings, Docket 12964. Statement of R. L. Burckhalter, Assistant General Manager, Southern Pacific Com-

LONG HAUL AND SHORT HAUL 105

pany; prepared for the San Francisco Consolidation Hearing, March 31, 1923. Introduction.
16. Interlocking Directors Wheeling & Lake Erie, and Trunk Lines, Finance Docket 3584, tr. pp. 584-585.
17. *Supra*.
18. *Supra*, tr. pp. 15-16.
19. *Supra*, tr. p. 17.
20. *Supra*, tr. pp. 21-22.
21. *Supra*, tr. pp. 438-439.
22. Construction by Pittsburgh & West Virginia Ry., Finance Docket 6229, tr. pp. 2148-2149.
23. *Supra*, tr. pp. 1252-1253, 1255-1256.
24. Unification of Southwestern Lines, Finance Docket 5679, tr. Letter dated June 6, 1926. Upthegrove to Loree.
25. *Supra*, exhibit no. 11.
26. Central Railroad of New Jersey *vs.* New York, New Haven & Hartford Railroad, Docket 16721, Brief for Central Railroad of New Jersey, p. 141.

CHAPTER V

CONNECTIONS AND COMPETITORS

Although striving for the long haul is the most vital, it is by no means the only factor in the carving out of the channels of trade and commerce. Some of the important routes carrying a heavy volume of business could not be satisfactorily explained by this factor alone. Few indeed are the important junctions from and to which only one road leads in either direction. The transcontinental lines, limited as they are in number by the available passages through the mountains, connect with numerous eastbound lines fighting for the business. Many of the eastern connections connect at a common junction. Such is the case at Omaha; here seven roads meet the Union Pacific. So it is at Twin Cities; here six roads join the Great Northern and the Northern Pacific all ready to haul expeditiously to Chicago. Many lines radiate west and southwest from New York City; most probably they haul many trains of westbound empties. All afford the New York, New Haven & Hartford a long haul on westbound carloads. Yet the New Haven's loaded cars with revenue-producing traffic transferred at New York City move in preponderant volume westbound over the lines of the Pennsylvania. The Erie, the Delaware, Lackawanna & Western, the Lehigh Valley, the Baltimore & Ohio, the Central Railroad of New Jersey get but little of this business.

CONNECTIONS AND COMPETITORS 107

The lines controlling traffic movements do not share their interchange ratably among the several connections which accord them the long haul. Indeed there is no particular reason for so expecting. And the necessity for such an obvious declaration can be justified only in the light of the existing misapprehensions on the subject. Many, including some in high positions of state, believe that the existing channels of traffic are natural, and the tentative report on Consolidation issued by the Interstate Commerce Commission establish and justify traffic channels because of the existing interchange among participating carriers, as if such interchange relationship were a conclusive demonstration of the inevitableness of the existing situation. Just the contrary may be the case. The significant interchanges between participating carriers at a particular gateway represent the practical consummation of the balancing of their business interests. And there is no particular public interest necessarily involved in their continuance. The public interest must be established separately in each instance.

Why, then, with the length of the haul the same, do carriers controlling the routing of traffic elect to give more to one line and less to another? Why should the Southern Pacific give more business to the St. Louis Southwestern than to the Missouri-Kansas-Texas on shipments bound to and beyond St. Louis? Both roads run eastward from Waco and Dallas; and the Southern Pacific could probably secure the same division and approximately the same standard of service from both lines. And why should the Missouri Pacific give the Chicago, Rock Island & Pacific less and the Wabash more traffic at St. Louis? The haul of the Missouri Pacific is the same.

Why the difference in treatment? The New York Central originates a large volume of bituminous coal traffic in the richly blest Clearfield coal region of northwestern Pennsylvania. Over 5,000,000 gross tons of this coal were delivered to the Philadelphia & Reading at Williamsport in 1920.[1] Part of this was delivered by the latter to the Central Railroad of New Jersey for local delivery; and a goodly part to connections: the Lehigh & New England, the Long Island, the Lehigh & Hudson River. The Pennsylvania also connects with the New York Central at Williamsport; it serves a wider distributing territory than the Philadelphia & Reading. Yet for a typical week in 1922 for which figures are available, the latter received six times as much traffic from the New York Central at Williamsport as the Pennsylvania did.[2]

These illustrations are not unusual. They are typical of the interchange at all important junctions. They cannot be explained by resort to the principle of the long haul. That explains why the business reached the gateway under consideration. It does not explain why at that gateway the carloads were transferred to road A instead of to road B.

At every junction some traffic must be delivered to each and every road. Each road serves local points not served by others; and traffic destined to these points must necessarily move over the local lines. The fate of these traffic movements is fixed. Regardless of the relation between the participating carriers, the local terminating line must be given a part of the haul. Beyond this local traffic, however, there is the through and overhead business. Every important carrier in the country, other than purely local feeders, serves as a part of routes which compete actively with other routes.

CONNECTIONS AND COMPETITORS 109

To a large extent, competition is purely regional. Every road within a particular region strives with others to carry traffic to a regional junction. There it unites with other properties that extend to distant markets of consumption or centers of production. They serve their own regions and do not penetrate into those served by their connections. At the Potomac River gateways the Seaboard Air Line and the Atlantic Coast Line serving southeastern territory connect with the Pennsylvania and the Baltimore & Ohio which serve trunk line territory. Both carriers realize their own business interests by consulting those of their connections. A carload of tobacco from the Carolinas expedited by the united efforts of the Atlantic Coast Line and the Pennsylvania to its destination to a cigar factory in Philadelphia benefits both carriers. Neither road competes with the other. The Pennsylvania could not have moved the tobacco up to the Potomac River; and neither could the Atlantic Coast Line have obtained the haul beyond the Potomac River to Philadelphia. Carriers so related to each other may for convenience be designated as friendly connections.

Competitive stress and the urge for expansion have created many interregional situations in most sections of the country. The railroad net is characterized by lines thrown beyond indigenous territories: territories that are unified by common traffic problems, and by substantial uniformity in rate scales. Roads thus radiating through two districts generate complex problems of interchange. They compete for business in transregional territories with roads that connect at their important interchange points. At points of traffic origin they compete for a line haul up to a common junction. Beyond the junction only one road extends. Their business interests are not complementary; for in serving each other they do not necessarily respond to the urge of their own exigencies. In transporting a shipment with speed and efficiency from a common junction a property may increase the competitive strength of its competitor at points of origin.

There are many railroad relationships of this character; and they represent the result of varying business considerations. The bold expansion of the Atchison, Topeka & Santa Fe in the late eighties across all its friendly connections from Kansas City to Chicago served temporarily to embarrass it in the next decade, but aided it in part to achieve its eminence among American railroads in the twentieth century.

The expansion of the Chicago, Rock Island & Pacific beyond its native territory in the Mississippi Valley was bungled by promoters who had had no previous experience in railroad life. Feeders were acquired in southern Arkansas and northern Louisiana that could give the system but a short haul, and a long line extending west of Memphis was acquired that possessed no sound relation to the rest of the system. It made no physical connection with the main line extending into St. Louis short of a point in central Oklahoma. This circuity made competition with the Missouri Pacific and St. Louis Southwestern for St. Louis business over its own lines legally impossible.

The Pennsylvania quickly abandoned an ill-fated venture into southeastern territory in the seventies;[3] and twenty years later the Philadelphia & Reading hurried itself into bankruptcy by its efforts to expand into New England.[4] On the other hand, the penetration of the New York Central into New England territory through its

CONNECTIONS AND COMPETITORS 111

acquisition of the Boston & Albany, and the expansion of the southwestern St. Louis & San Francisco system into Birmingham, Alabama, were attended with an unusual degree of success.

Whatever the historical causes may have been, it suffices for present purposes to recognize the existing interterritorial extensions, and to appraise their bearing on the formation of traffic routes and on the economics of railroad consolidation. A road thus extending between two traffic regions introduces complicated problems of railroad competition. It controls a route over which it possesses complete authority. The route is administered under the ægis of a single management from point of origin to point of destination. That management has a single and wholehearted interest in dispatching the business. It need not concern itself with the operating or traffic requirements of any of its connections. And it can, therefore, adjust its train schedules and all its other operating arrangements with the sole purpose of producing the highest possible standard of railroad service over the route in question. Further, it need not fret about delays in train movements due to interchange delays. Its trains need not be detained at junction points; no interchange records are needed; no switching to and from foreign tracks is required; no possible slowing up in train mileage need be anticipated due to pressure of compelling business interests of connections.

This efficient one-line service competes with multiline service. The Atchison, Topeka & Santa Fe, for example, affords oil refiners in Oklahoma a one-line service to Chicago; whereas the St. Louis & San Francisco and Missouri-Kansas-Texas rely upon connections at St. Louis for such shipments. In the southeast, all the properties depend on connections for shipments bound to St. Louis; the Southern Railway, on the other hand, extends beyond the conventional territorial gateways into St. Louis with its own lines. In New England, the New York Central through its controlled Boston & Albany provides the exception; its system lines run through the heart of the rich traffic-producing sections of the country all the way to Boston.

The competitors of the road controlling the one-line service must meet its standard of service. They must perfect business arrangements of a character to overcome the obstacles created by diversity of corporate identity. Two, three and frequently six and seven separate managements are involved. Contrasting traffic policies and operating methods may prevail. Two separate groups of administrators with varying standards of authority and responsibility must be handled. The standard of maintenance may be high on one property, and low on the other. A train speed of thirty miles an hour on the former may perhaps step down to a gait of twenty miles on the latter. Bridges adequate to carry the slight trainloads of one property may collapse under the burden of the heavy trainloads received from the other.

Nevertheless, these multiline routes must compete with the one-line routes. It is imperative that they overcome all obstacles to the rendition of a high-class service over roads under separate ownership, separate management and separate operation. This requires an extraordinary degree of coördination among the several carriers. To perfect a through schedule, in the language of an executive traffic official of an important eastern trunk line, "It takes co-operation of every road entering into the through transportation." [5]

It is in the operation of the trains, primarily in their transfer from the tracks of one road to those of another, that the greatest opportunity for a breakdown in service exists. And here exists, therefore, the opportunity to render a superior service capable of meeting that afforded by the one-line hauls. At interchange points cars must be placed on the interchange track by one road and removed by the other. Often an extensive switching service must be performed. Reports must be kept: the location of every owned car must be known; the waybills must be exchanged. In fact a code of rules has been established for many years to serve as a basis of uniformity in the conduct of interchange relationships.

Rules may be rules; and they may be good rules, but men must administer them. Each person charged with their administration is ordinarily an agent of his principal. If he is honest and capable, he strives for the interests of his employer. If participating carriers in a through route realize their long haul through a common junction, and if they do not compete for any important portion of the haul, then (in the absence of any other consideration) their business interests are common. Measures that profit one also profit the other. Their economic good fortune runs along the same paths of action or inaction. Good or bad service on particular shipments exert similar effects on their respective revenues.

A route composed of carriers so circumstanced and so minded can perform good service. If the economic interests of the carriers clash, however, the resultant service afforded by the route is likely to be adversely affected.

Short hauls and competitive loss of business are not the raw materials for the good-fellowship and the genuine spirit of coöperation essential for the efficient operation of railroad trains over two separately managed properties. "Service over a through route composed of two rival and antagonistic systems," states high operating railroad authority, "cannot stand comparison with service over a single system from origin to destination." [6]

If the two systems are not rivals in any substantial sense for any part of the haul performed by each other, then their interests are not antagonistic. Positive measures are then designed to overcome the seeming delays that appear to characterize a multiline service. Usually the important measures taken are of a technical operating character. Only those intimately associated with the operation of the properties are cognizant of their nature and extent. And as a result little is known of the definite tangible means whereby through routes composed of separately owned properties give excellent competitive service. Yet knowledge of these is important. Decreased rates and increased service (assuming for a moment their possible compatibility) are the eventually anticipated results of a sound national plan of consolidation. Yet excellent service can be effected without any unity of ownership or management. Unity in traffic interest may produce a superior service; even though consolidation may not necessarily improve service.

The internal structure of operating harmony underlying the smooth movement of business over multiline routes has been revealed to the curious layman by proceedings before the Interstate Commerce Commission in many of the construction and unification cases. The federal regu-

CONNECTIONS AND COMPETITORS 115

latory body has admitted into a public record almost everything submitted by the interested parties. Of all these cases—many of surpassing interest—perhaps the most dramatic embodies the measures taken by the Taplin brothers of Pittsburgh to make the Pittsburgh & West Virginia an essential part of a new competitive route from the Mississippi Valley to the Atlantic seaboard. Co-operation between the participating carriers—the Pittsburgh & West Virginia constituting a small fraction of the mileage of the proposed route—is vital to its success. A study of the problems of this line might possess additional flavor because of its possible bearing upon a current situation. And more than academic importance might not impair its illustrative value.

The Pittsburgh & West Virginia was built at a large cost some two decades ago to connect with the Wheeling & Lake Erie on the west and the Western Maryland on the east, to effect a new through route to the seaboard for the Gould system. The Wheeling & Lake Erie to Toledo, and the Wabash west to St. Louis established contact with the Missouri Pacific—the heart of the Gould group. The present Pittsburgh & West Virginia brought the system into Pittsburgh. The route from Pittsburgh to St. Louis was successfully established, although at a prohibitive cost which in about a decade after the construction of the Pittsburgh entrance, bankrupted the entire project.[7] Strategically, moreover, the system was never complete, for the connecting link between Pittsburgh and Connellsville was lacking. The Pittsburgh & West Virginia terminated at Pittsburgh, and the Western Maryland began at Connellsville.

After all the cards of receivership and reorganization

had been shuffled the destiny of the Pittsburgh & West Virginia turned out to rest in the hands of Pittsburgh financial interests who later sold out to the Taplin brothers. The ownership of the Wheeling & Lake Erie rested securely in the hands of the Rockefellers through the ownership of a substantial percentage of its senior class of stocks. Its management, however, was independent. The management of the Pittsburgh & West Virginia was in the hands of its proprietors; and this fortunate unity, altogether too rare in modern times of diffusion of ownership, conduced to vigor of managerial action. The road was handicapped by a poor traffic diversity, for most of its traffic consisted of bituminous coal. It did not enjoy access over its own lines to the heavy traffic-producing areas of the Pittsburgh district and to the centers for the manufacture of steel. Contact was made with the rich industrial region of the Monongahela Valley through physical connection with the Pittsburgh & Lake Erie. If some of this steel business bound for the Middle West could be made to move over the Pittsburgh & West Virginia, the latter would enjoy a long haul and a reasonable profit. The Pittsburgh & Lake Erie through its system affiliation with the New York Central and the Cleveland, Cincinnati, Chicago & St. Louis, however, had its own line to that region.

To make a bid for this western business it was vital for the Pittsburgh & West Virginia to render an unusually high-grade service. For the possible route between Pittsburgh and St. Louis now consisted of lines under separate ownership and management. Furthermore, the mileage of the proposed route was somewhat circuitous. Between Pittsburgh and St. Louis, the new route as eventually

CONNECTIONS AND COMPETITORS 117

established, consisting of the Pittsburgh & Lake Erie, the Pittsburgh & West Virginia, the Wheeling & Lake Erie, the Northern Ohio, and the so-called "Clover Leaf"—now a part of the New York, Chicago & St. Louis—ran for 649 miles as compared with 617 miles over the one-line route of the Pennsylvania.[8] To meet and, if possible, to beat competitive one-line direct routes, train movements had to be quickened at all points. Delay was intolerable. As the first step the Pittsburgh & West Virginia and the Wheeling & Lake Erie concluded an operating arrangement under which each road hauled through trains with its own engines and crews beyond its own termini on the tracks of the other to a convenient yard.[9] An economical engine haul of one hundred and four miles replaced what otherwise might have been two comparatively uneconomical engine hauls of fifty-five and forty-nine miles on the Pittsburgh & West Virginia and the Wheeling & Lake Erie respectively. Division point facilities on both roads were made mutually available to take care of train crews, inspections, and all other divisional point and terminal yard requirements. By this arrangement, from four to twelve hours were saved.[10]

Moreover, the car supply of both roads was pooled, and the equipment used as though it were common property. Thus, a further delay inevitable in operating under the rules of car interchange was eliminated.[11] Through this pooling arrangement considerable savings were effected. In 1926, for example, the Pittsburgh & West Virginia was short of one class of cars, and had a surplus of another. The former it obtained from the Wheeling & Lake Erie which the latter secured from the Wabash. Due to the coal strike, the Pittsburgh & West Virginia had a surplus of 1,400 gondolas entailing a large per diem loss. Through coöperation the surplus was reduced to 450.

With the coöperation of the western connections of the Wheeling & Lake Erie, a freight schedule was perfected not only equal to but superior to that afforded by either of the competitive trunk lines: the Pittsburgh & Lake Erie–New York Central system route, the Pennsylvania, or the Baltimore & Ohio. The new route, aided probably by freedom from terminal difficulties that delayed operations on the competitive trunk-line hauls,[12] made a one-day delivery schedule from Pittsburgh to St. Louis.[13] The Pittsburgh & Lake Erie, originating the preponderant volume of freight for the new route, could not make better than a second-day delivery. By active coöperation with the Pittsburgh & West Virginia it gave its patrons a high-class service not obtainable in any other way. The continued efficiency of the route depended upon an absolute coordination between all the participating carriers.

This westbound route became effective in 1923. During the succeeding three years the westbound traffic delivered by the Pittsburgh & West Virginia to the Wheeling & Lake Erie increased by almost 200 per cent.[14] Most of this was high-class iron and steel traffic carrying high rates and yielding a good net.

On eastbound business the Taplin brothers have not been so successful. The Western Maryland does not hook up with the Pittsburgh & West Virginia on the east as does the Wheeling & Lake Erie on the west. The eastern connecting link, the Pittsburgh & Lake Erie, competes vigorously for eastbound traffic with the Pittsburgh & West Virginia. The same even-handed service competition for eastern business is afforded by the Baltimore & Ohio

CONNECTIONS AND COMPETITORS 119

and the Pennsylvania. All of the trunk lines thus able to render satisfactory service over their own lines would be derelict to their own interests to surrender voluntarily any available business to their competitors. The Pittsburgh & Lake Erie, as a unit of the New York Central family, could not be expected to facilitate competition on business which its system can carry equally as well. It can afford its customers excellent service to Baltimore and other points reached by the Western Maryland equal to that afforded by the Pittsburgh & West Virginia. The New York Central has nothing substantial to gain by making competitive life easier for the Pittsburgh & West Virginia; that is, on eastbound business. It therefore refuses even to establish through rates with it, effective to and from its originating territory, and to and from eastern points.

Should the Pittsburgh & West Virginia succeed in soliciting an eastbound shipment originating on the Wheeling & Lake Erie, the New York Central system would not be adverse to participate and to obtain a bit of the haul from the eastern terminus of the Pittsburgh & West Virginia at West End, Pittsburgh, to the western terminus of the Western Maryland at Connellsville. Through rates have therefore been established, effective on eastbound business originating on the Wheeling & Lake Erie, moving over the Pittsburgh & West Virginia, Pittsburgh & Lake Erie, and the Western Maryland. Nevertheless, the Pittsburgh & Lake Erie's best revenue interests are not realized by pulling trainloads from Pittsburgh to Connellsville. It will gladly carry whatever traffic it gets at Pittsburgh; but there is no particular reason why it should go out of its way to encourage the movement of eastbound traffic in competition with the New York Central system.

The Pittsburgh & West Virginia, therefore, cannot expect to obtain the same coördinated service eastbound from the Pittsburgh & Lake Erie that it obtains from Wheeling & Lake Erie westbound. Westbound, the Wheeling & Lake Erie secures almost a full system haul on traffic received from the Pittsburgh & West Virginia; eastbound the Pittsburgh & Lake Erie receives only a very short haul on traffic received from that line. On the westbound movement the Wheeling carries traffic for which it cannot compete with the Pittsburgh & West Virginia; on the eastbound movement the Pittsburgh & Lake Erie, through its New York Central system affiliations, can compete and does compete for traffic originating in Ohio.

On the west, therefore, the Wheeling enters into unusual operating arrangements to insure the establishment of a high standard of service. This is necessary to enable the route composed of the Wheeling and the West Virginia (among others) to compete with the Pennsylvania. On the east, no such coördination can be expected. Here the observer is presented an entirely different picture. Here are three different train schedules of three different lines. The Western Maryland operates two trains eastward from Connellsville, one leaving at six in the morning, and the other at nine in the evening. The Pittsburgh & Lake Erie trains leave their Pittsburgh terminals at nine-thirty in the evening to connect with the Western Maryland morning train, and at six in the morning to connect with the Western Maryland evening train. The Pittsburgh & West Virginia operates on a third schedule, which brings its trains to the Pittsburgh yards after the Pittsburgh & Lake Erie trains have left to connect with the Western Maryland train which leaves Connellsville that

CONNECTIONS AND COMPETITORS 121

evening. The trains of the Pittsburgh & West Virginia then must lay over all the night. They cannot leave Connellsville over the Western Maryland until the following morning. As a result the Pittsburgh & Lake Erie–Western Maryland route makes a first morning delivery in Baltimore; the Pittsburgh & West Virginia–Western Maryland a second morning delivery.[15] And this difference is all-important in the determination of competitive strength.

Through coöperation in operation with connections the Pittsburgh & West Virginia offers excellent service on the west. Through noncoöperation with connections, it can offer only a poor service in the east. Produce a business background leading to the existence of a spirit of coöperation between participating carriers in a through route, and excellent service results. Excellent service will follow regardless of the number of lines involved in a through carriage. Seven roads with diversity of ownership and diversity of management combine to form an efficient route carrying a dense volume of coal from Baltimore & Ohio mines in West Virginia to New York, New Haven & Hartford consuming points in New England. Special operating arrangements are in effect to facilitate the smooth handling of this traffic. Proprietary frontiers give way to mutuality of business interests. Service reciprocity is established: the Philadelphia & Reading operating its engines far beyond its own boundaries at Shippensburg to Hagertsown and Martinsburg to interchange with connections; and the Western Maryland operating its engines beyond its terminus to the Reading's yards near Harrisburg.[16] A unity in traffic interest—a joint participation from the revenue derived from a given haul—creates a common business foundation. This is literally the stuff and substance out of which solid business foundations are reared. The excellent service resulting from such a combination of circumstances needs no governmental stimulation. The public interest is indeed truly benefited. Consolidations may perhaps realize the aspirations of those who expect better service as one of the important consequences. That may be, yet it is an open question whether similar results are not frequently obtained through coöperation between independent carriers, without assuming the grave risks which accompany a national rearrangement of proprietary equities.

The stimulus to efficient railroad operation afforded within recent years by changing methods of distribution requiring rapid train movement, and by the rivalry of competitive transportation agencies, has been reflected by increased coöperation between connections. The reduction of delay in terminals—a delay that necessarily develops in transferring cars from one railroad to another—has been emphasized as an important benefit of consolidation. Cars moving through gateways of interchange over a multiline route are usually placed on an interchange track. They are set off in the terminal yards, inspected, and then shunted out for transfer to the yards of the receiving carriers for further through movement. This procedure occasions considerable delay, particularly in the congested terminals. To meet the competition of the one-line routes which operate their trains without any transfer service at the terminals, many carriers forming parts of through routes have devised arrangements to expedite the road-to-road deliveries. Interchange by yard-to-yard transfer, whereby the delay occurring on the interchange track is avoided by transfer from the yard of one com-

CONNECTIONS AND COMPETITORS 123

pany to the yard of another, has been employed "with utmost satisfaction" between the Union Pacific and Southern Pacific at Los Angeles.[17]

The prime service to the shipping public flowing from a sense of common interests between connecting lines is thus usually achieved through a careful coördination of operating arrangements. Some illustrations have already been given; many more might be mentioned. Operating coöperation does not complete the entire picture. Valuable information might be exchanged, information calculated to improve the standard of service on traffic flowing over roads not under common ownership and operation. The efficiency of the five-line Pittsburgh-St. Louis route was aided by the distribution to the Pittsburgh & West Virginia of daily reports on expedited Wheeling & Lake Erie freight prepared by officers of the latter road. These reports known as symbol reports enabled the proper employees to ascertain the exact movement of freight from one station to another. The Pittsburgh & West Virginia could thus obtain accurate data on cars moving from its line to the Wheeling & Lake Erie. And it could therefore furnish its shippers with reliable information on the location of their cars.[18]

The substantiality of business interests between connections leads beyond the rendition of an excellent service on existing traffic. It naturally proceeds to the development of additional business. Every road of any consequence enjoys some strategic advantage, usually expressed through its possession of a short and direct line to and from important points. Perhaps the control of this route may have served as the genesis of its existence. Its salesmen solicit with especial success for the movement of traffic over it.

In their daily contacts they communicate with shippers who have shipments to points that the road, represented by the soliciting salesman, cannot carry. Its line to such points may be unduly circuitous. Because of provisions of the law it may not be able to compete under any conditions. Its participating connection in a through route may be able to carry the business; and the solicitor of one road passes on the information to the solicitor of the other, so that his line may get the business.

Active coöperation between friendly connecting carriers is essential to the formation of efficient traffic routes. Coöperation in through traffic is based on a community of interest which is a resultant of two factors: the long haul and the absence of any substantial volume of competition between connections. If a multiline route is compounded of a full measure of these elements, it can perform a service to the shipping public equal to that performed by an efficient one-line route. It is the presence of both factors to an unusual degree that justifies the traffic officials of both parties to the St. Louis Southwestern–Southern Pacific route in speaking of it in superlative terms. That of the former asserts unequivocally that it gives as good service as a one-line route;[19] while that of the latter states that it is "one of the most remarkable combinations of routes" that has come to his attention.[20]

Many interchange points, on the other hand, serve as foci for the meeting of particular lines under conditions which do not lead to the formation of through routes. The connecting carriers do not unite to form an effective channel of trade and commerce; and the route physically in existence carries but a trifle of the volume of traffic of which it is capable. The interests of the originating line in most, though not in all, cases dominate the situation. Under ordinary conditions it interchanges at a junction giving it its long haul, and with a road at that junction with which it does not compete. Competition may be the life of trade; but it is not an occasion for the surrender of trade secrets to competitors. And just this is the normal result of extensive traffic interchange between competitors. Effective coördination of efforts among participating carriers to insure good service requires among other factors an exchange or at least a mutual examination of waybills. Information with regard to the name and address of the consignor and consignee is thus revealed to the connecting line—a competitor, be it remembered, of the originating line.

What powerful counterbalancing interest should oblige the connection to refrain from soliciting the full haul from the consignor? Even the innocent daily symbol report furnished the Pittsburgh & West Virginia by the Wheeling & Lake Erie to enable the former to trace movements of cars on the latter's line represented an opportunity for competition that did not subserve the best interests of both lines. The latter early in 1927 had established a through route with the Baltimore & Ohio, giving it a longer haul than that realized over the Pittsburgh & West Virginia. The Wheeling & Lake Erie preferred to move the traffic it controlled over the Baltimore & Ohio via Terminal Junction. Prior to that time its best revenue was realized through interchanging with the Pittsburgh & West Virginia at Pittsburgh Junction, Ohio. The symbol report which showed each carload of freight that moved from Wheeling & Lake Erie points over trunk lines competitive with Pittsburgh & West Virginia routes, enabled the latter to solicit on Wheeling & Lake Erie territory against competitive trunk lines. This aided both lines, since both realized the longest possible haul under prevailing conditions.

The new Baltimore & Ohio–Terminal Junction route, however, gave the Wheeling & Lake Erie a longer haul via the Baltimore & Ohio interchange. The symbol report now became an engine of competitive advantage in the hands of the Pittsburgh & West Virginia. The latter's solicitors, armed with information on movements via the Baltimore & Ohio route, appeared in Wheeling & Lake Erie territory for the purpose of inducing shippers to route via a route which short-hauled the originating line. It might ask shippers to move traffic to Philadelphia via Wheeling & Lake Erie to Pittsburgh Junction, Pittsburgh & West Virginia to Pittsburgh, Pittsburgh & Lake Erie to Connellsville, Western Maryland to Shippensburg, and Philadelphia & Reading to Philadelphia. This routing would give the Pittsburgh & West Virginia a full line haul. But it obliged the originating line to surrender the traffic at Pittsburgh Junction when no particular reason existed why it should not pull the carload an additional twenty-eight miles to Terminal Junction for delivery to the Baltimore & Ohio, and realize the additional revenue. The Wheeling & Lake Erie within six months after the opening of the Baltimore & Ohio route discontinued the practice of furnishing the Pittsburgh & West Virginia with the daily symbol reports.[21]

This disinclination of competitors to interchange business represents the second pillar underlying the established routes and traffic channels—the desire of the long haul being the first. The universality of its existence can-

CONNECTIONS AND COMPETITORS 127

not be attested by any all-inclusive data. Accurate interchange figures are not published periodically. Their publication is not required by law. The first body of comprehensive data was made available by the consolidation proceedings before the Interstate Commerce Commission in connection with its efforts to prepare the final plan for consolidation. Further detailed information of varying importance was made available through subsequent proceedings relating to proposals for acquisition of control of railroad properties under the relevant provisions of the Transportation Act of 1920. Sufficient information is publicly available to enable an impartial observer to reach a conclusion that railroad consolidation presents its greatest benefits and its gravest dangers to the country's railroad net from the manner in which it adapts itself to the principles of the long haul, and of the competitive or non-competitive connection.

For consolidation inevitably must disturb traffic interchange between connections. This very disturbance is the prime purpose and effect of consolidation. An originating line acquires one of its connections and with but little delay a train of circumstances is put into effect to increase the volume of traffic moved over that connection. All the heavy weight of soliciting influence is thrown in favor of the new connection. Coöperation and coördination become the watchword; and in time service over the route composed of the acquiring and acquired line is distinctly superior to that offered by the acquiring line with any other connection. And because of the better service afforded, more and more business is attracted to the route.

A consolidation of lines, or a mere acquisition of proprietary interest in one line by another, can be considered successful from the business standpoint if followed by a substantial increase in traffic over the new system. Perhaps economies in operation and capital costs can be achieved. So much the better. Perhaps a better diversity of traffic may follow as an incidental result. Even that advantage is not to be sneered at. That might in time increase somewhat the investment prestige of its securities, and so enhance slightly the price realized from their sale. The public interest might also be served indirectly through the ability of the new system to distribute more equitably the rate burden among its shipping public. With a greater diversity it may be possible to reduce rates on staple products on which the rate represents a high proportion of its value, and increase rates on manufactured goods on which the rate represents a low proportion. It may even happen in the goodness of mankind that a financially weak short line may be acquired. Thus, abandonment of a property necessary to the weal of a considerable population may be prevented.

All these benefits may be realized. They are, however, auxiliaries to the main issue. If there is a heavy interchange between two connections, a community in proprietary interest is desired to insure the maintenance of the interchange. Vested property rights must be protected. If the interchange between connections is light, common proprietary interests are needed to stimulate a heavy interchange. Vested rights must be created that will subsequently call for adequate protection.

The major contention developed in the elaborate proceedings before the Interstate Commerce Commission to aid that body to prepare a complete plan of consolidation, as called for by the law, revolved around the two funda-

CONNECTIONS AND COMPETITORS 129

mental principles of traffic interchange. No railroad executive of a trunk line appeared to protest against a proposed alliance in the Commission's tentative plan because the anticipated economies resulting therefrom would not be equitably distributed among all lines. On the contrary, if a road believed that the acquisition of a particular property was adverse to its own traffic interests, it advocated its disposition to some other property because of economies likely to follow. Observe the solicitude of the Great Northern in recommending the extensive economies, estimated at $5,000,000, as justification for the union of the Chicago, Milwaukee, St. Paul & Pacific with the Northern Pacific.[22] And then consider the prediction of Northern Pacific counsel that even in the immediate future the St. Paul would be of more value to the Great Northern for moving its business than it would be to the Northern Pacific; and, "that if such economies were a factor of importance they would as likely be found in a combination of the Great Northern and St. Paul as in a combination of the Northern Pacific and St. Paul." [23]

Neither the Great Northern nor the Northern Pacific wants the St. Paul; both are agreeable to cede to the other all economies from the St. Paul marriage. Both want the Chicago, Burlington & Quincy—economies or no economies. Both interchange large volumes of traffic with that road. They realize that a union of either with the Burlington would give that road the Burlington interchange. At Billings, Montana, and at Minnesota Transfer, the Chicago, Burlington & Quincy delivers heavy tonnages to the Great Northern. Consolidate the Northern Pacific and the Burlington, and in time the latter as the originating line will divert most of this traffic to the former. The Great Northern, therefore, does not take kindly to the Commission's suggestion to place the Chicago, Burlington & Quincy and the Northern Pacific in one system, and the Great Northern and the Chicago, Milwaukee, St. Paul & Pacific in another. Great Northern's loss of Burlington interchange promises to exceed its gain from St. Paul interchange.

The Chicago, Burlington & Quincy on its side submitted comprehensive testimony through its then president to demonstrate the inequity, even the iniquity, of that part of the Commission's Tentative Plan relating to the disposition of its property. The Great Northern should continue its association with the Burlington, it was urged; the heavy traffic interchange between the two properties must be preserved. If any economies were expected from their continued association, they were not mentioned; except perhaps the resulting financial sterility of large capital investments made in terminals and other properties to move the traffic interchanged between both lines which under the new dispensation could not be used. The Colorado & Southern should not be handed over to the Atchison, Topeka & Santa Fe. That would unquestionably tend to disrupt the interchange between the Burlington and the Colorado & Southern. There may be—undoubtedly are —many economies arising from the control of the latter by the former. And there may be other advantages. But they were not uppermost in the mind of Hale Holden, then president of the Chicago, Burlington & Quincy.

The Union Pacific argued the advantages accruing from its union with the Chicago & North Western. An important interchange of traffic east and west between the two

CONNECTIONS AND COMPETITORS 131

roads at Omaha would be preserved. The Southern Pacific opposed both the union of the Colorado & Southern with the Atchison, Topeka & Santa Fe to the northwest, as well as the union of the St. Louis Southwestern with the Missouri-Kansas-Texas to the northeast. The Santa Fe competes with the Southern Pacific; the latter could not depend on the former, in command of the Colorado & Southern, to give it excellent service on traffic coming to and from Gulf ports destined to Colorado and interchanged at Fort Worth. Neither did the Southern Pacific believe it could depend upon the Missouri-Kansas-Texas—a vigorous competitor in southern Texas—in control of the St. Louis Southwestern, for reliable coördinated service on business to and from Texas and St. Louis and points beyond. The same basis of discussion prevailed in the east. Both the Baltimore & Ohio and the New York Central sought control of the Central Railroad of New Jersey, not primarily to achieve any economies, nor to aid in the development of systems of substantially equivalent earning power; but rather to serve their particular traffic interests.

It would be monotonous to run the gamut of the Consolidation Proceedings for further illustrations. It is substantially correct to state that in the consolidation plans of privately owned and operated railroads in this country traffic considerations are paramount. The long haul and the friendly connection dominate the movement of interchange traffic; and each road in fighting for its share of available business must respect these two principles. Subject to notable exceptions, the large stakes in railroad consolidation are those of traffic interchange.

NOTES TO CHAPTER V

1. Consolidation Proceedings, Docket 12964, Brief for Reading Company, p. 112.
2. *Supra*, Tabulated Statements, New York Central Lines, pp. 15-16.
3. Stuart Daggett, *Railroad Reorganization*, pp. 146-148.
4. *Supra*, pp. 122-123.
5. Proposed Construction, by Pittsburgh and West Virginia Railway, Finance Docket 6229, tr. pp. 2165-2166; O. S. Lewis, Freight Traffic Manager, Baltimore & Ohio R. R.
6. Consolidation Proceedings, Docket 12964, Brief for Great Northern in support of consolidation of Chicago, Burlington & Quincy, Great Northern, Northern Pacific and subsidiaries, p. 73.
7. Wabash–Pittsburgh Terminal Investigation, 48 I.C.C. 97.
8. Proposed Construction by Pittsburgh and West Virginia Railway, Finance Docket 6229, tr. pp. 1355-1356.
9. Interlocking Directors of Wheeling & Lake Erie and Trunk Lines, Finance Docket 3584, tr. p. 755.
10. *Supra*, p. 755.
11. *Supra*, p. 765.
12. Proposed Construction by Pittsburgh and West Virginia Railway, Finance Docket 6229, tr. pp. 1355-1356.
13. *Supra*, pp. 416-417.
14. *Supra*, exhibit no. 54.
15. Proposed Construction by Pittsburgh and West Virginia Railway, Finance Docket 6229, Brief for Intervener, New York, Chicago and St. Louis, p. 47; *supra*, Brief for Applicant, p. 40.
16. Lease of Lehigh & New England Railroad, Finance Docket 5639, Brief for Reading Company, p. 18; also *Supra*, 124 I.C.C. 85.
17. Proposed Construction by Sacramento Northern, Finance Docket 6633, Brief for Southern Pacific Company, Intervener, pp. 26-27.
18. Proposed Construction by Pittsburgh and West Virginia Railway, Finance Docket 6229, Brief for Baltimore & Ohio, pp. 22, 91; *Supra*, Brief for Wheeling & Lake Erie, p. 10.
19. Unification of Southwestern Lines, Finance Docket 5679, tr. p. 1185.
20. *Wall Street Journal*, September 28, 1928, quoting Lewis J. Spence of Southern Pacific.
21. Proposed Construction by Pittsburgh and West Virginia Railway, Finance Docket 6229, Brief for Baltimore & Ohio R. R. Intervener, p. 91.
22. Consolidation Proceedings, Docket 12964, Brief for Northern Pacific in support of Commission's Tentative System, no. 14, p. 74.
23. *Supra*, p. 141.

CHAPTER VI

DIRECT AND INDIRECT ROUTES

The principles discussed in previous chapters by which traffic developed by an originating line is transported for its long haul, and delivered to its noncompetitive connections for further carriage to destination, seems to be challenged by a set of traffic considerations alleged to derive distinctive advantages from railroad consolidations. Promiscuous competition, it is argued, has created a large number of competitive routes through the main traffic lanes of the American railroad net. Many of these lines are long and roundabout; many others are short and direct. But if a road owns the long route and not the short one, it will move its business over the former; and except in case of an unusual circuity, the law protects the routing over the long line.

This practice represents an economic waste. Many train-miles of transportation service are uselessly performed. If the traffic be moved over the shorter routes, the same service to the public could be given at a lower cost. This ideal is to be realized by consolidation. "As a part of that idea of avoiding unnecessary duplication," states the General Counsel of the Association of Railway Executives, "there should be considered . . . the question of a given system being able to do a business on its own lines by shorter hauls. A railroad man having business wants to carry it on its own lines, and perhaps will carry it by a longer route. Now if we had [there were] available lines by which they could do the same service and carry by a shorter route, the cost of the hauling would be less."[1] And the even higher authority of the opinion of Henry C. Hall, a former member of the Interstate Commerce Commission, is warrant for the assertion that one of the advantages of consolidation "is that there being brought into one system various lines, other things being equal, the shortest route from that system would be the best route in that system for the purpose of getting a carload of goods from one place to another."[2] Edward Chambers, the able traffic executive of the Atchison, Topeka & Santa Fe, has claimed even more for consolidation. "It would enable," he states, "the discontinuance of back hauls and permit hauling via most direct rails and would enable the nonuse of many junction points and permit the use of the most natural and economic junction."[3]

The case for consideration of direct routing seems to be further strengthened by the traffic advantages adduced in the railroad unification programs laid before the Interstate Commerce Commission. Almost every proposal to acquire majority stock control, or to lease another line— or even the acquisition of a minority stock control requiring representation on the directorate of the road the stock of which has been acquired—has been supported by an exposition of the new and direct routes to take the place of existing routes. Many able and veteran traffic officials have submitted charts, exhibits, distance tables, maps, etc., to indicate the saving in mileages particular consolidations would effect. With an almost surprising degree of unanimity short, direct, and natural routes seem to flow as an inevitable consequence of corporate unification. The

DIRECT AND INDIRECT ROUTES 135

very first unification—the Missouri Pacific lines—formed with the Commission's approval under paragraph two, section five, of the Transportation Act, achieved a short route from the Rio Grande Valley to the middle west;[4] (see map on page 283) the other major southwestern grouping involving the Missouri-Kansas-Texas, the Kansas City Southern, and the St. Louis Southwestern, was to result in the formation of a shorter route to St. Louis from many points in the southwest, and a shorter route to Port Arthur from many points in Texas, Oklahoma and Missouri.[5] Both of the so-called Nickel Plate cases, representing the most important unification plan developed in eastern territory, were featured by the description of new routes that the plan was to realize. A new route over system lines via Columbus and Marion, Ohio, for the transportation of westbound West Virginia coal to Chicago was to replace the Chesapeake & Ohio route over its own Chicago division. A composite Erie–Nickel Plate route on Ohio–New York City traffic was to replace the existing unsatisfactory Erie route; and numerous new and short routes were to be established between central western and southeastern territory.[6]

The monumental mass of interesting and accurate data furnished to describe and explain the new routes in these and other cases seems apparently to convince the observer; and if consolidation so convincingly eliminates unnatural, uneconomic, and circuitous routing, one would reasonably expect the existing strong systems to be free of such wastes. The facts, however, confound the implication. There is, perhaps, no rail carrier that does not send part of its traffic by long and circuitous channels. And, on the other hand, there is perhaps no carrier of any importance that does not control a number of short and direct routes over which a heavy volume of traffic moves.

Indeed this may be said to be the natural evolution of the American railroad net. Each important property was originally conceived to connect particular areas of traffic production and traffic consumption. The carrier that first built through this region naturally selected the most favorable route. It controlled the short line between two or more important points to and from which a profitable volume of business moved. If the business proved sufficiently lucrative, competition was invited. Other roads were formed to carry business between the same points. The shortest and most favorable route having been preempted, the next best was selected. It is even possible that the latter—the less favorable route—may have succeeded in giving a superior grade of service. Perhaps through better management and efficient coördination with connections it moved its trains faster and on better schedule than its more favored competitor. In that case it carried more traffic. The probabilities are, however, that the pioneer line, if allowed a sufficiently long period to consolidate its traffic position, would, as the originating line, have commanded the haul on the greater portion of the available traffic.

Strange as it may seem, the pioneering line—and perhaps the major originating line—in a particular territory may not control the direct short route. Economic geography constantly changes and with it the major channels of trade and commerce change. A road builds through a region in directions that are based on trade trends then existing and that appear likely to continue. The Chicago, Milwaukee & St. Paul builds west of the Missouri River

DIRECT AND INDIRECT ROUTES 137

on the assumption that heavy immigration will continue into the northwest, and that the movement of eastbound lumber from that section will continue. Who can predict a new Congressional concept of immigration policy and its economic effects? And what economic or political wizard can foretell of the amazing growth in eastbound Panama canal traffic? And who can even now foresee the ultimate consequences of the growth of the Gulf ports with the accompanying increase in the volume of north and southbound traffic?

Every road in the country, except the short-line stub-end feeders, controls some short route connecting important traffic centers. This represents its chief claim to existence, and, together with its power to originate valuable traffic, its important strategic value. The Pennsylvania, with the New York, New Haven & Hartford, controls the short route from Pittsburgh to Boston; and with the Delaware & Hudson, the short route from Pittsburgh to Montreal. Over its own lines it controls the short route from such basic points in the Middle West as Chicago, Cleveland and Cincinnati to New York.[7] In western territory the Chicago & North Western controls the short line between Chicago and Omaha; the Atchison, Topeka & Santa Fe, the short line between Chicago and Kansas City; the Chicago, Burlington & Quincy, the short line between Kansas City and Omaha; the Chicago Great Western, between St. Paul and Omaha; the Chicago, Rock Island & Pacific, between St. Paul and Kansas City; the Wabash between St. Louis and Omaha; the Chicago & Alton between St. Louis and Kansas City; the St. Louis & San Francisco between St. Louis and Forth Worth; etc.[8]

The ownership of short routes is thus fairly widely scattered among different carriers. Almost every important property controls some short line between some points. And it also follows that that same property controls some indirect line between other points. Unless the circuity is too great, all carriers compete for traffic between important centers of production and consumption. The existing law sets a dead line of 15 per cent; competitively uniform rates cannot be established over lines with a mileage circuity beyond that limit. Within that limit the longer line competes strongly and successfully with the short line.

Many of the longer routes exceed the short routes by only a few miles, and perhaps the latter may make deliveries a few hours ahead of the former. But expedited railroad service is not measured by hours. The business day starts in the morning; and the arrival of a shipment at one or two o'clock in the morning produces no differential service advantage over one that arrives at five. Unless a one-morning-earlier arrival service can be rendered, the short line cannot attract a large volume of traffic towards its line.

And, it must be emphasized, carriers consolidate with other lines—be they long or short—to capture added traffic. The mainspring of business interest does not rest on an apparent saving in mileage that may be effected by a particular acquisition. The economy is small in any event. The saving in expenses can be effected only if, as indicated hereafter, many other factors are favorable. If a carrier originates desirable traffic, the long haul of which can be made to flow over a particular carrier, that particular carrier will move to acquire it—providing the ac-

DIRECT AND INDIRECT ROUTES 139

quisition can be made on reasonable terms. For everything has a price.

Under these circumstances, it is extremely doubtful whether consolidation necessarily results in the increasing utilization of short routes with resultant benefits to the public interest. The incidental character of this aspect of consolidation was thrown into bold relief by the action of the Interstate Commerce Commission on the proposal of the Chicago, Rock Island & Pacific to acquire stock control of the St. Louis Southwestern. The former serves territory in Arkansas and Louisiana. Besides its Choctaw main line running west from Memphis, Tennessee, it reaches local traffic producing territory in Arkansas with a number of branch lines. Another branch line operates south through northern and central Louisiana. This territory has within recent years developed a considerable tonnage of oil and bauxite to add to the lumber which is the staple commodity, although the movement of the latter has been declining in recent years. The consuming markets in St. Louis and points east can be reached only over an extraordinarily circuitous route of the Rock Island. The Rock Island system runs due west from St. Louis paralleling its Choctaw line. There is no physical connection between these two lines short of a point in central Oklahoma. To reach St. Louis from Arkansas, the Rock Island traverses three sides of an approximate parallelogram. To go east to St. Louis it first goes west along the Choctaw line to El Reno, Oklahoma; it then moves northward through Wichita and Herington, Kansas, to Junction City; there it turns east to Kansas City and St. Louis. (See map on page 141.)

An available supply of system empties moves over another trilinear route. The Rock Island carries cotton, wheat and miscellaneous products south to Fort Worth and to the Gulf through its semicontrolled Trinity & Brazos Valley, and other connections. Northward it carries much less. A supply of empties accumulates at Fort Worth. Three hundred and twenty-seven miles to the east the St. Louis Southwestern connects at Fordyce, Arkansas, with the north and south Arkansas-Louisiana line of the Chicago, Rock Island & Pacific. That line carries a preponderant tonnage of northbound business. To convey the empty cars from Fort Worth to Fordyce over the Rock Island requires a northward movement from Fort Worth, Texas, to El Reno, Oklahoma, an eastward movement from El Reno to Little Rock, Arkansas, and a southward movement from Little Rock to point of traffic origin, a total distance of 627.5 miles.[9]

The St. Louis Southwestern extending, as its name indicates, southwest from St. Louis, fits in nicely with the Rock Island lines in Arkansas, Louisiana and Texas. Its lines connect the two parallel east and west arms of the Rock Island running west from St. Louis and Memphis respectively, and it operates due east from Fort Worth to a connection with the Rock Island lines in southern Arkansas. Combination of these carriers represents the possibility of short-routing on an extensive scale. On traffic moving from St. Louis and beyond via the Rock Island to destinations on its lines in Arkansas, Louisiana, and some points in Oklahoma, the haul on the average is twice as long as the haul via the St. Louis Southwestern.[10]

This combination was effected early in 1925 through the acquisition of stock control of the St. Louis South-

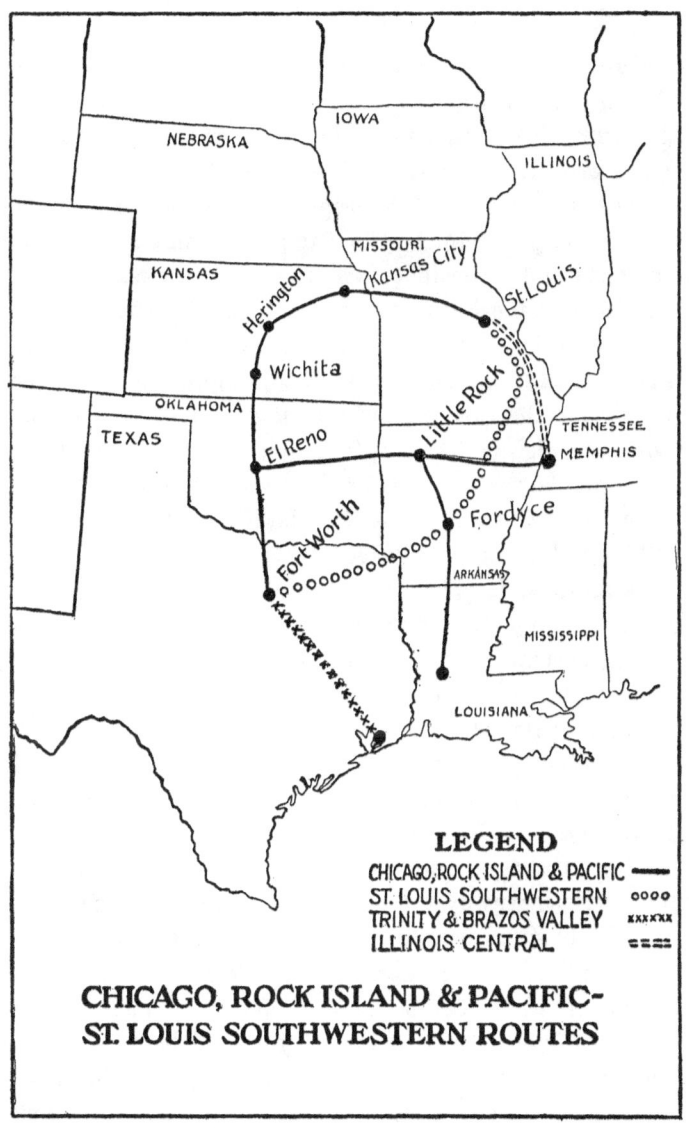

western by the Chicago, Rock Island & Pacific. The potential reduction in wasteful mileage resulting from this unification of railroads was clearly explained to the proper governmental authorities. The Commission's examiner quite properly expressed the opinion that elimination of circuitous routing did not represent a sufficient contribution to the public interest to warrant the union of railroad interests under consideration. Further facts were needed, particularly those bearing upon the possible effects on the destiny of the St. Louis & San Francisco, before any intelligent conclusion could be reached. The examiner recommended to the Commission that it disapprove of the proposed acquisition; and before that recommendation was acted upon, the Rock Island's share interest in the St. Louis Southwestern was sold to the Kansas City Southern.

The reduction in mileage that this combination might have afforded is not so great in practice as it appears to be on the map. It demonstrates again the difficulty, if not the downright danger, of drawing conclusions with respect to the advantages of consolidations. The reduction in train miles that might have ensued from the Rock Island's acquisition of the St. Louis Southwestern through the elimination of the former's route from St. Louis via El Reno to Arkansas and Louisiana points is largely hypothetical. Only a trifling volume of traffic between these territories moves over this route. The route is legally incapacitated from carrying any business. Its excessive circuity precludes it from quoting the low competitive rate to and from St. Louis unless it quotes similar rates to the many intermediate points en route. It being unprofitable and perhaps illegal to adopt such a policy, the Rock Island moves none of this business over its own circuitous

DIRECT AND INDIRECT ROUTES 143

lines. It transfers lumber and oil originating in Arkansas and Louisiana, bound for St. Louis and beyond, to the Illinois Central and the St. Louis & San Francisco at Memphis, Tennessee.[11] The Rock Island thus performs the unenviable task of short-hauling itself. The proposed union of the Rock Island with the St. Louis Southwestern accorded strictly with the established principles of traffic diversion. The former acquired the latter to improve its competitive position in southwestern territory, and to divert traffic so far as possible from its then Memphis connections to its own system lines.

Had the Rock Island shifted its Memphis-St. Louis traffic from its former preferred connections—the Illinois Central and the St. Louis & San Francisco—to its new partner in interest, the St. Louis Southwestern, it would have realized a long haul for its system lines. That this would have benefited the public interest is open to question. The short lines between Memphis and St. Louis are the St. Louis & San Francisco and the Illinois Central with distances respectively of 306 and 310 miles. The route of the St. Louis Southwestern is unduly circuitous, aggregating 400 miles.[12] To the extent that the proposed Chicago, Rock Island & Pacific–St. Louis Southwestern union would replace the Illinois Central and the St. Louis & San Francisco route on St. Louis–Memphis business by the St. Louis Southwestern, it would increase circuitous routing. On the other hand, the same corporate association would replace long by short routes on traffic to and from St. Louis and points in eastern Arkansas, Oklahoma and Louisiana.[13]

The diversion of traffic from existing connections to other connections incorporated within the new system—

the diversion that constitutes the ultimate aim and effect of every consolidation—may thus bring in its train the elimination of some long routes. And it may also conceivably eliminate other short routes. If a particular route-on-paper is unduly circuitous, extralegally so, then it moves no traffic. The route is purely an academic concept. If it does move a profitable volume of business there is nothing in the rate and cost situation that would exert overwhelming pressure to move that traffic artificially over a short route. If the short route is part of the system, well and good. It would be a fatal indictment of the management, indeed, if it did not realize the saving by performing the greatest volume of ton miles with the least possible number of train-miles. But it would be equally fatal to the efficiency of the management to sacrifice ton miles over its own lines to the so-called public interests which appear to require the movement over a short line not included in the system's mileage.

The unifications effected under the spur of private competitive interest since 1920 is a clear demonstration of the contradictory reaction of long and short routes. The Missouri Pacific system, the first organized with the official blessing of the Interstate Commerce Commission, was characterized by that body as being in the public interest partly because it provided "the shortest route from Brownsville, Houston and Galveston to St. Louis, Chicago and various eastern points." [14] The same system, however, provided a new and comparatively circuitous route from points in north Texas via Waco to Beaumont and Port Arthur to compete with the short route of the Southern Pacific.[15] Prior to the formation of the Missouri Pacific system, the Gulf Coast Lines achieved their traffic

DIRECT AND INDIRECT ROUTES 145

destiny by routing traffic eastward for interchange via Louisiana gateways. As a part of the Missouri Pacific, the system interests turned its traffic star northward via interchange with the affiliated International Great Northern. That produced, as noted by the Interstate Commerce Commission, a short route to many northern Mississippi and Ohio Valley points. But it also established a circuitous route from Texas originating points to Kansas City and other Missouri Valley points.

To take another illustration in the southwest: the union of the Kansas City Southern and the St. Louis Southwestern would give the former a short route to St. Louis from Texas and Louisiana points,[16] and the latter a short route to Kansas City from its Texas and Louisiana points. But this same union would afford circuitous routes to important destinations in central and southern Kansas, as compared with a route formed by a union of the St. Louis Southwestern with the Chicago, Rock Island & Pacific.[17]

In the east, Commission consideration has been given to the consolidation of the Baltimore & Ohio with the Philadelphia & Reading and the Central Railroad of New Jersey. The latter two carriers ship many cars of anthracite coal west to Buffalo and beyond from the Mahanoy and Shamokin regions via Newberry Junction. This is the "short, direct and economic route."[18] The Baltimore & Ohio in control of these two lines would be recreant to its best interests if it did not exert all legitimate means as the originating property to swerve this traffic over its own lines. A waste in mileage would then inevitably result. And the late A. H. Smith, former president of the New York Central, urged vigorously in the Consolidation Proceedings before the Commission, that control of the Central Railroad of New Jersey by his road would not lead to the perpetuation of the short interior Shippensburg route for the movement of Baltimore & Ohio soft coal into New York City. The New York Central in control of the Central Railroad of New Jersey would not grant the Baltimore & Ohio trackage rights from Allentown, Pennsylvania, to Bound Brook, New Jersey. It would grant trackage over the Bound Brook-Jersey City line. The Baltimore & Ohio, if it desired to compete with coal hauled by the New York Central from the Clearfield coal district, would be obliged to move its coal over the long and congested seaboard route through Baltimore and Philadelphia.[19]

It is fairly probable that no important unification or consolidation can be effected, nor any reasonably practical one suggested, which will not, to some extent, present similar situations of long and short routes, of direct and indirect routing. In any event the measure of possible loss or gain in transportation cost cannot be computed by a comparison of distances alone. The transportation service involves the creation of ton miles. The mileage in a route tells only a part of the story of transportation cost. A particular unification produces some short and some long routes. The ultimate saving in transportation costs, however, depends in part upon the relative volume of traffic carried over the several routes. A union based on the elimination of a long route but little used, as illustrated by the Rock Island route from Arkansas and Louisiana to St. Louis, is suggestive of little savings. It bears a negligible relation to the public interest which requires efficient service at reasonable rates.

DIRECT AND INDIRECT ROUTES 147

Even more significant are the unifications considered —and in some cases approved—by the Commission which directly promote roundabout routing. The most notable, perhaps, was the proposed lease of the Buffalo, Rochester & Pittsburgh by the Delaware & Hudson. The former is a bituminous coal carrier traversing the Clearfield coal district of western Pennsylvania, while the latter is an anthracite carrier serving the Wyoming coal field in the northeastern part of the same state. The properties do not connect physically; and the distances over intermediate connections approximate, by the Delaware, Lackawanna & Western, 158 miles; by the Lehigh Valley, 163; and by the Pennsylvania, 228 miles. A considerable volume of the anthracite of the proposed lessee moves to Buffalo and to Canada via the Lake Ontario ferries. The proposed lessor enjoys access to both of these gateways.

The Delaware & Hudson negotiated a trackage arrangement with the Pennsylvania—the most circuitous connection, be it noted—for the purpose of forming a through route over its own system lines. Anthracite coal formerly moving over the Lehigh Valley or the Delaware, Lackawanna & Western to Buffalo was now to move over the Delaware & Hudson–Buffalo, Rochester & Pittsburgh, with Pennsylvania trackage. While the route from the anthracite region to Buffalo via the Lehigh Valley was 272 miles; and via the Delaware & Hudson in conjunction with the Lehigh Valley 314 miles; and via the Lackawanna, 253 miles; the distance via the new trackage route was to be 405 miles.[20] The proposed lessee expressed its intention of doing all it possibly could to divert the anthracite coal traffic from its short route competitors to its own long trackage route. (See map on page 149.)

The unification through lease of these two carriers was disapproved by the closest possible vote of six to five. One commissioner concurred in the rejection solely on the ground that the disposition of the lessor road should await the formulation of a more comprehensive plan for the consolidation in eastern trunk line territory. The expression of dissent from the majority view completely ignored the considerations bearing on direct and indirect routing. It favored the unification because the two lines did not compete; because their unified operation would result in some economies; because the rental was not excessive; because there were no unjust or unreasonable provisions in the trackage and lease contracts; and finally because the shippers favored the arrangement.[21] But not a word on the desirability, to say nothing of the necessity, of direct routes.

That railroad consolidation necessarily leads to direct routing is in substance based on a misconception of the impelling forces behind the movement. Direct routing may or may not be an accompanying incident. Direct routing is not in all cases in the public interest. It may not lead to better service or more reasonable rates. Costs of transportation do not consist of distance factors exclusively. Grades and curvatures exert an effect on operating and capital costs out of all proportion to distance. Hardly an important carrier of the country exists which has not sacrificed distance to good grades. The increasingly heavy trainload of the modern era of transportation imperatively demands low grades for economical operation. And when heavy grades limit the trainload, new routes involving longer distance are used; or what is even more common, expensive cut-offs compelling heavy

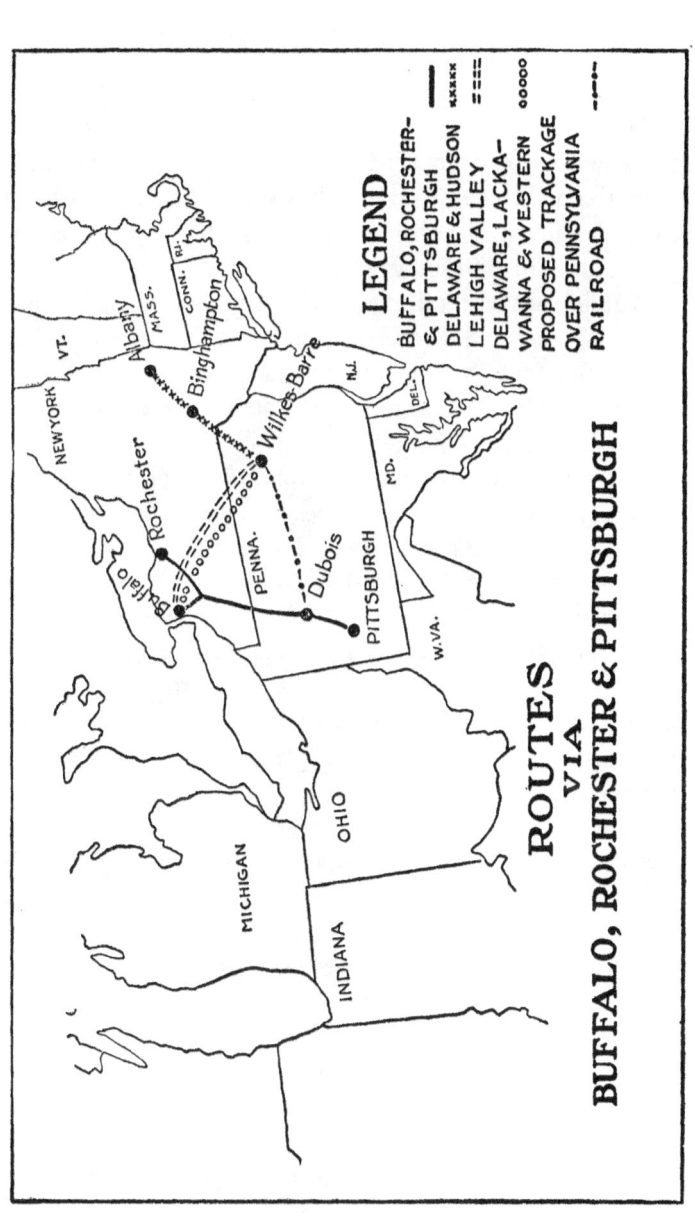

capital expenditures are constructed. Both the Baltimore & Ohio and the Pennsylvania have, within recent years, built cut-offs and reduced grades on an extensive scale. The Magnolia cut-off on the Baltimore & Ohio, with its small saving in distance, justified its cost only by the 50 per cent reduction in grade.[22] The reduction in grades by 70 per cent on its line near Canton, Ohio, by the Pennsylvania, achieved a trifling reduction in distance; but the $5,000,000 investment, due largely to grade reduction, realized a handsome annual saving in train operating costs of over $550,000.[23]

The Pennsylvania uses circuitous routes on some of its most important lines. It sacrifices distance to grades. Right in the heart of its system from Pittsburgh to Conemaugh just east of Johnstown, it uses a line extending north from Pittsburgh along the west bank of the Monongahela River, which crosses the river at right angles and then follows two small streams, until it joins the main line east of Johnstown. This low grade line is 18 miles longer than the southern shorter but high grade line over the Ohio Connecting Bridge.[24]

Between Baltimore and Harrisburg, the Pennsylvania reduces its operating costs by using its low grade Columbia & Port Deposit line. The additional 29 miles is "vastly more than compensated for by the greater tonnage which can be handled over the lower grade." [25]

The Lehigh Valley built a roundabout route to its Tifft Farm Terminal at Buffalo in order to avoid congested conditions on its direct route; and the Pennsylvania makes a wide detour at Horseshoe Curve to gain distance in climbing the mountain.[26]

Shorter routes are therefore not more economical

DIRECT AND INDIRECT ROUTES 151

routes; and a saving in distance is not always equivalent to a saving in costs. Indeed a saving in mileage may be dearly purchased by a more than compensating loss due to excessive grades. Out of the amazingly elaborate record in the numerous unification cases that have passed in review before the Commission—a goodly part of it filled with minutiæ bearing only on specific private interests—only a small amount of consideration has been given to the transportation costs over various routes. The surprising paucity of the record upon which the formation of the Missouri Pacific system, the acquisition of the St. Paul's interest in the Chicago, Milwaukee & Gary and in the Chicago, Terre Haute & Southeastern, etc., was approved represents an excellent illustration of the extent to which the public interest is or can be considered in technical proceedings. Only infrequently did the stimulus of private interest produce any data of great value on the subject of comparative cost of different lines. A rather notable situation developed from the recommendation of the Interstate Commerce Commission in its Tentative Plan of Consolidation that the Northern Pacific be allied with the Chicago, Burlington & Quincy, and the Great Northern with the Chicago, Milwaukee & St. Paul. The Burlington is financially a strong road and pays good dividends, and the St. Paul is financially a weak road and pays no dividends. The St. Paul and the Northern Pacific parallel each other for many miles in Montana. Competition is close; and on the other hand their unification would promote many economies in operation. The Great Northern in the Consolidation Proceedings naturally invited the Commission to consider these economies, particularly in the light of their bearing upon a union of the Chicago,

Milwaukee & St. Paul with the Northern Pacific rather than with itself.

It therefore prepared a detailed statement of savings certain to ensue, it was alleged, from the union of the St. Paul with the other property. Through the utilization of short routes and the abandonment of 372 miles of road, a total annual saving of over $5,000,000 was predicted.[27] Operating and other costs would be reduced to this aggregate amount because of a reduction of 583,500,000 net ton miles, and 1,190,338 passenger train miles.

The Northern Pacific then undertook to show that long and expensive mileage routes might be low grade and economical transportation routes. Low grades so reduced operating costs that the net savings from the use of direct routes was materially revised.[28] In one particular case the Northern Pacific had, paradoxically enough, built a cut-off in northwestern Montana at "a very heavy expenditure," which increased the mileage between two points from 68 miles to 100 miles. Over the long line, however, one engine could handle 50 per cent more tonnage than two engines could over the short line.[29]

The clash of opinion between the experts developed another significant line of reasoning. Divert traffic to the short line from the long line. That might produce savings arising from the use of the short line. But what of the capital investment in the long line and in the accompanying yard and terminal facilities? This capital investment must be amortized. How will this loss compare with the operating savings realized from the use of the short route? Suppose that that part of the route slated for abandonment is held under contract with other properties subject to a financial arrangement obliging each road

DIRECT AND INDIRECT ROUTES 153

to pay a fixed sum regardless of use. In discussing the consolidation of the Northern Pacific and the Chicago, Milwaukee & St. Paul, it was proposed that the latter abandon the use of certain tracks used jointly with the Oregon, Washington Railroad & Navigation Company. Some of the tracks are owned by the latter and leased to the St. Paul; some are owned by the latter and leased to the Oregon Company. The Spokane terminals are jointly owned, and were constructed as a joint undertaking. The invested capital approximates $10,000,000.[30] If, as has been urged, the St. Paul abandon the use of this property, what will be the total annual loss; and how will it compare with the total annual savings realizable from such abandonment?

And this is not all. The long line may carry a heavy volume of traffic, and the short line a light volume. That situation looks ideal. It represents the railroad condition in the northwest. The short line, the St. Paul, carries little traffic; the long line, the Northern Pacific, carries much traffic. But what is the physical condition of the short line? What facilities does it own to enable it to carry the increased volume of business? If its facilities are insufficient, what investment will be required to enable it to furnish the public with adequate service? And how much invested capital on the long line will be lost to provide transportation service on the short line? Existing yards, stations, sidetracks and the other appurtenances of the railroad business will be junked on the long line; and new appurtenances of a similar character must at the same time be provided for on the short line. In no important unification case have these considerations been adequately presented to the Interstate Commerce Commission; and in no important case has the Commission developed them on its own initiative.

Suppose on the other hand that the long line carries a light volume of traffic and the short line a heavy volume. Would it be in the public interest to force traffic over the short line up to and beyond its capacity? Indeed, if the long line is not congested and has fairly smooth grades, the question is raised whether short-line routing is not distinctly against the best interests of the public. Representatives of both private and public interests have frequently stressed the avoidance of congestion as one of the benefits of consolidation. Edward Chambers of the Atchison, Topeka & Santa Fe, a man of wide experience in the railroad business, has stated as one of the benefits of consolidation the "taking advantage of each opportunity to go around congested terminals." [31] Professor William Z. Ripley, in his Report to the Interstate Commission on the Consolidation of Railroads, considered "the encouragement of alternate routes and gateways in order to relieve present or prospective congestion at the great railway meeting points," as a "general principle constantly [to be] kept in mind in connection with consolidation and having substantial effect upon it." [32]

Under conditions which are not by any means unusual, circuitous routing may be economically justified. Short and direct routes frequently pass through congested terminals. Transportation costs are excessive, and service is slow and unsatisfactory. Plant expansion is particularly expensive. The cost of land—if land be available—is high, and perhaps prohibitive. Taxes are high, and so are wages.

Noncongested lines, regardless of their circuity, moving around large terminals rather than through them,

DIRECT AND INDIRECT ROUTES 155

have become more and more valuable within recent years. The St. Paul's acquisition of the Chicago, Milwaukee & Gary is due in part to the former's desire to control a belt line around rather than through the Chicago terminal area.[33] The control of the Ann Arbor by the Wabash was to some extent prompted by a similar desire of the latter road to avoid the terminal delays in Chicago. The distance between such representative points as Toledo, Buffalo, Detroit on one hand, and St. Paul on the other via the translake ferries is only slightly less than the distance via Chicago. Yet it has been reliably stated that under normal conditions the car ferry route makes "three days' better time" than is made through Chicago.[34]

The increasing congestion through the nation's metropolis has occasioned numerous official investigations and has produced a number of administrative public bodies specially qualified to deal with the problem.[35] A considerable proportion of the traffic that crowds the New York Harbor is destined for New England. Much of it can reach the consignee through the noncongested Delaware Valley tracks of the Lehigh & New England and the Lehigh & Hudson. Yet they are but little used for this purpose. Except for some local cement and some bituminous coal emanating from mines on the Baltimore & Ohio system and the Western Maryland, the Lehigh & New England cannot be utilized for New England traffic. The lack of through rates closes the line for most of this business.[36] The Lehigh & Hudson is freely used for this purpose by the Central Railroad of New Jersey. The latter does so, however, only under business compulsion. It would rather use New York Harbor; but the New York, New Haven & Hartford refuses to establish through rates for this purpose. It closes this gateway against the movement of any Central Railroad of New Jersey traffic coming from any point west of a line drawn through Allentown, and Harrisburg, Pennsylvania, and Martinsburg, West Virginia. All the lines originating New England-bound traffic control lines to New York Harbor. They prefer to haul traffic to the very end of their lines and thus realize their long haul.

It may be suggested that the circuity, amounting to about 15 per cent of the Delaware Valley route over the New York Harbor route, might prevent the rendition of an adequate standard of service. This is not the case. The train time may be slightly longer. The terminal time is much less. The New York, New Haven & Hartford has advised the Interstate Commerce Commission that the movement via the circuitous route "requires thirteen hours less time in the case of local merchandise than via New York Harbor; twenty-four hours less time in the case of overhead merchandise; and from thirty-seven to thirty-nine hours less time in the case of anthracite coal. Generally speaking, in other words, merchandise takes from one-half a day to a day longer to move through New York Harbor than through Maybrook (the circuitous route), while coal takes over a day and a half longer." [37]

These small, noncongested lines possess strategic importance. They represent a valuable prize in the consolidation contest. The Philadelphia & Reading wants to acquire exclusive possession of the Lehigh & New England. Its proposal to lease the property was rejected by the Interstate Commerce Commission.[38] The Pennsylvania wants it; and it does not want the Philadelphia & Reading to have it.[39] Professor Ripley in the appendix to the Tenta-

DIRECT AND INDIRECT ROUTES

tive Consolidation Plan of the Commission, expressed the opinion (impliedly at least) that neither should have it; it should be controlled by a trunk line either at its northern or southern end.[40]

It is agreed on all sides that additional traffic should move over this interior route. The trunk line carriers think so, providing they are not short-hauled; the Interstate Commerce Commission thinks so. The Port of New York Authorities, charged with the efficient administration of the Port, think so: "freight, alien to it [the New York Harbor] in origin and destination," it states, "which can be routed via other natural gateways . . . should be so routed, so as to provide ample and adequate capacity in all local harbor terminals for handling the traffic, which must of necessity pass to, from or through this port." [41]

The interior route may be indirect from Easton, Pennsylvania to New England destinations. But it is direct in connection with the Baltimore & Ohio, Western Maryland, and Philadelphia & Reading from the former's coal mines in West Virginia to Easton. It is shorter than the Baltimore & Ohio route to New England via Philadelphia and New York Harbor. More than that, it is a more economical route. It passes through no congested terminals. It possesses ample spare capacity for the carriage of additional business. It performs better service.

Here is a route, therefore, that is dual in nature. It is short in part and long in part. Its circuity, however, is in the public interest. Its use, rather than the use of the harbor route, seems more likely to lead to more economical transportation costs, and this is the best assurance of excellent service at adequate rates.

NOTES TO CHAPTER VI

1. Hearings before the Senate Committee on Interstate Commerce, 68th Congress, 2d session on S. 2224, Part 2, p. 68.
2. *Supra*, 69th Congress, 1st session, on S. 1870, p. 106.
3. *Supra*, p. 97.
4. Control of Gulf Coast Lines by Missouri Pacific R. R., 94 I.C.C. 199.
5. Unification of Southwestern Lines, 124 I.C.C. 418.
6. Nickel Plate Unification, Finance Docket 4643, 4671, Brief for Applicant, Abstract of Evidence, Vol. II, pp. 28-37.
7. Construction by New York, Pittsburgh & Chicago Railroad, Finance Docket 4741, Brief for Applicant, p. 12.
8. Consolidation Proceedings, Docket 12964, Brief for Great Northern Railway in support of consolidation of Chicago, Burlington & Quincy, Great Northern, Northern Pacific and subsidiaries, p. 139.
9. Control of St. Louis Southwestern, Finance Docket 4809, Brief for the Chicago, Rock Island & Pacific, p. 44.
10. *Supra*, p. 22.
11. This was the situation, at least, prior to the acquisition of a minority share interest in the Chicago, Rock Island & Pacific by the St. Louis & San Francisco, and the creation with approval by the Commission of interlocking directorate interests between the two roads.
12. Acquisition and construction of lines in southeastern Missouri and northeastern Arkansas, Finance Docket 7031, 7032, Brief for Applicant, Abstract of Testimony and Exhibits, p. 23.
13. Control of St. Louis Southwestern, Finance Docket 4809, Brief for the Chicago, Rock Island & Pacific, pp. 21-23.
14. Control of Gulf Coast Lines by Missouri Pacific, 94 I.C.C. 199.
15. Construction by W. B. T. & S. R. R., Finance Docket 3197, 5104, Brief for Applicant, Statement of Case and Abstract of Evidence. Part II, p. 128, 137-138, 157, *supra*, 124 I.C.C. 806-807.
16. Unification of Southwestern Lines, Finance Docket 5679-5680, Brief for Applicants, Vol. II, p. 91.
17. Control of St. Louis Southwestern, Finance Docket 4809, exhibit no. 7.
18. Consolidation Proceedings, Docket 12964, Statement of Agnew T. Dice for Reading Company, May 7, 1923, p. 73.
19. *Supra*, Brief for Port of New York Authority, pp. 64-65.
20. Control of Buffalo, Rochester & Pittsburgh, Finance Docket 5656, 6147, Brief for Baltimore & Ohio, Intervener, p. 87.
21. *Supra*, 131 I.C.C. 750.
22. Proposed Construction by Pittsburgh & West Virginia Ry., Finance Docket 6229, Brief for Baltimore & Ohio, Intervener, p. 109.
23. *Supra*, tr. p. 2229.
24. *Supra*, tr. p. 2216.
25. *Supra*, Brief for Pennsylvania, Intervener, p. 21.

DIRECT AND INDIRECT ROUTES

26. *Supra*, p. 53.
27. Consolidation Proceedings, Docket 12964, Brief and argument in opposition to choice of Great Northern rather than Northern Pacific for separation from Chicago, Burlington & Quincy and association with the Chicago, Milwaukee & St. Paul, tr. p. 67.
28. *Supra*, Brief for Northern Pacific in support of Commission's System No. 14, pp. 77, 108-111.
29. *Supra*, pp. 106-107; tr. p. 1989.
30. *Supra*, pp. 92-93.
31. Hearings before the Senate Committee on Interstate Commerce, 69th Congress, 1st session, on S. 1870, p. 97.
32. Consolidation of Railroads, 63 I.C.C. 484.
33. Control of C., M. & G. Ry. by Chicago, Milwaukee & St. Paul Ry., 71 I.C.C. 124.
34. Acquisition of Ann Arbor, Finance Docket 4942, tr. p. 28.
35. New York Harbor Case, 47 I.C.C. 643; see Port Authority Statutes published by the Port of New York Authority; see also the valuable annual reports of the Port of New York Authority.
36. Lease of Lehigh & New England, Finance Docket 5639, Brief for Reading Company, pp. 22-23.
37. Central Railroad of New Jersey *vs.* New York, New Haven & Hartford, Docket 16721, Brief for Respondents, p. 90.
38. Lease of Lehigh & New England, 124 I.C.C. 81.
39. *Supra*, Finance Docket 5639, Brief for Pennsylvania R. R., pp. 14-16.
40. Consolidation of Railroads, 63 I.C.C. 521.
41. Port of New York Authority, Annual Report for 1925, p. 30.

CHAPTER VII

CLOSED AND OPEN ROUTES

Railroad traffic moves on a simple basis. A shipment between points on one road is local traffic, and one over two or more roads is through traffic. A shipment in the latter class may be assessed the local rate on each road—what is known in the technical language of the rate experts as a combination of locals. Most shipments over two or more lines pay a rate lower than the latter. Such rates are known as through or proportional. With these as a solid foundation there has been erected a vast superstructure of highly technical rates and charges. The rapidly changing economic and business needs of the country have necessitated constant and multitudinous adjustments. And the rate structure has been molded accordingly.

If two or more roads physically connecting do not wish to move any of their traffic over each other's lines, they usually establish local rates. They move traffic on a combination of locals. They cannot lawfully refuse to move any traffic offered for carriage. The originating road therefore assesses a local rate for movement towards the junction with one connection, and a through or proportional rate for movement towards the junction with some other connection. The latter rates are almost always lower than the former; and little traffic moves over a route that pays a combination of locals—a higher rate. Such a route

CLOSED AND OPEN ROUTES 161

is said to be "closed," while a route privileged to forward business on through or proportional rates is said to be "open."

The great volume of freight traffic interchanged among American railroads moves over open routes. Each road at the confines of its territorial jurisdiction, at its many junction points, provides facilities for the transfer of the loaded or empty freight car to the tracks of its neighbor. The car is moved, repairs are made, the accounting is rendered on the basis of rules to which all Class I roads give their approval. The rate from origin to destination is paid by the shipper to the originating road; and the latter accounts to the participants in the transportation service on the basis of "divisions" mutually agreed upon. This is the normal method of interchange.

Open routes—meaning thereby through rates, ordinary interchange, and reasonable divisions—are established among carriers between which some traffic is expected to be interchanged. Closed routes, on the contrary, are established to choke off traffic between connections. If a route is such that a flow of business over it might tend to deprive one of the carriers of its long haul, the closing of the route would eliminate such business. The Union Pacific, the Northern Pacific, and the Great Northern have for many years refused to establish through rates via Washington junctions with the Chicago, Milwaukee, St. Paul & Pacific on a large share of the latter's traffic bound for Portland, Oregon. That point the St. Paul does not reach. But they all agree to receive this business on through rates at eastern junctions: the Union Pacific at Omaha, and the other lines at gateways in Minnesota and North Dakota. The St. Paul may, if it chooses, carry traffic to the Portland lines for delivery at Washington junctions. Traffic so delivered is carried at local rates from the latter points to destinations. Competition demands the lower through rates; and so the St. Paul must take the short haul on any business it moves to Portland. In the words of its former president, the St. Paul is "shut out of the Portland business, except to take it to Omaha and send it around the short route. Although originated on our railroad, we are unable to take it on the long line." [1]

Here is a simple expedient to enable the controlling line to capture all available business for its own haul. Close the route to competitors, to all roads that short-haul the line dominating the traffic movements. Why cannot all the roads follow the policy of the New York Central in refusing to grant the Pittsburgh & West Virginia through rates on business moving from points west of Toledo to Baltimore? The Western Maryland is equally as anxious to carry to Baltimore traffic received at Connellsville from the Pittsburgh & West Virginia as it is to carry traffic received from the Pittsburgh & Lake Erie (a New York Central controlled line) at the same point.

But there is no sound reason why the New York Central system lines should not get the haul that the Pittsburgh & West Virginia seeks. The former therefore "closes" this route to the latter. And similarly with the Pennsylvania, the Pittsburgh & West Virginia cannot interchange except to strictly local points served by it.[2]

And why is it not, generally, financially profitable and accordingly desirable for roads acquiring others to capture the latter's traffic forthwith by closing the latter's routes to its competitors? This is sometimes done, particularly when short feeders are acquired. The St. Louis

& San Francisco pursued this policy when it acquired additional lines in the fertile St. Francis basin. The announcement of the purchase of the St. Louis, Kennett & Southeastern and the Butler County was accompanied by an unambiguous statement of purpose. "We are buying them," stated the assistant freight traffic manager of the acquiring line (and) on its behalf, "to use as a part of the Frisco and as being a part of the Frisco we expect to secure the maximum haul on all the traffic we produce on these lines outbound, and also to secure the maximum haul over the Frisco on all the inbound traffic to points on those roads. It will be our purpose to close the Piggott gateway." [3]

The acquisition of control of another feeder—the Jonesboro, Lake City & Eastern—by the St. Louis & San Francisco was followed by such an elimination of routes that appeared likely to impair the business prospect of another short line, independently controlled. The latter's property consisted of two disconnected lines, which the line of the Jonesboro tied up. Logs cut on one part of the road moved to the sawmill on the other via the Jonesboro. The St. Louis & San Francisco in control of the latter closed this route. It assessed rates on the basis of a combination of locals, thus increasing the rates by approximately 130 per cent.[4] The short line that was so unceremoniously treated had been delivering part of its traffic to the St. Louis Southwestern for the long haul to market. The St. Louis & San Francisco, by closing the routes of the short line, succeeded in diverting its long haul traffic to its own lines, and away from the St. Louis Southwestern.

It seems such a simple process for the controlling line to chop off the head of its competitor that one is led to inquire why that practice has not been more universally followed. Perhaps it might not be too far from the truth to say that possible retaliatory decapitation by the decapitated has been the chief deterrent. The development of the railroad net in this country has precluded the adoption of any such policy. Railroad lines were laid out under the stimulus of an era of free competition. Free competition implies equal opportunity. It does not imply equal ability; nor does it imply equal access to the same fund of capital. Some projects were initiated and nurtured by men of outstanding ability: the Chicago, Burlington & Quincy by C. E. Perkins; the Pennsylvania by Edgar Thompson and Thomas A. Scott; the Atchison, Topeka & Santa Fe by William B. Strong and E. Z. Ripley, etc. They or their successors managed to complete their projects on a nation-wide scale. They built or expanded by absorption until they connected vast areas of production with corresponding markets for consumption.

Other projects started nobly, but failed for want of able and energetic management or for lack of capital. The St. Louis & San Francisco and the Texas & Pacific, bound for destinations well indicated by their ambitious titles, halted far in the interior. The collapse of the Gould hopes for a coast-to-coast system left many unconnected lines suspended on the railroad map: the Wabash stopping at Toledo; the Pittsburgh Terminals beginning in Pittsburgh and petering out in western Ohio; the Missouri Pacific with its unproductive bridge line reaching out from eastern Kansas to lock hands at Pueblo with the Denver & Rio Grande Western, the control of which fluctuated so uncertainly for many years. Excessive competition and successive corporate failures produced the stub ends of the

CLOSED AND OPEN ROUTES 165

Chicago Great Western and the Chicago & Alton at the Missouri River; and Chicago & Eastern Illinios at the Mississippi.

These smaller roads are found in all sections of the country. Some are small; some are large. Some are prosperous and some not so prosperous. Except for the small feeder lines, however, almost all of them participate in the carriage of through freight. Over their own lines they do not unite important points of traffic origin with markets of consumption. One penetrates the nation's fruit supply, but does not reach the important consuming markets; while another serves the markets but not the fruit orchards. Therefore the Southern Pacific and the St. Louis Southwestern form practical through routes for the transportation of fruit from the Imperial Valley to the Mississippi Valley.

In Colorado the Chicago, Burlington & Quincy, the Chicago, Rock Island & Pacific, and the Missouri Pacific reach but do not cross the mountain barrier. The Union Pacific, however, cuts clear across it to Seattle, Washington, and Portland, Oregon, on the north and Los Angeles on the south. The Union Pacific can, if it chooses, close its route to the Chicago, Burlington & Quincy. It can refuse to establish through rates from points on its line to destinations reached competitively by the Chicago, Burlington & Quincy and its own lines. It would thus force its shippers to forward freight over its own tracks as the originating road. It might thus increase its volume of eastbound freight; and traffic now moving over the Burlington from Denver to Council Bluffs might move over the Union Pacific.

The former, however, carries considerable westbound

freight bound for points beyond the Rockies. West from Denver extend the lines of the Denver & Rio Grande Western, and the Western Pacific. The former reaches Ogden, Utah; and beyond that are tracks of the Western Pacific. The Chicago, Burlington & Quincy can deliver the westbound business it controls as an originating line either to the Union Pacific or to its competitors. The Union Pacific wants a share of this business. Should it close its routes to the Burlington on eastbound business, the latter is likely to close its routes to the Union Pacific on westbound business. Both, therefore, open their routes to each other. The one-line route from the Pacific coast to the Missouri River encounters competition of a multi-line route. This competition forces it to trade openly with its competitors.

A similar major situation prevails at Kansas City. The one-line route of the Atchison, Topeka & Santa Fe connects the rapidly growing southwest with Chicago and the middle west. Kansas City is a great railroad frontier. Middle western lines like the Chicago, Milwaukee, St. Paul & Pacific; the Chicago Great Western; and the Chicago, Burlington & Quincy terminate there from the east; a transcontinental line, the Union Pacific, from the west, and a southwestern line, the Kansas City Southern, from the south. From Kansas City south and west, such lines as the Missouri Pacific, the Missouri-Kansas-Texas, and the St. Louis & San Francisco operate.

Under these circumstances it would be questionable business policy for the Atchison, Topeka & Santa Fe to close its routes to its competitors. Theoretically, it could advise its shippers in Oklahoma and Texas of the unavailability of through routes for the carriage of freight

CLOSED AND OPEN ROUTES 167

to Chicago via Kansas City and the Chicago & Alton. The latter could then advise its shippers in Illinois and Missouri of a similar unavailability of routes for the southwest via Kansas City and the Atchison. It could transfer traffic for Fort Worth and Dallas to the St. Louis & San Francisco; for Houston and Galveston to the Missouri Pacific, and for Beaumont and Port Arthur to the Kansas City Southern. Competition thus compels free and open routing at the Missouri River.

Open routes based on the establishment of through routes and through rates are general throughout the country. Many large systems throw open stations on their lines for movement of business by competitors. The originating line—the line controlling the movement of traffic—does not always choke off competition through the cancellation of through rates via competitive rails. Indeed the major changes in corporate ownership and operation of American railroads during the last quarter of a century have exerted little effect on the status of open routes. Railroad men can assert with full confidence that trading at the strategic junctions have been free and open. Consolidations, community of interest, ordinary corporate acquisitions have not led to any disturbance of the rights of shippers in routing traffic. Their legal privileges to route traffic over any and all connections have rarely been disturbed.

Witness the development of the New York Central system. Control of the Michigan Central and the Lake Shore & Michigan Southern was acquired in 1898 through the purchase of a majority of stock by the New York Central & Hudson River Railroad. No competitive routes were closed. All of the joint rates and through

168 RAILROAD CONSOLIDATION

routes for the handling of business over the competitive routes were continued. These included the Lake Shore & Michigan Southern and the Pennsylvania via Erie, Pennsylvania; and those of the Lake Shore & Michigan Southern and the Michigan Central with the Delaware, Lackawanna & Western and the Lehigh Valley via Buffalo.[5]

The Boston & Albany was leased in 1900. No routes or gateways were closed then or have been closed since. The Boston & Albany in fact has now more routes competitive with the New York Central than it had in 1900.[6]

In 1909 the Toledo & Ohio Central was acquired. Because of the previous participation in its ownership by the Pennsylvania, the Erie, the Baltimore & Ohio, and the Chesapeake & Ohio, it had perhaps an unusually large number of open routes. None of these routes have ever been closed.[7]

Taking another major situation: in 1901 the Great Northern and the Northern Pacific acquired control through stock ownership of the Chicago, Burlington & Quincy. The lines of both proprietary roads terminate at St. Paul from the north. From that point the acquired line operates southward to Chicago. The Chicago, Milwaukee, St. Paul & Pacific operates a competitive line between St. Paul and Chicago. This road competes also with the parent properties northwest beyond St. Paul. The joint control of the Chicago, Burlington & Quincy did not lead to the cancellation of routes and rates with the system competitive both to the acquiring and the acquired lines. Despite the intensifying of competition occasioned by the Pacific coast extension of the St. Paul lines, the president of the Chicago, Burlington & Quincy could correctly say in 1923: "The St. Paul gateway is wide open. It is not

CLOSED AND OPEN ROUTES

closed. . . . The St. Paul gateway is not dried up. The Northern Pacific as well as the Great Northern interchange is very large . . . the gateway is open, because joint through rates apply via other lines to Chicago as well as via the Burlington."

And a representative of the Northern Pacific, referring to the same situation, stated positively that, "There is no suggestion in the record [the record in the Consolidation Proceedings] that the division of rates or that the through service was different at St. Paul as between the northern lines and the Burlington, from the rates and through service as between those two lines and the other Chicago roads reaching St. Paul." [8]

Whether routes with connecting competitors are closed or opened is a question of business expediency. The maintenance of an open route by an originating line leads directly, to the extent of the traffic carried by a competitor, to the loss of business. The originating road will not ordinarily short-haul itself unless it believes it can secure some advantage in return. If circumstances are such that this result is not reasonably warranted, it is questionable whether open traffic routes will be maintained. Frequently, the acquisition of short-feeder lines is followed by a cancellation of rates with competitive connections. A terminating line may occasionally find it necessary as sound policy to oblige its connections to short-haul themselves. The closing of the Harlem River route by the New York, New Haven & Hartford to the Central Railroad of New Jersey has been noted in another connection. The delivering line in its own interests short-hauls the originating line.

Under conditions of particularly vigorous competition it is doubtful whether competitors will concur in the establishment of through rates. The Boston & Albany's lease to the New York Central did not prevent the maintenance of many open routes with the latter's competitors. Nevertheless the Delaware & Hudson has never been able to negotiate joint rates for bituminous coal delivery via the Boston & Albany.[9] The New York Central originates a large tonnage of bituminous coal in northwest Pennsylvania. This moves to New England markets over the Philadelphia & Reading–Central Railroad of New Jersey via Newberry Junction and Haucks to Jersey City, thence via New York Central system lines. The latter, apparently, desire to invite no unnecessary competition in its New England territory from coal carried by the Delaware & Hudson. The added miscellaneous traffic that the Boston & Albany can expect from granting the Delaware & Hudson the privilege to move bituminous freely into New England over an open traffic route cannot be large. Another New England carrier, the Boston & Maine, interchanges traffic reciprocally with the Delaware & Hudson; and the majority of what little miscellaneous traffic New England-bound the latter carries, it must perforce deliver to the Boston & Maine for a haul. That is so, since that road in turn delivers its high-grade manufactured goods westbound to the Delaware & Hudson.

It is therefore not always certain whether particular traffic conditions will lead a property to open or close a route. An important decision of traffic policy is usually made when the corporate control of a road changes hands. An independently owned and operated carrier furnishes a satisfactory originating or terminal service. It may develop a substantial tonnage of desirable business. In so far as possible, it carries the traffic for the long haul;

CLOSED AND OPEN ROUTES 171

and exchanges freely with its connections. It may furthermore be strategically situated; it controls a direct line between important traffic centers, and so is able to perform a profitable through business. Its own lines, however, do not command access to the markets that absorb the goods produced in its own territory. Its connections carry the goods to market.

One of these acquires control of the road. The controlling trunk line may or may not close the open routes that the acquired road maintained with its trunk line connections. The latter compete with the line acquiring the independent property. The connections may be fearful that the new interests may close routes and divert traffic formerly moving over their lines. They, therefore, oppose the contemplated change in control. Under the existing law, the program of the acquiring line must be submitted to the Interstate Commerce Commission for its approval. The competitors of that road appear before that body and urge the rejection of the proposed unification program on the ground that its consummation might lead to the disturbance of existing channels of trade and commerce. Traffic flowing to and from the carrier proposed to be acquired, and to and from designated connections, will now flow over the line of the acquiring line. Such a diversion in the movement of traffic is a disturbance of existing trade channels, and per se a violation of the law.

This reasoning the Commission has respected. Occasionally it has carried this reasoning to its logical conclusion and rejected proposed unifications because of possible disturbance of existing routes. The proposed share control of the International & Great Northern by the St. Louis & San Francisco and the lease of the Virginian

Railway to the Norfolk & Western Railway was disapproved because of the prospective disturbance of existing traffic routes. This course, however, is drastic, and has not been frequently resorted to. Indeed, the two cases mentioned are the only important ones on record in which Commission disapproval of proposed unification was based squarely on anticipated eliminations of channels of trade and commerce. In the practical administration of this phase of the law the Commission early discovered another one of those paradoxes that seem to result from the effort to conventionalize large business operations. A unification eminently desirable in other directions appears likely to upset existing railway routes. As presented to the Commission the proposal will, however, if effected, salvage a financially weak line rendering a poor standard of service. Its acquisition by a strong trunk line will raise the standard of service over the acquired line and, perhaps, reduce expenses of operation. Or the acquisition will contribute to the vigor and vitality of interrailway competition; not, be it noted, between a weak and strong road, but between two healthy properties.

The Commission cannot well refuse its assent to such proposals so conducive to the promotion of the public interest. Confronted with these situations the Commission early decided to broaden its administrative functions. The provision of the law bearing on consolidations gives the Commission power to approve and authorize acquisitions "on such terms and conditions as shall be found by the Commission to be just and reasonable in the premises." Acting under this grant of authority, the Commission proceeded to condition its approval with provisos calculated to keep existing gateways open for the movement of traffic

CLOSED AND OPEN ROUTES 173

by all connecting lines. This significant extension of administrative regulation of private property interests was first elaborated in a case presented to the Commission within a short time after the passage of the Transportation Act. The New York Central requested permission to acquire control of the Chicago River & Indiana Railroad and the Chicago Junction Railway. These two properties furnish a terminal service in Chicago to numerous trunk line connections. Their acquisition by the New York Central was opposed by competitive trunk lines: the Baltimore & Ohio, the Erie, and the Pennsylvania. They believed their interests threatened by the prospective diversion of traffic from their own routes to those of the New York Central.

The Commission approved the project, subject to no less than seventeen conditions. Some were of only incidental importance to the subject under discussion. The second condition, embracing the real substance matter, endeavored to insure the "present neutrality of handling traffic inbound and outbound by the Junction and River road organization . . . so as to permit equal opportunity for service to and from all trunk lines reaching Junction rails, without discrimination as to routing or movement of traffic which is competitive with the traffic of the Central and without discrimination against such competitive traffic in the arrangement of schedules." [10]

In subsequent cases in which the preservation of existing gateways for the interchange of traffic was an issue, the Commission usually, though not consistently, authorized changes in corporate control subject to substantially similar conditions. The lease of the strategically located Carolina, Clinchfield & Ohio by the Alantic Coast Line–

Louisville & Nashville system was opposed by the Seaboard Air Line, a connection of the lessor, which competed with the lessees. It contended that the proposed lease would unquestionably increase the traffic interchange between the lessor and the lessees, and reduce that interchanged between the lessor and itself. The Commission approved the lease on condition that existing routes between the lessor and other carriers be preserved and that existing gateways for traffic interchange between these carriers be maintained. The lessees were definitely required to continue the traffic neutrality of the Clinchfield "so as to permit opportunity for service and routing or movement of traffic which is competitive with traffic of the applicants (lessees) to and from all connecting lines reached by the line of the Clinchfield companies, without discrimination in service against such competitive traffic."

The Carolina, Clinchfield & Ohio, the Commission stated, "shall be maintained as an open route equally available" to all its connections for traffic moving over routes between designated points. These are routes of which the lessor is an essential part. To secure control of the lessor, the lessees definitely undertook not to "discriminate as to rates, fares and charges" against other carriers participating in routes with the lessor.[12]

The lease of the Alabama & Vicksburg and Vicksburg, Shreveport & Pacific—the two lines generally known as the Vicksburg route—to the Illinois Central was vigorously contested by numerous trunk line connections of the former. The competitive situation was unusually keen. Lines east and west of the Mississippi River carried traffic to, from and over the Vicksburg route to and from southeastern, southwestern, and middle western territory.

CLOSED AND OPEN ROUTES 175

The prospective lease of the Vicksburg route by the Illinois Central, it was contended, would divert traffic over Illinois Central routes to the detriment of routes composed of the lines of its competitors. Here again the Commission, convinced that the proposal was "in the public interest," authorized its consummation on condition that the acquired line be maintained as an open route. The acquiring line was ordered by the Commission to "maintain existing gateways for the interchange of traffic" with the other connections of the acquired line; and to "continue the present neutrality of handling traffic by the Vicksburg Route, so as to permit equal opportunity for service and routing or movement of traffic which is competitive with traffic of the" acquiring line; and "without discrimination in service against such competitive traffic."

The Commission employed unequivocal language in directing the Illinois Central to permit the Vicksburg route to be used as a link for through traffic to those of the latter's connections who "may desire to participate in through routes and joint rates" to and from points on the Vicksburg route and its connections.[12]

It cannot be concluded, however, that administrative insistence upon open routes is an inevitable concomitant of each and every unification proposal. The desirability of open routes for all connections occasionally gives way to other considerations. A recent acquisition by the St. Louis & San Franciso of a short line in southeastern Missouri which was opposed by the St. Louis Southwestern may serve as an illustration. The acquired line participated in a through route with both of the trunk line carriers. The route established with the St. Louis Southwestern offered excellent service; and that carrier asked the Commission to oblige the St. Louis & San Franciso, as a condition precedent to the acquisition desired, to maintain the open route between the short line and itself. The acquiring line assured the Commission that it could meet any schedule the St. Louis Southwestern might have, "if it be found necessary and economical to do so, and that it proposes [proposed] to cancel the existing through rates and to operate the Southeastern [St. Louis, Kennett & Southeastern] as an integral part of the Frisco [St. Louis & San Francisco] system." The Commission declined to impose the conditions requested by the St. Louis Southwestern; and approved unqualifiedly the acquisition of the short line by St. Louis & San Francisco.[13]

The short line was financially a weak carrier. The consolidation of a property of this character with a trunk line was one of the major objectives of the national consolidation program. The St. Louis Southwestern had declined to acquire this property. In the Loree Southwestern Unification case, its status had been considered. The short line had intervened, asking the Commission to condition its approval of the proposed Southwestern system upon its acquisition by the St. Louis Southwestern. The St. Louis Southwestern, after an examination of the property, could not, however, appreciate its value as an integral part of its system. The assurance of the permanency of a short line as a constituent part of a trunk line carrier was apparently, in the opinion of the Commission, worth the price of an open route.

The controlling conditions in this case may explain, if perhaps they do not justify, the exception to the rule. With minor exceptions of this nature, the Commission has heeded the protests of carriers whose traffic interchange seemed threatened by a proposed change in control of a connection. It has usually imposed conditions to its approval of proposed acquisitions or unifications designed to insure the maintenance of open routes. Generally, the railroads concerned have accepted the conditions. In no case have any proposals been dropped because of dissatisfaction with the Commission's conditions relative to the continuance of open gateways. Even more surprising, on the face of things, is the maintenance of open routes by controlling carriers with competitive connections in the years before Commission regulation of consolidation. Well-planned unifications conceived on sound business lines have as their primary objective an increase in the flow of business from and to the acquired line over the acquiring line. The seemingly promiscuous maintenance of open routes threatens the fulfillment of this purpose. Existence of through routes and through rates from and to the acquired road and lines competitive with the acquiring road, permits shippers to route traffic over competitive lines. Such routing propensities, if persisted in, would defeat the chief business aim of consolidation.

Frequently the willingness of a road to maintain through routes and through rates may be explained by sound business considerations. The ready compliance with the "open gateway" dicta of the Interstate Commerce Commission, however, casts suspicion upon the presumption that any substantial volume of traffic is diverted to competitors as a result. The ability of an initial carrier to forward traffic over favored routes is in no substantial way associated with rate differentials; and the equivalence of through rates over competitive lines does not seriously retard this ability. The existence of "open routes" via the important traffic gateways gives the shipper the opportunity to route freight beyond the gateway over the lines of road which compete with the initial carrier. The competitor of the latter can enter its home territory and solicit for the business available.

The dependence of the ordinary shipper upon the home road for adequate service is not materially lessened thereby. To that road the shipper must still look for spotting privileges, for trap-car service, for switching facilities; that is the road which builds the spur or private sidetrack so necessary for the receipt and delivery of the shipper's freight. That is the road to which appeal must be made for a supply of cars. And in times of a general car shortage it is difficult to induce the initial carrier to move empties from the junction with the competitive connection to the spur or industrial track, or the team track of the originating carrier. The available through route and through rate may open to the shipper the privilege to route over a competitive connection beyond the common gateway. It only rarely contributes to his best business interests to elect to accept that privilege.

To measure even with approximate accuracy the volume of traffic that shippers route through "open gateways" over the lines of connections not favored by originating carriers is a work attended with considerable difficulty. Some traffic must be interchanged even between the keenest competitors. Traffic destined to a point local to one road must move over that road. Certainly no business arrangement can be effected which would prevent a shipper from receiving freight. That is evident. And yet that may be the only kind of traffic traded between competitive carriers at an "open gateway." Hale Holden, one of the foremost railroad men of the west, has stated that, "The St. Paul gateway is wide open. It is not closed because there are other railroads coming to St. Paul. Of course, the Burlington, the Northern Pacific, and the Great Northern work preferentially together, but a further examination of the figures will show that it has not excluded any of the other lines, and the gateway is open, because joint through rates apply via other lines to Chicago, as well as via the Burlington, and there is a very large interchange between the Northern lines and other St. Paul–Chicago lines." [14]

How much of this interchange constitutes local traffic that must necessarily move over lines other than the Burlington cannot be accurately deduced from available data. Only an examination of waybills could produce the information. In no other way could the exact destinations be ascertained. It is significant, therefore, that one of the St. Paul–Chicago lines competitive to the Burlington officially states that in so far as it is concerned, "except where routing is controlled by the shipper, the interchange between the Milwaukee [Chicago, Milwaukee, St. Paul & Pacific] and each of the Northern Lines [Northern Pacific and Great Northern] is largely confined to traffic to or from local points on one line or the other." [15]

The open gateway maintained at Buffalo between the New York Central and its connections contributes little, other than the inevitable local traffic, to the interchange business of the Delaware, Lackawanna & Western. "Prior to the consolidation of the Lake Shore with the New York Central," declares the official statement of the Delaware,

Lackawanna & Western presented before the Interstate Commerce Commission in the Consolidation Proceedings, "very considerable traffic was interchanged between the Lake Shore and the Lackawanna at Buffalo. Since such consolidation very little traffic is interchanged except at *local* points on the Lackawanna system which cannot be reached by New York Central lines." [16]

Competitive or local traffic, moreover, is not readily identified as such. Competitive traffic may be considered in the broadest sense as business which could be handled physically by another carrier; or as a service performed which could have been performed by another carrier. The existence of an alternative pair of tracks between common points does not always measure a corresponding degree of competitive ability. A road may match another in the possession of an adequate line between two particular traffic centers. It may not, however, command a similar ability of service to the shipping public. Here is a road, the New York, Chicago & St. Louis for example, owning team tracks in Cleveland so located as best to serve the shippers' convenience. Similar facilities of the Wheeling & Lake Erie are not so located. The facilities of the former cannot be used by the latter under the usual reciprocal switching arrangements.[17] Such team track business is substantial in volume. Of the tonnage of the New York, Chicago & St. Louis that originated or terminated at Cleveland during November, 1926, 21.3 per cent "was loaded or unloaded on team tracks or through freight houses of the Nickel Plate [New York, Chicago & St. Louis] in the Cleveland district which could not be reached by the Wheeling [Wheeling & Lake Erie] under reciprocal switching arrangements." [18] Can the Wheeling & Lake

CLOSED AND OPEN ROUTES 181

Erie be said to enjoy the ability to compete with the New York, Chicago & St. Louis for this class of traffic? Yet the latter maintains "open routes" with the former to all points. "It does not attempt to shut out the Wheeling & Lake Erie from any business which we could handle as a one line road by using our own line individually." [19]

Other forms of denial of use of facilities of one carrier to another were considered in a previous chapter. These restrictions tend to indicate that, in practice, competitive traffic cannot embrace all business that on the face of things can be handled physically by two or more carriers. Open routes, to points served by carriers subjecting the use of their facilities to such limitations, are not widely "open" to the movement of competitive traffic.

Neither is traffic "open" for movement to those roads with excessively circuitous lines between particular points. Many are the important competitive points connected by roundabout carriers over the tracks of which the transportation of freight is legally prohibited. To enable a road to compete in common markets with another road, rates must be uniform. The road controlling the circuitous line to the common competitive market does not enjoy full liberty of action in meeting the rate set by the short line. The long line must consider the rates charged to intermediate points; and only under particular conditions, and with Commission approval, can it meet the low competitive rate without lowering the rate to intermediate stations. The profits that might develop from the carriage of freight to the competitive markets may be smaller than the corresponding losses on business to intermediate points; that is, assuming that rates to the latter would be lowered to the level of the rates in the far-off markets.

In many cases, therefore, carriers will not reduce intermediate rates. It is common knowledge that many transportation properties thus surrender their opportunities to do business to and from competitive points even though their lines are *physically* capable of rendering the service in question.

Also on overhead traffic, all of which appears to be strictly competitive, it sometimes happens that competitive ability is peculiarly encouraged to one line and discouraged —perhaps even denied—to another by specific business arrangements. The Wheeling & Lake Erie, for example, for the control of which the eastern trunk lines have been contending for over two years, competes for overhead traffic (among other lines) with the New York, Chicago & St. Louis. The recent order of the Interstate Commerce Commission directing the disposition by the latter of its share holdings in the Wheeling & Lake Erie was justified in part by the probability of the undue lessening of competition between these two lines. Part of the various species of competition consists of the carriage by the Wheeling & Lake Erie of overhead traffic between Cleveland and Toledo interchanged with the New York Central at both points. The New York, Chicago & St. Louis controls a short line between Cleveland and Toledo. Yet, because of the absence of any working business arrangements, it cannot participate in this New York Central interchange. It cannot compete with the Wheeling & Lake Erie.[20]

Because of these and certain other considerations there is a wide difference of opinion with regard to the traffic competitive between the New York, Chicago & St. Louis and the Wheeling & Lake Erie. The traffic authority of the

CLOSED AND OPEN ROUTES

latter considers traffic competitive if the service performed by one line could have been *physically* performed by another. The traffic manager of the former qualifies his concept of competitive traffic. So that for 1926 the latter deduces a total of 27,456 cars carried by the Wheeling & Lake Erie as competitive with the New York, Chicago & St. Louis; whereas the traffic expert of the Wheeling & Lake Erie arrives at the figure of 57,101 cars.[21]

In the determination of what traffic is competitive, the most important factor remains still the persuasion that the owning—the originating—line can exercise upon shippers located in its territory. This was sketched in a previous chapter and requires no further consideration. It is sufficiently significant to raise this question in intensely practical form: What proportion of competitive traffic do owning carriers lose by the maintenance of open gateways, either voluntarily or through Commission compulsion? The heart of the problem resolves itself into the primary factor of service. Rates for transportation between two points are uniform. Competition between carriers revolves around service; and that carrier which furnishes the best service obtains the major part of the business. The availability of through routes and through rates over a particular carrier does not, in and of itself, contribute to the increase in the standard of service rendered, and the "open route" does not diminish the power of the originating carrier to render shippers in its territory a superior grade of service. It does, however, give the competitive line the opportunity to solicit business in the territory of the originating line. It does so at a distinct advantage, and the volume of business it wrests away from the home line is not substantial. The management of an originating line which, through the maintenance of an open gateway, voluntarily surrenders a substantial portion of traffic to its competitor would indeed be derelict to its shareholders. And yet a railroad executive of the caliber of A. H. Smith, the late president of the New York Central lines, in the Consolidation Proceedings before the Interstate Commerce Commission, affirmed positively that it had been its policy "to rely upon its service to secure the long haul and not upon restrictions of routing, or the abolition of competitive gateways."

This observation is pregnant with truth. The open gateway is maintained; the routing right of the shippers is untrammeled. The rates being the same, the road that offers the best service carries the business. And who offers the best service in New York Central territory? In New England the system lines consist of the Boston & Albany. System control dates back to 1900. No through routes with connections have been cancelled, and additional routes have since then been added. The Boston & Maine contending for trunk line control of New England roads in the Consolidation Proceedings denied the contention that such control would lead to diversion of the traffic flow from the acquiring trunk line road, and away from the former trunk line connections of the acquired road. The Boston & Maine cited the "open routes" the Boston & Albany maintained with its connections after its lease to the New York Central. Note, however, its further significant assertion that while this was true, "excellent service is [was] afforded along the system line, and as a result most of the traffic is [was] attracted to it [Boston & Albany]." [22]

Toledo, Ohio, is another important "open gateway" maintained by the New York Central. Toledo is an im-

CLOSED AND OPEN ROUTES 185

portant junction. The major trunk lines pass through from east to west. In addition a number of small lines terminate at that point from different directions. Their joint lines connect important producing and consuming regions. The Toledo & Ohio Central and the Hocking Valley carry bituminous coal from southern Ohio to Toledo; and the Ann Arbor and the Wabash reaching Toledo from the north carry that commodity to consuming markets in Michigan. Here certainly is the basis of a through route, of a "channel of trade and commerce." Another line, the former Cincinnati, Hamilton & Dayton, connects the southeastern carriers at the Ohio River with the east and west trunk lines operating through Ohio. It also provides the roads terminating at Toledo from the north with a direct connection to the Ohio River and with the southeastern carriers operating therefrom.

For many years these small Ohio lines joined with the northern lines at Toledo in the formation of traffic routes carrying large volumes of freight. "The Toledo & Ohio Central," states the traffic manager of the Ann Arbor Railroad, "at one time was a feeder and a good connection of the Ann Arbor Railroad." The Cincinnati, Hamilton & Dayton, according to this traffic expert intimately familiar with local conditions, represented at one time "one of the best known well-established traffic routes in the United States." [23]

Since 1910 these north and south extensions in Ohio have been acquired by other lines: the Toledo & Ohio Central by the New York Central, the Hocking Valley by the Chesapeake & Ohio and the Cincinnati, Hamilton & Dayton by the Baltimore & Ohio. Important through routes and through rates have not been eliminated. The gateway has remained "wide open" for competitive trading. The many connections of the Toledo & Ohio Central, competitive with the New York Central, have been invited to interchange freely. It is doubtful, however, whether the system lines have lost much traffic by this invitation. "The delivery of coal to the New York Central Lines is mostly made through Toledo, at which point the Toledo & Ohio Central interchange with the New York Central Lines averages 65 per cent of its total." At that same gateway during the first twelve years of its control by the New York Central system, the deliveries of freight other than coal by the Toledo & Ohio Central to the former average more than four times the deliveries to the three foreign roads. And during the same period the New York Central lines delivered to the Toledo & Ohio Central nearly two and one-half times as many cars of other freight as were turned over to it by foreign lines.[24]

It is thus fairly clear that acquisition of the Toledo & Ohio Central and the other Toledo-bound lines has been followed by the usual business results. The Toledo & Ohio Central, the Hocking Valley, and the Cincinnati, Hamilton & Dayton have been absorbed into the system lines. The through routes, of which these independent lines were a part, have, in the language of the traffic manager of the Ann Arbor, "all disappeared. The Toledo & Ohio Central at one time was a feeder and a good connection of the Ann Arbor Railroad. We do not expect them to work with us. The same is true of the Hocking Valley and the Cincinnati, Hamilton & Dayton."[25]

The gateway, in other words, is gradually drying up. The system lines divert more and more of the traffic of

CLOSED AND OPEN ROUTES 187

the acquired road over their own routes. The acquiring system need commit no overt act. It closes no routes. It cancels no rates. In the language, again, of the traffic expert of the Ann Arbor already quoted: "The rails of the Cincinnati, Hamilton & Dayton are still there. The rates are there. The divisions are there, but it does not mean anything in traffic, because there is not that compelling competitive spirit. They have other interests that drain the traffic away in other directions." [26]

An "open route"—as that term is conventionally used—may be one over which, theoretically, competitive traffic may move. In business life, however, the competitive traffic which replaces a similar volume of system traffic is strictly regulated in the interests of system welfare. Traffic local to a competitor must move. It is to interests of the acquiring system and to the best interests of the public as well, that this traffic move expeditiously. Additional traffic—traffic clearly competitive in character—may be permitted to move over competitive routes. The originating line may frequently short-haul itself to give a competitor a part of the haul. It may do this to enable it in turn to secure traffic from the competitive carrier. The principles underlying short-hauling have already been considered in a previous chapter.

Beyond this a connection may even invade foreign territory and successfully solicit business. The Chicago Great Western, for example, controlling a circuitous route from Omaha to Chicago, receives little eastbound business from the Union Pacific at the former point. The Union Pacific interchanges mostly with the Chicago & Northwestern and secondarily with the Chicago, Milwaukee, St. Paul & Pacific. The Chicago Great Western, a financially weak road, is greatly in need of additional business. It originates comparatively little freight. In 1925 the business received from connections represented 63.6 per cent of the total carried. The business interests of its connections being such that they do not find it profitable to give it traffic, it is imperative that it invade their territory and induce shippers to route freight over its lines.

"All of the business of the company," states the president, "except that originating on its lines necessarily is received from connections and is consigned over the Great Western as the result of *personal solicitation*. Our strongest competitors, through close alliances with roads west of the Missouri River, and, in some cases, east of Chicago, are able to secure business that we cannot reach." [27]

This policy is expensive and develops only a relatively small tonnage. Other properties solicit vigorously for a share of through traffic on foreign soil. Weak carriers like the Gulf, Mobile & Northern, and the Georgia & Florida have through direct solicitation increased their through traffic somewhat in recent years.

Subject to these limitations, "open routes" are only a whit less effective for the diversion of competitive traffic to the routes of the acquiring line than closed routes. "Closed routes" are the sharper tool. It produces more immediate results. But the results are not thereby any more definite and certain. Hanging dispenses quickly with convicted criminals. Electrocution, perhaps, produces even quicker results. The strangling processes of the Inquisition were undoubtedly slower; but the victim was just as certain to be dispatched. So an acquiring line may forthwith cancel tariffs of the acquired line with competitive connections, and oblige shippers to forward their freight

CLOSED AND OPEN ROUTES 189

over the acquiring line. Or it may continue all the routes in full effect and institute a gradual, but certain, throttling process of traffic diversion. The method adopted represents a genuine choice of sound business policy, or it may be forced upon an acquiring property by Commission mandate. Whatever the form, the substance remains the same. Open routes or closed routes produce similar results; and, in the language of the able chairman of the Wabash and the Missouri Pacific lines, "as lines have been absorbed by other systems, gateways or interchange points previously existing have, in a large measure, continued to dry up and new ones be formed." [28]

NOTES TO CHAPTER VII

1. Consolidation Proceedings, Docket 12964, Statement of Harry E. Byram, Nov. 20, 1922, p. 1704.
2. Proposed Construction by Pittsburgh & West Virginia Ry., Finance Docket 6229, tr. pp. 1268-1269.
3. Acquisition of St. L., K. & S. E. R. R., Finance Docket 6244, Brief and exceptions for Intervener to report of Examiner, p. 8.
4. Construction of Lines by St. Louis Southwestern Ry. Co., Finance Docket 7031, 7032, Abstract of Testimony and Exhibits, pp. 86-87.
5. Consolidation Proceedings, Docket 12964, Brief for Port of New York Authority, p. 369.
6. *Supra.*
7. *Supra.*
8. *Supra*, Abstract of evidence relied upon by Chicago, Burlington & Quincy, p. 94.
9. *Supra*, Statement of L. F. Loree, p. 14.
10. Chicago Junction Case, 71 I.C.C. 639-641.
11. Clinchfield Railway Lease, 90 I.C.C. 133.
12. Control of A. & V. Ry., and V. S. & P. Ry., 111 I.C.C 178-179.
13. Acquisition of St. Louis, K. & S. E. R. R., 131 I.C.C. 110.
14. Consolidation Proceedings, Docket 12964, Abstract of evidence relied upon by Chicago, Burlington & Quincy, etc., p. 94.
15. Great Northern–Northern Pacific merger, Finance Docket 6409, 6410. Reply Brief for Applicants, p. 74.
16. Consolidation Proceedings, Docket 12964, Statement for the Delaware, Lackawanna & Western, May 16, 1923, p. 8.

17. Interlocking Directors of Wheeling & Lake Erie and Trunk Lines, Finance Docket 3584, Brief for Walter L. Ross, etc., pp. 19-20.
18. *Supra*, p. 58.
19. *Supra*, tr. p. 389.
20. *Supra*, Brief for Walter L. Ross, etc., p. 33.
21. *Supra*, p. 61; exhibit no. 7.
22. Consolidation Proceedings, Docket 12964, Brief for Boston & Maine, p. 44.
23. Interlocking Directors of Wheeling & Lake Erie and Trunk Lines, Finance Docket 3584, tr. p. 739.
24. Consolidation Proceedings, Docket 12964, Statement of Alfred H. Smith, May 16, 1923, p. 19.
25. Interlocking Directors of Wheeling & Lake Erie and Trunk Lines, Finance Docket 3584, tr. p. 739.
26. *Supra*, p. 740.
27. Annual Report, 1928, Chicago Great Western, p. 5.
28. Consolidation Proceedings, Docket 12964, Statement of William H. Williams, May 18, 1923, p. 45.

CHAPTER VIII

CHANNELS OF TRADE AND COMMERCE

The operation of the underlying business principles previously discussed tends to direct the flow of railroad traffic over particular lines and away from other lines. The originating carrier in large measure dominates the traffic movement. It bends its energies to realize its long hauls and highest revenue. Short hauls it may indulge in for sound business reasons which may lead to a higher net in the aggregate. And under normal conditions, it prefers to interchange with complementary rather than with competitive connections. Within the confines of these broad business factors, many others exert their various effects. The ability to obtain a supply of empty cars or a return movement of loaded cars from one particular connection will entitle that carrier to receive more business from the traffic-controlling line than another connection. Or another connection may exchange valuable trackage rights in return for a greater flow of interchange business.

Under the driving impetus of these business operations, traffic tends to flow along many well-defined channels. The business-getting organizations of American railroads route the available business over their own lines as far as possible; and then over such connections as are imperiously dictated by the soundest business rule of all: that of the highest profit on invested capital. The resultant "rivers of commerce" may not "become delimited and fixed," [1] as claimed by reliable railroad authority. That is, not necessarily so. But the prospect of large volumes of traffic moving regularly year after year over specific carriers to the exclusion of others does seem to carry with it, certainly to the uninitiated observer, some element of superior merits and of definite finality. A large volume of traffic moves regularly into New England over the New York, New Haven & Hartford, via the Pennsylvania Railroad; another portion over the Boston & Albany via the New York Central; and another over the Boston & Maine via the Delaware & Hudson. Similar regularities of traffic movements characterize every important region in the country. And it would seem to the outsider that natural forces are operating to produce these phenomena. The traffic flows along natural lines in accordance with the wishes and the best business interests of the shippers.

The grave necessity of the retention of these routes—of these channels of trade and commerce as they have been officially designated—appealed to the legislators in 1920. Those who drafted the law wrote into it the remarkable provision that consolidations must adapt themselves to the maintenance of "the existing routes and channels of trade and commerce": a sort of Article X of the Covenant of the League of Railroads. "Wherever practicable," the existing routes and channels must dominate the scene of consolidation. The vista of ideals, of rearranging the nation's carriers so as to produce a few strong competitors equally capable of earning a fair return from uniform rates fixed by government authority with the single view of the public interest, was to be realized only if consistent with the maintenance of existing routes and channels.

Its position of paramount significance in the law renders it imperative to define clearly the exact nature of a channel of trade and commerce. Fundamental to all discussion is the certainty that the opportunity of a shipper to reach his accustomed markets should not be restricted. No consolidation should interfere with the right and privilege of a shipper in Chicago and St. Louis to forward his wares to Pittsburgh, Baltimore, Philadelphia or New York. And providing the service is the same, what difference should it make to him whether it is carried by one of four, five or more systems? Yet the law implies there is a difference. Regardless of any substantiality of service as between different lines, the traffic must be carried over "existing routes and channels of trade and commerce." Do the existing channels in eastern territory consist of four systems as is urged by New York Central, the New York, Chicago & St. Louis and the Baltimore & Ohio? of five systems as is argued by the Wabash? or of even more systems as is suggested by the tentative plan of the Interstate Commerce Commission?

And how can a channel of trade and commerce be defined; how can its existence be determined? Just how do the people of the country secure better service at reasonable rates through the retention of an existing trade channel? In what way does the disturbance of an existing channel, and perhaps its replacement by a new one, impair the standards of good service or increase a reasonable rate? Public discussion has done little to clarify the subject. The monumentally industrious report of Professor Ripley, accompanying the tentative report on consolidation issued by the Interstate Commerce Commission, sheds but little light on the problem. The legal desire of maintaining "the existing routes and channels of trade and commerce" is explained by Professor Ripley as implying "not the preservation of merely artificial currents and conditions." The statute should be construed to contain an "invitation to consider these carrier corporations in their basic relationship to the welfare, present and prospective, of the country. Viewed in this larger sense the act is at once an invitation and an opportunity. It calls for an analysis of the commercial geography of the United States, in its relation to the layout of its railway net. For, unless the location of its railways conforms to the commercial requirements of the country, there can be no permanent prosperity for either." [2]

The same thought, that railway routes should be natural, is expressed perhaps more specifically by Dr. C. S. Duncan, a representative of the carriers. He insists that "the public shall not, by any system of consolidation, be deprived of any existing opportunity by rail to reach present markets; that existing trade centers shall not be unfavorably affected by the merger of roads, and that commodities shall continue to move to and from such centers as at present, or as they would move *naturally* in the future under changing economic conditions." [3]

This idea with its emphasis on natural as against artificial railway routes is not particularly novel. A generation ago Judge Cooley, the outstanding member of the Interstate Commerce Commission at that time, expressed a somewhat similar thought. In the course of a decision interpreting that section of the law forbidding discrimination between connecting lines, he stated that a dissimilarity between connections sufficiently substantial to justify a dissimilarity in treatment must be one that "arises from

CHANNELS OF TRADE AND COMMERCE 195

physical conditions and not from business motives."[4] If physical conditions may be assumed to be natural, then it may be averred that Judge Cooley urged the formation of railway routes based on "natural" conditions.

It becomes necessary, therefore, to examine the conditions under which and the extent to which consolidations produce natural channels of trade and commerce, and the extent to which such routes naturally formed lead to better transportation service at reasonable rates.

Routes may first be examined from the standpoint of transportation costs. Short, direct and noncongested routes are cheaper to operate than routes that are long, indirect and congested. And routes operating over level plains are less expensive to operate than routes crossing the mountains. Routes, furthermore, with low grades and light curvature produce a transportation service at lesser expense than that afforded by routes with unfavorable grades and curvatures. Theoretically, it may be possible (although this may be seriously challenged) to devise paper consolidations to facilitate the formation of the most economical routes. It has already been indicated that in actual practice it is extremely difficult to decide what particular routes are the most economical. The short route from most of trunk line territory to New England cuts directly through New York Harbor. But this route is most congested. The long and circuitous route up the Delaware Valley is little used; it is noncongested. And it makes up in greater train speed what it loses in additional train miles. The Pennsylvania is the short line between Chicago and New York. It, however, crosses a summit of 2,180 feet; while the New York Central, controlling the longer line between these two cities, operates at water-level grades. It is a pretty problem, indeed, to decide what line produces the most economical transportation service. And the solution is not simplified by the circumstances that per unit transportation costs so greatly depend upon traffic density.

The control of a direct and low cost line is not in most cases the ultimate objective of a particular consolidation. Occasionally a noncongested line may be desired to enable the acquiring carrier to divert some business away from the congested line. This represents the business justification of the Pennsylvania's interest in the Lehigh & New England; and perhaps also the New York Central's interest in the Central Railroad of New Jersey. Generally, however, a road is wanted because of the additional profit it might bring to the parent property. If the acquired line, in addition, be a low cost line, so much the better. But the point of emphasis is the increased gross, and not the decreased cost.

Not wholly irrelevant in this connection is the observation that high public authority frowns upon consolidations that might produce low cost channels of trade and commerce, because of competitive disabilities. The Baltimore & Ohio–Western Maryland union (now in the making) is being questioned by the Interstate Commerce Commission on grounds of possible illegality. The Clayton Act, with its prohibition of any substantial diminution of competition, may prevent the public from receiving the benefits of whatever lessening in transportation costs that consolidation might achieve.

Even more pertinent and significant is the conclusion of that able representative of public interest, Professor Ripley, that the Northern Pacific–St. Paul merger should not receive official approval because of competition between the two lines. Yet the St. Paul runs directly east from Ellensburg in central Washington to Missoula in western Montana, and over favorable grades as well. The Northern Pacific, on the contrary, runs southeast, though it swerves due northeast to Spokane and beyond; and then it turns southeast again. The Consolidation Proceedings were enlivened by a merry battle between experts of the Great Northern and the Northern Pacific, each struggling to establish that the St. Paul would be an excellent prize for the other. Nobody would gainsay, in abstract, the advantage of a direct, low-grade, noncongested and low cost line. In the world of business life, however, it happened that this line carried little business. The St. Paul's line west of the Missouri River had only recently been constructed. Most traffic-producing industries were located on the lines of its competitors; and in accordance with well-established principles already discussed they obtained the long haul for their own lines. Little traffic was thus left for the St. Paul. Its competitors may want a low cost line; but they want traffic more. They cannot afford to pay for additional low-cost carrying capacity which they do not need; particularly so when they have ample leeway on their own lines.

A consolidation does not always produce low-cost railway routes. Low costs are desirable, highly desirable. But sound railroad business judgment and well-informed and authoritative public opinion recognize that they must frequently give way to other factors. The maintenance of the present volume of traffic and the prospect of an increase, and not the potential reduction in costs, is the driving force behind consolidations, conceived and executed on the basis of business self-interest. On the other hand, the maintenance of interrailway competition is still sufficiently vital in the minds of representatives of the public interest to overcome, with its many possible advantages, those flowing from low-cost transportation channels.

Routes may also be examined from the standpoint of service to the shippers. The contention that existing channels of trade and commerce provide shippers with a service they cannot afford to lose and in which they enjoy a legitimate right is widely urged. Through the use of existing routes, shippers reach competitive markets. Rates and services are reasonably satisfactory. Over the course of many years shippers have accustomed themselves to the use of these routes. They feel that in some way or other they represent a natural adjustment to the economic scheme of things. The argument is unusually attractive when its full force is concentrated on the welfare of a particular community. The recommendations of Professor Ripley, that the southwestern lines be extended from St. Louis to Chicago, called forth vigorous objections from the trade interests of the former community. Consolidations of that scope, they confidently asserted, would lead the new consolidated systems to carry their traffic to Chicago; the new routes would impair, if not destroy, the existing routes based on St. Louis; and would make St. Louis a mere stopping point on the main line to Chicago.

Shippers' access to desirable markets on the basis of reasonably good service—and this is the substance of their vested interests—is represented by the railroads as being tied up with the maintenance of the channels of traffic via routes of which their lines form an essential part. The suggestion to break up the Hill lines is opposed because it might "prove detrimental by depriving shippers in some

CHANNELS OF TRADE AND COMMERCE 199

cases of a route which gives them access to markets they have developed, and by substituting in other cases a less efficient route than the one which has had the benefit of the test of long experience." [5] Traffic received from shippers in the northwest by the Great Northern now moves to the Twin Cities, and thence south and east predominantly over the Chicago, Burlington & Quincy. The Commission's suggestion that the Great Northern and the St. Paul unite might lead the Great Northern's traffic to move via the St. Paul, instead of via the Burlington.

That this would operate to modify the earning power of all affected carriers is fairly certain. That it would deprive the shippers of substantial rights is less certain. Under the new dispensation suggested by the Commission the St. Paul, instead of the Burlington, would move the Great Northern's traffic from the Twin Cities to Chicago. How this might hurt the shippers was not made clear. No word was said of the relative train service via the two lines. Nothing was said of their train schedules, nor of their relative access to the terminal facilities at Chicago. Let it be assumed that the one line can render equally as good service as the other. Then wherein is the shipper injured?

The assumption of fairly equivalent service over both routes is by no means forced. A road acquires another to increase the volume of system traffic, or perhaps to prevent any substantial reduction—a reduction which might occur by consolidation of any part thereof with some other road. The acquiring road then would be derelict to its own best business interests not to give excellent service. Increased traffic is in part the result of good service; without it shippers could not effectively compete with other shippers located on roads that rendered high-class service.

It is by no means obvious or "natural" that existing routes afford the shipper better service and more markets than those obtainable over other routes. The Chicago, Burlington & Quincy is without question an excellent engine of transportation service. But that it affords Great Northern shippers a service superior to that which the St. Paul affords its shippers, or that which would be afforded Great Northern shippers after its consolidation with that line, cannot be assumed. It must be established by reference to the facts of this particular situation. If it were indeed so, it would not reveal any general truth. Under another set of circumstances a new route formed through readjustment of corporate ownership might give better service than the former route. The trunk line control of the Wheeling & Lake Erie might create new routes. Some Ohio traffic, Baltimore-bound, now moves over Wheeling & Lake Erie–Pittsburgh & West Virginia–Pittsburgh & Lake Erie–Western Maryland. Under new ownership it might move Wheeling & Lake Erie–Baltimore & Ohio. Here it is decidedly evident that the existing route, the existing channel of trade and commerce, would not give the shippers any better service nor access to any more or better markets than those which might be furnished by the new route.

It is important to make at least passing mention of the fact that no acquisition case before the Commission has produced a careful and comprehensive study of the merits of alternative routes available to the shipper. There have been many partial studies, all approached from the standpoint of the carrier. The Nickel Plate Unification case developed the comparative capital and operating costs of the Chesapeake & Ohio–Chicago division route and of the Chesapeake & Ohio–Hocking Valley–Erie route to Chicago.[6] The proposed lease of the Virginian, by the Norfolk & Western, was featured by a study of the operating conditions over the Virginian–Chesapeake & Ohio route via Deepwater and the Virginian–Norfolk & Western route via Matoaka.[7] Numerous cost studies of this nature have been made. It is believed, however, that no unification case has called forth an exhaustive study of the advantages and disadvantages of alternative routes, from the shipper's standpoint. Many are the cases which have described the new one-line markets available to the shipper, as a result of particular unification proposals. A bituminous coal shipper on the Chesapeake & Ohio now finds his market in Michigan over a route consisting of the originating line and the Pennsylvania. It is proposed to unify the operations of the Chesapeake & Ohio, the Hocking Valley and the Pere Marquette. The shipper on the Chesapeake & Ohio will then have available what is known as a one-line route to carry his shipments to market. These one-line routes are said to be of great public advantage. Some railroad men have gone so far as to say that "much of the efficiency to be expected from consolidation would be destroyed if the effort were made to preserve existing routes crossing over from one system to another. The very terms of the statute as to routes and channels of trade contemplate that the through routes will be developed within the limits of the respective systems rather than through a miscellaneous crisscrossing from one system to another." [8]

There is in this a sufficient substance of fact to give it a semblance of truth. A one-line movement is under one complete corporate management from origin to destination. The management controls every detail of service, and at no time does the shipment leave the confines of the property over which the management exerts control. A multi-line shipment is handled by various separate managements. Each time the car crosses a railroad frontier, a delay occurs. Elaborate rules of car interchange and car inspection must be complied with. Records must be compiled; the exact location of each foreign car in transit must be known; bills for car repairs must be forwarded; compensation for use of another road's equipment must be made. If the connecting lines are competitors for the same traffic, if their business interests are not common, then every point of contact invites opportunity for delay and obstruction. Service over a route composed of antagonistic lines is not good. A one-line route to replace such a multi-line route would be productive of great good to a shipper.

If, however, the route consists of complementary, non-competitive lines, whose real business interests do not conflict, then a multi-line route can give excellent service. The various methods by which independently owned and operated properties can coöperate to produce good service have already been discussed. Good service, access to markets, and movements of commodities "as they would move more naturally in the future under changing economic conditions," to use the expression of Dr. Duncan, are assured to many shippers who do not receive the benefits of one-line service. The Southern Pacific reaches no middle western markets over its own lines, yet its shippers are not heard to complain that their competitive disability suffers as a result. How such high-grade service is rendered to Southern Pacific shippers is therefore of un-

CHANNELS OF TRADE AND COMMERCE 203

usual significance; and the conclusions of Lewis J. Spence, the recently resigned able traffic executive of the Southern Pacific lines, possess corresponding merit. ". . . it seems to me," he stated in the Consolidation Proceedings, "that that objective is not so much the creation of a line under a single management between two objective points, as it is the preservation of a through route, or different groups of through routes between those points. The units in each of those through routes need not be under one management, in order to preserve them. In other words, if groups are created whose interests beyond the point of connection do not conflict, those two groups can preserve that through route and channel of trade and commerce just as well as a complete line of which all the units are under the same management." [9]

The traffic manager of the St. Louis Southwestern, which forms a through route with the Southern Pacific on a large volume of freight bound for St. Louis and beyond, expresses a similar opinion. The service over the route composed of these two lines is as adequate and efficient as that rendered over a one-line route.[10]

Many of the largest and strongest systems are satisfied with the service rendered over two-line routes. They have therefore refrained from expanding into noncompetitive territory. The Southern Pacific and the Union Pacific in transcontinental territory do not reach St. Louis or Chicago. The former is satisfied with the service received from the Chicago, Rock Island & Pacific, the St. Louis Southwestern and their connections; and the latter with that received from the Chicago & Northwestern and the Chicago, Milwaukee, St. Paul & Pacific. Both prefer to retain their independent status and bargain for traffic with their connections. Neither has made any move to acquire any of their connecting lines with which they exchange so much valuable traffic.

Channels of trade and commerce thus formed through the use of numerous system lines frequently render service equally as good as that rendered by the one-line routes. The rendition of a superior grade of service is frequently effected through a route crisscrossing from one system to another. The public interest in adequate service may positively call for routes composed of independent lines. The five-line route from Pittsburgh to St. Louis provides better transportation service than any one-line route. The seven-line interior route from Baltimore & Ohio coal mines to New England consuming territory is imperatively required by the public welfare. Congestion through New York Harbor sets a limit on the value of traffic passing through that gateway.

Existing channels, the retention of which is required by statute, may thus be measured either by the economy in transportation costs, or by the standard of service to shippers with the resultant accessibility to markets. Each test has been used at times. Only under exceptional circumstances has the economy of a transportation route been advocated as a justification for a proposed consolidation. The increased standard of service to the shipping public is a necessary result of those unifications, which bring short and financially weak lines under the ægis of the well-established trunk lines of the country. And the realization of superior one-line routes have been the results of the same class of unifications. Illustrations of acquisitions of such weak lines abound: the control of lines in the St. Francis Valley by the St. Louis and San Francisco [11] and by the St. Louis & Southwestern; [12] the extension of the Southern Pacific southward into the Rio Grande Valley through the San Antonio & Aransas Pass, [13] and northward through the Texas midland; [14] the absorption of feeder lines by the Seaboard Air Line; [15] the acquisition of the Atlanta, Birmingham & Atlantic by the Atlantic Coast Line; [16] etc.

These considerations have also had some little weight in discussions bearing on the *major* consolidations. If a specific proposal promised to produce shorter mileage routes between two or more points, it was elevated into a position of prominence. With a limited number of notable exceptions, the discussion halted at that point. Comparative grades and curvatures, comparative volume of traffic movements and other similar factors—all necessary to the determination of a well-balanced conclusion—were not referred to.

These factors, however, insensibly fade into the background in the discussions leading to the determination of channels of trade and commerce. All parties seem to have tacitly agreed that the volume of traffic interchanged between any connections represents the acid test of a "natural" trade channel and of a "natural" railway route. If a heavy tonnage is interchanged between any connections it indicates that a route formed by, with and over these roads, is one that represents the working of underlying conditions. It is a "natural" and not an "artificial route." If at a particular junction, say at Omaha, the traffic interchanged between the Union Pacific and the Chicago & Northwestern is greater than that interchanged between the Union Pacific and the Chicago, Milwaukee, St. Paul & Pacific, then the route formed by the former two lines is "natural," and the route formed by the latter two is "artificial."

That traffic interchanges constitute the best measure of the routes and channels of trade and commerce was the deliberate assumption underlying the very first important official document on consolidation produced after the passage of the Transportation Act. The law required the Commission to agree upon a tentative plan of consolidation, presumably to serve as a basis for a discussion. The Commission engaged Professor William Z. Ripley of Harvard University to prepare a report on the subject. A report with specific recommendations for consolidation of the country's railway properties was duly made, and the Commission, with some notable exceptions, followed these recommendations in its Tentative Plan for Consolidation. Professor Ripley's report,[17] published in the summer of 1921, within eighteen months after the passage of the Act is, broadly speaking, a geographical and traffic analysis of American railroads. It is a bold attempt to rearrange the corporate ownership of the country's railways, in accordance with the country's economic needs. "For, unless the location of its railways conforms to the commercial requirements of the country, there can be no permanent prosperity for either." [18]

Commercial requirements call for the maintenance of "existing routes and channels of trade and commerce." These routes do not imply the preservation of merely artificial currents and conditions. They dictate the preservation of "natural" currents of railway traffic. And the existence of "natural" conditions is indicated by traffic interchanges. That is the substance of the reasoning of Professor Ripley's report.

It is significant that almost all of the important decisions bearing on the specific allocation of a particular property to one consolidated system or another hinged around considerations of traffic interchange. Shall the Philadelphia & Reading go to the New York Central or to the Baltimore & Ohio? The interchange of the Reading with surrounding trunk lines is examined. While establishing "the substantial interest of the three great trunk lines, it also makes plain the predominant interest of the Baltimore & Ohio. The Reading received almost 40 per cent more cars from the Baltimore & Ohio than from the New York Central and its deliveries were almost double." [19] These facts then constitute one valid reason for the assignment of the Reading to the Baltimore & Ohio.

To what road shall the Boston & Maine go? Look at the interchange data for one answer. In 1919 it received from the Delaware & Hudson about 50 per cent more loaded cars than it received from the New York Central. "And it delivered to the Delaware & Hudson just about an equal preponderance of tonnage, as compared with the New York Central. The *natural* relationship of the Boston & Maine to the Delaware & Hudson among all the other trunk lines west of the Hudson River is quite evident. Such an affiliation, in the case of the adoption of a trunk line plan for New England, is self-evident."

If the trunk line allocation of New England roads be adopted as a sound policy, shall the New York, New Haven & Hartford be assigned to the Pennsylvania? Again the traffic interchange is the line of analysis. The former interchanges at two gateways. At the Harlem River the Pennsylvania enjoys an "overwhelming preponderance."

But the interchange at Maybrook, the other gateway, is "entirely inconclusive as to its relative affiliation with the other trunk lines." [20]

Shall the Chicago & Northwestern merge with the Union Pacific? The decision is based largely on Union Pacific interchange at Council Bluffs. "The outstanding fact is the preponderance of the Chicago & Northwestern. Excepting the St. Paul, the Northwestern exchanged more cars than all the rest of the lines put together." Another factor supports this alliance, but it merely "fortifies substantially the recommendation for merger based upon interchange traffic." [21]

How shall the Union Pacific reach St. Louis over its own rails? The best line for this purpose is the Wabash. And why? Because the interchange relationship between the two roads, particularly at Kansas City, makes "it obvious again that a natural current of traffic here exists." [22]

Which of the other two Hill lines shall merge with the Chicago, Burlington & Quincy? The interchange at Billings, Montana, partly points the way to a solution. It indicates "that the Burlington received from the Northern Pacific in 1919 much more than double the tonnage received from the Great Northern, and that it delivered to the Northern Pacific almost three times as much traffic as to the Great Northern." Therefore, "there can be no doubt as to the course of this *natural* current of traffic to the Northwest." [23]

These selections typify the report of Professor Ripley. Here and there other factors creep in—the avoidance of terminal congestion, the economics of double tracking, the utilization of direct routing, etc. But the central point of

CHANNELS OF TRADE AND COMMERCE 209

analysis is the traffic considerations: competition must be preserved and existing channels of trade and commerce must be maintained. And the existing channels are measured by the traffic interchanges between the carriers participating in a particular route.

The publication of the Tentative Plan of Consolidation and Professor Ripley's accompanying report was followed by hearings held in all parts of the country for the purpose of obtaining the views, of all those interested, on the subject of consolidation. The data thus gathered by the Commission and the opinion and views expressed before it were to aid that body in the perfection of a final and all-embracing plan of consolidation. The country's railway properties were to be readjusted in such a way that direct fee ownership would eventually rest in a limited number of corporations—nineteen, according to the tentative Plan of the Commission.

The Commission, in the hearings on the so-called Consolidation Proceedings, built up a record aggregating sixty-seven volumes of testimony and exhibits. Channels of trade and commerce were analyzed with a thoroughness—even if with the partiality occasioned by the character of the proceeding—obtainable only by years of active experience. The line of reasoning adopted by Professor Ripley was zealously pursued by railroad traffic men. Trade channels suggested in the tentative report which met with the approval of all interested parties were not thoroughly discussed. But those suggested that tended to upset any important vested rights were attacked and analyzed with the vigor and vehemence characteristic of the defense of business perquisites.

The discussion of the subject by able and experienced

railroad men tended to indicate the tenuous character of the reasoning underlying Professor Ripley's report. It developed first that traffic interchanges justifying (apparently) the existence of a channel of trade and commerce were frequently due to temporary factors. The Billings interchange of the Chicago, Burlington & Quincy (already noted) exhibiting a heavy preponderance in favor of the Northern Pacific as against the Great Northern, and therefore supporting the alliance of the former two properties, included data up to 1919.[24] Traffic interchange for the following two years completely reversed the relationship. During the period of Federal Control in 1918 and 1919, the United States Railroad Administration had routed tonnage originating on Great Northern rails and bound to the Chicago, Burlington & Quincy at Billings, via the Northern Pacific, from Spokane to Billings. Abnormal conditions, which operated in favor of the Northern Pacific in 1918 and 1919, operated against that same road in favor of the Great Northern in the two succeeding years.[25]

The Billings interchange, moreover, is only one of the important interchange contacts between the Great Northern and the Northern Pacific on the one hand, and the Chicago, Burlington & Quincy on the other. At the Twin Cities the interchange has always been substantially greater between the Great Northern and the Burlington than between the Northern Pacific and the Burlington.[26] The Great Northern (but not the Northern Pacific) and the Chicago, Burlington & Quincy, furthermore, connect at Sioux City, Iowa; and there interchange a substantial volume of traffic. A study of traffic interchange between the three Hill lines from 1908 to 1921 (and 1908 is used as a point of departure because of the construction in that year by the Great Northern of its Great Falls–Billings extension to a connection with the Burlington) reveals an interchange with the Burlington by the Great Northern and Northern Pacific respectively of 28,094,105 tons and 25,760,796 tons. "It will be observed," concludes the author of this traffic study, "that the Great Northern and the Burlington have established an interchange greater than that between the Northern Pacific and the Burlington, thereby maintaining, to a greater extent, a route and channel of trade and commerce." [27]

A study in the Great Northern–Northern Pacific merger case reveals that this Great Northern preponderance had continued through 1926. The loaded car interchange for that year between the Burlington and the Great Northern amounting to 101,612 cars substantially exceeded the corresponding interchange of 85,972 cars with the Northern Pacific.

And another analysis of the interchange in tons and revenue between the three lines of January, April, July and October for the year 1924; February, May, August and November of the year 1925; and March, June, September and December of the year 1926 exhibits a similar tendency. The Great Northern interchange amounted to 2,090,093 tons and realized $23,898,087 in revenue; while that of the Northern Pacific realized corresponding results of only 1,705,140 tons and $21,816,220 in revenue.[28]

So that Professor Ripley and the Great Northern, by using data for different years and for different junctions of interchange, reach diametrically opposite conclusions on the determination of the existence of a channel of trade and commerce. To the former the channel is over the

Northern Pacific, and to the latter it is over the Great Northern, and the Burlington.

The paucity of reliable interchange data dictates the exercise of great caution and circumspection in the measurement of trade channels on the basis of interchanged traffic. The business traded at specific junctions among all connections is frequently guarded—and perhaps legitimately so—as a business secret. The absence of complete information led Professor Ripley into a serious error on the Hill lines' interchange relationships. Almost all of the interchange figures in his report to the Commission, not only on the Hill lines, but for other lines as well, were expressed in terms of carloads or tons. The Commission at the hearings held in connection with the preparation of a plan of consolidation called for interchange data expressed in similar terms. It is decidedly questionable, however, whether the gross volume of business interchanged (either in tons or in carloads) constitutes an accurate index of the measure of the public interest in the resulting channel of trade and commerce. Ton miles, and not tons alone, reflect the volume of railroad service. A large tonnage transferred from one road to another at a particular junction may be hauled for a short distance. Conceivably this traffic may be of the very class which, in order to serve the public best, had better be transported by motor truck. It is the kind of traffic, in any event, for the carriage of which the truck most successfully competes.

Regardless of the competition of the motor truck, it still remains true that the better measure of the public transportation service is represented by ton miles rather than by tons or carloads interchanged. It is therefore signifi-

CHANNELS OF TRADE AND COMMERCE 213

cant that neither the report of Professor Ripley nor the vast mass of testimony and exhibits introduced in the subsequent Consolidation Proceedings contained any considerable analysis of interchange on a ton-mile basis. To this generalization there is one important exception. The report of Professor Ripley had recommended the allocation of the Philadelphia & Reading and the Central Railroad of New Jersey to the Baltimore & Ohio. The car interchanges had shown that the latter trunk line had interchanged more with these two terminal lines than did the Pennsylvania and the New York Central.[29] The report had nevertheless recognized the strategic importance to the New York Central of the east and west line of the Central Railroad of New Jersey–Philadelphia & Reading from Jersey City through Easton, Allentown, and Haucks to Newberry Junction. Bituminous coal from western Pennsylvania mines located in New York Central territory moves over a direct route via the latter junction to local Philadelphia & Reading and Central Railroad of New Jersey territory, and some to tidewater at Jersey City. Considerable anthracite coal, originating at mines in Central Railroad of New Jersey territory, moves over the full length of the line of the latter road to Jersey City for interchange with the New York Central.

The long haul thus given the Central Railroad of New Jersey by the New York Central is not matched by similar results from Baltimore & Ohio traffic. Most of the latter's traffic moves for short distances over the lines of the Central Railroad of New Jersey; from Allentown to the Lehigh and New England connection at Bethlehem, a distance of 5 miles; from Allentown to the Lehigh and Hudson connection at Easton, a distance of 16 miles, and from Bound Brook to the Baltimore & Ohio connection at Cranford Junction, a distance of 15 miles.[30]

The long haul of the New York Central and the short haul of the Baltimore & Ohio's traffic interchanged with the Central Railroad of New Jersey modifies the interchange picture. The results of a ton-mile study of the traffic moving over the line of the latter property from Haucks to Jersey City for the year 1921 are summarized as follows: [31]

	Tons	Per Cent	Tons, One Mile	Per Cent
Baltimore & Ohio..........	8,099,862	27.6	240,509,877	13.8
Philadelphia & Reading	4,282,000	14.6	140,657,449	8.1
TOTAL B. & O. and Reading	12,381,862	42.2	381,167,326	21.9
Western Maryland	1,133,800	3.9	76,526,929	4.4
TOTAL via Reading	13,515,662	46.1	457,694,255	26.3
New York Central	2,393,200	8.2	314,110,342	18.0
All others	13,373,650	45.7	971,327,231	55.7
TOTAL Haucks to Jersey City	29,282,512	100	1,743,131,918	100

The "predominant interest" [32] of the Baltimore & Ohio evident to Professor Ripley on the basis of car interchange data now becomes obscured. Crediting the Baltimore & Ohio with coal traffic carried via the Shippensburg route by the Philadelphia & Reading from the latter point to Allentown, its ton miles exceed those of the New York Central by less than 4 per cent.[33]

While the hearings in the Consolidation Proceedings were still in progress, carriers had applied to Commission for approval of proposed acquisition through share con-

CHANNELS OF TRADE AND COMMERCE 215

trol and lease contracts. The central position given in the statute to the necessity of the maintenance of existing channels of trade and commerce obliged the applicants to emphasize the traffic phases of railway consolidation. Adopting the standards laid down by Professor Ripley in his report to the Commission, the Missouri Pacific successfully urged the existing interchange relationships as indicative of the existence of a needed trade channel. Traffic had for many years moved between Houston and the Middle West over the International Great Northern to Longview, thence over the Texas & Pacific to Texarkana and beyond to St. Louis over the Missouri Pacific. So intimate had been the traffic relationships between these properties for many years that "the Missouri Pacific system, the Texas & Pacific Railway and the International Great Northern had, in many cases, their joint commercial and traffic agents to solicit business; not only in this country, but in Mexico. For quite a while, the Missouri Pacific, Texas & Pacific and International Great Northern had one general traffic manager." [34] The proposal of the St. Louis & San Francisco to acquire the International Great Northern had been officially disapproved because of the certain resulting disruption of this route.[35]

This was all well and good. A system had been created which maintained an existing channel of trade and commerce, and the existence of that channel could be easily established by the considerable volume of traffic interchanged between its constituent members. Successive unification programs promulgated thereafter did not present such clear cases. Shortly before the approval of the organization of the Missouri Pacific system, the Van Sweringen brothers of Cleveland announced their plans involving the formation of a new trunk line in eastern territory. Using the New York, Chicago & St. Louis as a nucleus they had managed to gain a sufficient degree of proprietary interest in a number of properties to insure their working control. In consonance with well-established financial principles they then devised a holding company scheme to insure the perpetuation of full control in their hands. This plan was subsequently presented to the Commission for its official consent. The financial methods did not accord with the views of the Commission; and it refused to approve the unification.

As a transportation machine, however, the Commission pronounced it unobjectionable. Had it not been for its financial set-up, the Commission made it clear, the proposal probably would have been sanctioned. The system as first presented (and as it still exists, despite Commission disapproval) associated the New York, Chicago & St. Louis, the Erie, the Pere Marquette, the Chesapeake & Ohio and the Hocking Valley into one transportation unit. It was not a completely unified system in fee ownership. It had its minority shareholders; it had its separate operating and traffic officials for its constituent units. In these respects it was on no different basis than the New York Central lines. That system consists of roads controlled by share ownership (the Cleveland, Cincinnati, Chicago & St. Louis, the Michigan Central, the Cincinnati Northern) which are individually officered and managed. And the New York Central also has its minority shareholders, who incidentally are fairly vigorous in the assertion of their vested interests that are contradictory to those of the controlling power. This is well exemplified

CHANNELS OF TRADE AND COMMERCE 217

by the opposition of the stockholders' protective committee of the Cleveland, Cincinnati, Chicago & St. Louis to the proposal of the New York Central to lease the property. The combined properties nevertheless represent, for most practical purposes, a well-unified transportation system.

Of the carriers embodied in the new eastern trunk line system, the Chesapeake & Ohio is financially the strongest. Yet its traffic and routing problems are presented as the motivating reasons for its acquisition of control of the Erie and the Pere Marquette.

The Chesapeake & Ohio is predominantly a bituminous coal carrier, almost 93 per cent of its originated traffic in 1926 consisting of products of mines.[36] Of its revenue coal tonnage, 70 per cent moves to connections and more than 90 per cent of this moves in approximately equal amounts via Cincinnati & Columbus to Central Freight Association Territory.[37] Within recent years the Columbus route has carried the larger part of the coal traffic.[38] It controls also a system line to Toledo through its majority share ownership of the Hocking Valley. Its line to Chicago is handicapped by excessive grades and curvatures; and can be fitted for economical transportation of coal only by large capital expenditures.

At Toledo, Cincinnati and Columbus connection is made with many lines, including the three major eastern trunk lines: the Pennsylvania, the New York Central and the Baltimore & Ohio. Destination territory of Chesapeake & Ohio westbound coal is generally in territory served by these lines. Large amounts of coal have been delivered by the Chesapeake & Ohio to these carriers. In 1922 the former delivered to the latter more than 42 per cent of the loaded cars delivered to all of its connections. Due partly to operation of business principles attendant upon a community of traffic and proprietary interest established between the Chesapeake & Ohio and other lines the percentage has since declined, reaching approximately 33.5 per cent in 1926.[39]

The car deliveries of the Chesapeake & Ohio to the lines which it proposes to acquire are only nominal. Its deliveries to the Erie and Pere Marquette from 1920 to 1926 did not exceed respectively 4 per cent and 2 per cent of its total car deliveries to all connections.[40]

The car interchange of the two other important units in the new system presents a similar aspect. The interchange of the Erie with constituent lines in 1926 amounted to 66,256 cars and with other lines 1,801,655 cars, while the Pere Marquette's interchange with constituent lines amounted to 58,676 cars and with other lines 753,146 cars.[41]

If traffic routes are based on existing interchange, there would appear to be no room for any reasonable doubt that the constituent lines in the new system do not form important channels of trade and commerce. The Chesapeake & Ohio's westbound soft coal traffic, which has increased so rapidly within recent years, has successfully reached its destination over the lines of its trunk line connections. There has been some congestion and delay at Cincinnati. This may be due to inadequate terminal facilities; or it may be due to the reluctance of trunk line connections to expedite movement of Chesapeake & Ohio's coal—coal which competes with that produced by mines located in the territory of the trunk lines. No accurate and satisfactory data were produced to permit one to reach a well-matured judgment on this point. Suffice it to say that, despite scat-

CHANNELS OF TRADE AND COMMERCE 219

tered statements of dissatisfaction, traffic in increasing volume moved over Chesapeake & Ohio lines to consuming territory located on the line of the Pennsylvania, Baltimore & Ohio and the New York Central. The light traffic interchanged among the constituent lines of the new system would hardly warrant a demand for unification based on existing channels of trade and commerce. The proponents of this unification could not justify its formation under the statute on the basis of reasoning adopted by Professor Ripley in his report; the reasoning used by almost all important carriers in the definition of trade routes in the Consolidation Proceedings, and the reasoning that underlay the Commission's sanction of the Missouri Pacific unification.

Necessity is the mother of invention in business, as well as in science. Being unable to point to any established interchange in order to justify the existence of trade channels required by accepted standards of the public interest, the carriers devised a new denominator. The Commission was advised that "certain changes in routing over the unified lines will occur. Traffic will be rerouted, wherever possible, so that it will move over the lines of the Unified System, which have the lowest grades, least curvature, greatest capacity and least congestion, which will avoid crowded terminals and which will otherwise be helpful in improving and expediting service and reducing operating costs." [42]

While no route will be closed and interchange at all junctions will be freely encouraged, the new system will open new routes for the movement of traffic. Chesapeake & Ohio coal, formerly moving to Chicago over its Chicago division, will in the future move over the Chesapeake &

Ohio, via Ashland, Kentucky, north over its line to Waverly, Ohio, and over a new line recently constructed to Columbus; thence via Marion and westward over the Erie. Many other new routes will be formed, six being denominated as particularly important by the traffic manager of the Chesapeake & Ohio.[43]

This modified concept of the nature of the channels of trade and commerce, the preservation of which was enjoined by the law, was accepted *in toto* by the Commission. "One of the most important factors in the Unified System," stated that body in its decision in the first Nickel Plate Unification case, "will be the movement of traffic over the most economical routes, having regard to density of traffic; congestion at terminals and grades." [44] And further, "While traffic will be routed so as to avoid congestion at terminals and otherwise improve and expedite service and reduce operating costs, there is no indication that any existing route will be closed." [45]

The single concession to the earlier concept is contained in the last phrase of the above quotation; that is, that no route will be closed in the course of the rerouting process. Whatever significance the latter phrase may have, it is obvious that the opening of new routes will divert traffic from existing routes. The interchange between roads participating in existing routes will decline. Be that as it may. The point is that channels of trade and commerce are recognized as existing over routes which move large volumes of traffic and over routes which move but a nominal volume.

The conclusion relating to this confusion of ideas that has found lodgment in the mind of the Commission is not based exclusively on a comparison of these two cases. The

CHANNELS OF TRADE AND COMMERCE 221

history of Commission consideration of railroad unification during the past eight years evidences a continuous and progressive adaptation of the statutory standard to the practical exigencies of each situation. The 50 per cent stock interest in the Denver & Rio Grande Western by the Missouri Pacific met with Commission approval partly because of the large volume of interchange between the two roads. The latter's share in the former's interchange at its eastern gateways of Denver, Colorado Springs and Pueblo exceeded one-third of the total. The Commission found that the route formed by these two lines, over which a substantial amount of traffic moves, has been in existence for more than thirty years.

During the same month the Commission gave approval to the joint lease of the Carolina, Clinchfield & Ohio, by the Atlantic Coast Line and the Louisville & Nashville. The preponderant interchange of the acquired line was with the Southern Railway. The Commission found that over a period of eight and two-third years the Southern gave the Clinchfield more than 40 per cent of the latter's traffic received from connections and that the Clinchfield gave the Southern almost 50 per cent of the traffic it delivered to connections. The interchange between the Clinchfield and one of the joint lessees, the Louisville and Nashville, was infinitesimal; while the interchange with the other lessee, the Atlantic Coast Line, was comparatively small. The lessees' acquisition promoted the public interest because of the opening up of a *new* route for coal from Kentucky to the Carolinas, and of a *new* competitive merchandise route between the northwest and the southeast.[46]

Other illustrations abound: the proposed unification

(approved by the Commission purely as a transportation proposal) of the St. Louis Southwestern, the Kansas City Southern, and the Missouri-Kansas-Texas between which the interchange amounted to approximately 2 per cent of their total interchange, and which they did not expect greatly to increase;[47] the proposed lease of the Buffalo, Rochester & Pittsburgh by the Delaware & Hudson (the two lines being separated from each other by over two hundred miles), proposing to substitute circuitous routes for existing direct routes, which was rejected by a close vote of six to five, the deciding vote being cast by a Commissioner on the general ground that *any* allocation of the lessor road in advance of a more comprehensive consolidation proposal in eastern territory was immature;[48] the acquisition by the Illinois Central of the Alabama & Vicksburg and the Vicksburg, Shreveport & Pacific, the traffic of the acquired lines moving largely northward over lines other than the Illinois Central,[49] etc.

It would serve no useful purpose to examine these and numerous other situations minutely. It would develop no new principle. Sufficient has been said to advance the conclusion that one of the safeguards thrown around consolidations is not serving its purpose well. Channels of trade and commerce may have some meaning. If they do, the regulatory authority charged with the administration of the law regarding consolidations has done nothing towards their clarification.

It is questionable indeed whether government authority can do much to regulate the formation of railway routes, if for a moment one may assume the identification of that term with channels of trade and commerce. Railway

CHANNELS OF TRADE AND COMMERCE 223

routes are established to enable the participating lines to carry traffic. Once the routes are in existence, traffic moves in accordance with established business principles already discussed: the line in the territory in which the traffic originates ordinarily, with the consent of the shipper, decides the route over which the traffic moves; it insures to itself the long haul so far as is possible, and at its long haul gateway it trades out the traffic with a view to the furtherance of its best business interests. It selects a complementary line, rather than a competitor; it directs more traffic to that line which gives it more in return; it exchanges loaded carloads for supplies of empties.

This is the stuff from which railway routes—channels of trade and commerce—are made. If existing routes carry large volumes of traffic, then the constituent lines which propose to unify their corporate ownership and operation desire to retain them. Therefore, the Great Northern, the Northern Pacific and the Chicago, Burlington & Quincy, which interchange extensively, find it profitable to consolidate. They want to retain the present available business interchanged between them. And they resolutely propose to defend their interchange from invasion by the Chicago, Milwaukee, St. Paul & Pacific. That would be the inevitable result of the carrying out of the suggestion of the Commission in its tentative plan to align that property with one of the Hill lines.

Similarly, the Union Pacific and the Chicago & Northwestern trade extensively at the Missouri River. Any proposal, such as made by Hale Holden, formerly of the Chicago, Burlington & Quincy, to ally the Northwestern with some other property is certain, as it did, to meet with the opposition of the Union Pacific.

If, on the other hand, the constituent lines interchange little traffic, their union is effected for the purpose of increasing its volume. Unification may contribute to increased interchange along internal system routes. The new Nickel Plate System is an excellent illustration. The important Chesapeake & Ohio coal traffic moving over trunk line connections is to be moved over the Erie west to Chicago and east to the Mahoning Valley. And traffic formerly moving over trunk lines to Michigan is to move via Toledo over the Pere Marquette. Or, as in the case of the so-called Loree southwestern unification, the primary purpose may be to increase traffic drawn from other roads.

The fundamental aim in all consolidation is to increase the traffic moving and to be moved over the lines of the consolidated system. There is no preference for existing railway routes as against new ones. Whether new routes will be needed depends upon the traffic characteristics of each separate situation. If new routes will attract more business, they will be formed. And it is only proper that they should be formed. To move a profitable volume of business over the new routes, however, requires a high standard of service performed at a reasonable cost. Without the former, the business could not be obtained, and without the latter, roads could not afford to carry it. The new routes, therefore, must enjoy good grades and curvatures; they must be properly maintained and steadily improved. The point at which physical, operating and traffic conditions, over an existing or proposed route, permit satisfactory service at rates reasonable to the shipper and remunerative to the carriers is a vital question of business judgment. The Commission, or any other regulatory body,

CHANNELS OF TRADE AND COMMERCE 225

can be of little assistance in aiding the management in reaching a sound conclusion.

The formation of railway routes—of channels of trade and commerce—proceeds along business lines. These are "natural" in the best commercial sense of the word. For they express the constant adaptation of genuine competition in railway service to the requirements of the shipping public. Railway routes come and go, as the public demand requires. The formation of important routes receives exhaustive consideration. They require the investment of large amounts of capital. And the business prospects for the new routes are accurately weighed in the balance. These considerations are frequently reflected in written documents, ordinarily known as traffic agreements. And to these attention will now be turned in the next chapter.

NOTES TO CHAPTER VIII

1. Control of Erie Railroad and Pere Marquette Railway, Finance Docket 6113-6114, Brief for Chesapeake & Ohio, Vol. I, p. 35.
2. Consolidation of Railroads, 63 I.C.C. 477.
3. Hearings before the House Committee on Interstate Commerce, 69th Congress, 1st session, on H.R. 11212, May 27, 1926, Part IV, p. 94.
4. N. Y. & N. R. Co. *vs.* N. Y. & N. E. R., 3 I.C.C. 542
5. Consolidation Proceedings, Docket 12964, Brief for the Great Northern Railway in support of the consolidation of the Chicago, Burlington & Quincy, Great Northern, Northern Pacific and subsidiaries, p. 78.
6. Control of Erie Railroad and Pere Marquette Railway, Finance Docket 6113-6114, Brief for Applicants, Vol. I, p. 41; Vol. II, p. 66.
7. Control of Virginian Railway, 117 I.C.C. 67.
8. Consolidation Proceedings, Docket 12964, Brief for the Great Northern Railway in support of the consolidation of the Chicago, Burlington & Quincy, Great Northern, Northern Pacific and subsidiaries, p. 73.
9. Consolidation Proceedings, Docket 12964, Statement by Lewis J. Spence on System No. 17, February 26, 1923, p. 44.
10. Unification of Southwestern Lines, Finance Docket 5679, 5680, tr. p. 1185.

226 RAILROAD CONSOLIDATION

11. Control of Jonesboro, Lake City & Eastern, 99 I.C.C. 753; Acquisition of St. Louis, Kennett & Southeastern, 131 I.C.C. 105.
12. Construction of lines by St. Louis Southwestern Ry. Co., 150 I.C.C. 685.
13. Control of San Antonio & Aransas Pass Railway, 94 I.C.C. 701; Construction of Extension by San Antonio & Aransas Pass Railway, 124 I.C.C. 513.
14. Acquisition by Southern Pacific, *et al*, 138 I.C.C. 205.
15. Control of Charlotte Harbor & Northern Railway, 105 I.C.C. 249; Control of Tavares & Gulf, 105 I.C.C. 383; Acquisition of Jacksonville, Gainesville & Gulf Railway, 124 I.C.C. 623; etc.
16. Reorganization of Atlanta, Birmingham & Atlantic Railway, 117 I.C.C. 181, 439.
17. Consolidation of Railroads, 63 I.C.C. 465.
18. *Supra*, p. 477.
19. *Supra*, p. 492.
20. *Supra*, pp. 512-513.
21. *Supra*, p. 575.
22. *Supra*, p. 575.
23. *Supra*, p. 591.
24. *Supra*, pp. 590-591.
25. Consolidation Proceedings, Docket 12964, Brief and Argument in opposition to choice of Great Northern rather than Northern Pacific, for separation from Burlington and association with St. Paul, p. 7.
26. *Supra*, p. 7-8.
27. *Supra*, tr. Vol. II.
28. Great Northern–Northern Pacific merger, Finance Docket 6409, 6410, Brief for Applicants, Vol. I, p. 71.
29. Consolidation of Railroads, 63 I.C.C. 492.
30. Consolidation Proceedings, Docket 12964, Statement of A. H. Smith, May 16, 1923, pp. 35-37, 39-40; Brief for Baltimore & Ohio, pp. 20-21; Brief for Port of New York Authority, p. 352.
31. *Supra*, Brief for Baltimore & Ohio, pp. 20-21.
32. Consolidation of Railroads, 63 I.C.C. 492.
33. This comparison is not entirely adequate, since the car interchange data of Professor Ripley relates to the Philadelphia & Reading for October, 1920, whereas the study in the Consolidation Proceedings relates to the Central Railroad of New Jersey's Haucks-Jersey City Line for 1921. It is believed, however, that the inadequacy of the available data will vitiate neither the strength nor the accuracy of the point under discussion.
34. Consolidation Proceedings, Docket 12964, Vol. XXI, tr. p. 2957.
35. Control of International Great Northern by St. Louis-San Francisco Railway, 79 I.C.C. 438.
36. Control of Erie Railroad and Pere Marquette Railway, Finance Docket 6113-6114, Brief for Interveners, Henry W. Anderson, *et al*, Vol. I, p. 179.
37. Nickel Plate Unification, Finance Docket 4643, 4671. Report and order proposed by Applicants, p. 25.

CHANNELS OF TRADE AND COMMERCE

38. Construction of line by Chesapeake & Hocking Railway, 117 I.C.C. 120.
39. Control of Erie Railroad and Pere Marquette Railway, Finance Docket 6113, 6114, Brief for Interveners, Henry W. Anderson, *et al*, Vol. I, p. 83.
40. *Supra*, p. 188.
41. *Supra*, Brief for Chesapeake & Ohio, Vol. I, p. 44.
42. Nickel Plate Unification, Finance Docket 4643, 4671, Brief for Applicants, Vol. 2, p. 67.
43. Control of Erie Railroad and Pere Marquette Railway, Finance Docket 6113, 6114, Brief for Chesapeake & Ohio, Vol. II, p. 38.
44. Nickel Plate Unification, 105 I.C.C. 433.
45. *Supra*, pp. 437-438.
46. Clinchfield Railway Lease, 90 I.C.C. 121, 126.
47. Unification of Southwestern Lines, 124 I.C.C. 414-415.
48. Control of Buffalo, Rochester & Pittsburgh Railway, 131 I.C.C. 750.
49. Control of Alabama and Vicksburg Railway, and Vicksburg, Shreveport & Pacific Railway, 111 I.C.C. 178.

CHAPTER IX

TRAFFIC AND TRACKAGE AGREEMENTS

The legal opportunity for free trading among all connections which "open routes" afford, does not lead to corresponding traffic results. Through routes and through rates enable each carrier to carry business at equal rates; but, even assuming an equivalence of service, it does not follow that all connections enjoy some substantial share of the available business. Each carrier, of course, obtains the strictly local interchange—that part of the traffic which originates on or is destined to points reached exclusively by its lines. Through and overhead traffic is, to a greater or lesser degree, competitive. It may move alternatively over one line or another, or over one combination of lines or another. The shipper at important junctions is presented with a strikingly rich selection of routes. Trading at the primary gateways of Kansas City and St. Louis is particularly free and open. From the former to an important city like Beaumont in southeastern Texas, there are 16 competitive routes; to Dallas 15; to Houston 13; to San Antonio 12. And from St. Louis to Beaumont 18 routes; to Dallas 41; to Houston 31; to San Antonio 23; while to Greenville, Texas, a seemingly unimportant point in eastern Texas, there are 54 routes. And all these routes are, on expert authority, declared to be competitive.[1]

A shipper on the Boston & Maine can, if he desires,

TRAFFIC AND TRACKAGE AGREEMENTS

route his Chicago traffic over this road, thence over the New York, New Haven & Hartford to the Harlem River gateway and over the Pennsylvania. Or he can order the business moved westward via Mechanicville and the Delaware & Hudson; and beyond the latter road, he can, if he wishes, direct that the shipment be moved over the Lehigh Valley and the Wabash; or the Lehigh Valley and the New York, Chicago & St. Louis; or the Lehigh Valley and the Grand Trunk; or the Erie; or the Delaware, Lackawanna & Western and the Wabash; or the Delaware, Lackawanna & Western and the New York, Chicago & St. Louis; or the Delaware, Lackawanna & Western and the Grand Trunk.

Also, the shipper may, in the contemplation of the law, direct the movement of his business via Rotterdam Junction and the New York Central system. He may also route over a number of northern Canadian routes via White River Junction and the Central of Vermont.

Despite this extraordinary superfluity of choice available to the shipper, he moves the brunt of his business over a few well-established routes. Every line participating in each route endeavors to secure the longest possible haul. Each one solicits the business of the shipper. But, as already discussed in detail, the originating road—that one which furnishes the shipper directly with team tracks, industrial tracks and other terminal facilities—is most successful in the solicitation process. The shipper routes the traffic over those lines and connections which tend to promote the best business interests of the originating carrier. The "open route" at the interchange point permits the shipper to send his freight over some line or route which short-hauls the initial carrier. And sometimes he exercises that right, particularly so, in the case of the larger shippers. That privilege is denied him if the route is "closed." The restrictions on the routing freedom of the originating line are not, however, sufficiently important to disturb seriously its ability to capture the preponderant volume of business.

At the free trading point the initial carrier meets many connections anxious to secure a share of its controlled traffic. The mere existence of an "open route"—of a through route and a through rate—over a particular connection does not necessarily mean that any traffic will be interchanged. That line may be a keen competitor of the originating carrier; so that in accordance with the considerations already touched upon, the latter will strongly resist any tendencies to effect a transfer of traffic to and from the former. The initial line may decline to interchange with another connection, and for a different reason. That road may control little traffic movements; it may originate but little traffic on its own lines. It may carry only a comparatively small volume of overhead business. There may be another connection which may enjoy a relatively large volume of business both originating and that received from its connections.

Witness the Union Pacific: it controls a large tonnage of eastbound business. The fruit from California, the lumber from Oregon, the potatoes from Idaho, and the wheat from Kansas it can carry no farther than Omaha. Most of its traffic is, however, destined for points beyond. Many carriers are willing and able to carry the business east to Chicago. It is not surprising that the Chicago, Burlington & Quincy, and the Chicago, Rock Island & Pacific get little of this business. To a greater or less degree, they com-

TRAFFIC AND TRACKAGE AGREEMENTS 231

pete west of the Missouri River. But why should the Chicago & North Western get so much and the Chicago Great Western so little? This query was propounded by the then member of the Interstate Commerce Commission, John J. Esch, at one of the hearings in the Consolidation Proceedings:

Q. (By Commissioner Esch). There are half a dozen roads between Council Bluffs and Chicago of almost equal mileage and you distribute some of that freight and receive some of that freight from these several lines? Why, with those conditions, should the North Western receive and deliver so much more than any other carriers connecting with the Union Pacific at Council Bluffs?
A. That is in line, Mr. Commissioner, with the policy of the Union Pacific Railroad covering coöperation at the Missouri River with its eastern connections. We have made a perfectly fair and neutral attempt to divide our unrouted eastbound tonnage in the proportion that they deliver us westbound tonnage. So that by giving us a stronger westbound business they would naturally build up that reciprocal relation.[2]

The Chicago & North Western gives more westbound and receives more eastbound. The Chicago Great Western gives less westbound and receives less eastbound.

Business is business, and a fair trade is no robbery. An eye for an eye and a tooth for a tooth may not be good biblical virtue. It is good business; and an exchange of a ton for a ton carries with it the implication of undoubted fairness. This substantial equivalence of tonnage in trading has been elevated by veteran railroad authority into an axiom. William H. Williams, the guiding hand in the destinies of the Wabash and the Missouri Pacific, has expressed it as follows: "If your traffic eastbound and westbound exactly balanced, you would be entitled to a car for each car that you gave the other line. If, on the other hand, the traffic in one direction was twice as much as in the other, with the direction of the prevailing load, for every two cars you gave the other line you would be entitled to one in return." [3]

At the Mississippi River gateway the proportion is different. Here, for example, the St. Louis & San Francisco gives the Chicago & Eastern Illinois three cars of freight for every one that the Chicago & Eastern Illinois gives to the St. Louis & San Francisco.[4]

And another experienced expert, the traffic manager of the Virginian Railway, has afforded the laymen an inside view of the situation. "It is a common practice," he recently stated, "for a carrier to periodically call the attention of its connections to the amount of business given them and asking for a corresponding amount in return; that is, if the interchange with the line addressed does not happen at the time to be breaking evenly." [5]

As the tonnage controlled by the initial line increases, the volume of return traffic received from connecting lines increases. Growth begets more growth; and as the originated business increases, so the interchange business increases. Indeed the underlying force of this tendency constitutes part of the motive impelling carriers under private ownership towards corporate consolidation. The concentration of the traffic formerly moving over several lines independently controlled into the hands of one party gives the latter a bargaining power with connections superior to that enjoyed by the constituent lines. The major eastern consolidation proposal—that involved in the pro-

TRAFFIC AND TRACKAGE AGREEMENTS 233

posed linking of the New York, Chicago & St. Louis, the Chesapeake & Ohio, the Hocking Valley, the Pere Marquette, and the Erie—was urged by T. C. Powell, formerly vice president in charge of traffic of the Erie and now president of the Chicago & Eastern Illinois on the ground that, "The greater volume of interchange traffic will induce a greater return of traffic from connecting lines. The combined solicitation will secure traffic that may be moving via other routes and, in some instances, traffic that is not moving at all." [6]

L. F. Loree, who is generally credited with being the main figure behind the proposed association of the Missouri-Kansas-Texas, Kansas City Southern, and the St. Louis Southwestern, supported that grouping because of its resultant ability to secure more tonnage from lines operating north of Kansas City and St. Louis such as the Chicago, Burlington & Quincy, Chicago, Milwaukee, St. Paul & Pacific, the Chicago Great Western, the Wabash, and the Chicago & Alton, than they could obtain if operated separately.[7]

At the southeastern terminus of this proposed southwestern system, at Memphis, Tennessee, similar results were expected by C. Haile, then vice president in charge of traffic of the Missouri-Kansas-Texas. At this point the Southern, the Louisville & Nashville, and the Nashville, Chattanooga & St. Louis interchange considerable business. Their business from the southeast is handled at this gateway rather than at St. Louis because of their greater earnings through the Memphis gateway. "The Missouri-Kansas-Texas," said Mr. Haile, before the Interstate Commerce Commission, "now has [then had] no influence with the Louisville & Nashville, or with the

Nashville, Chattanooga & St. Louis, practically none with the Southern Railway, . . . but if we can show that the very greatly increased mileage would be available to them, through our solicitation, combined with that of the Cotton Belt, I think that would excite an interest and disposition to work in our interest, that is entirely lacking now." [8]

The exact nature and measure of the traffic—the business—interests of connecting lines at the large gateways are not easily determined. One line may control a good tonnage, and will distribute it among lines that will best serve its own business aims. At one junction, trading in traffic among particular lines is dominated by the principle of the long haul. At another, the principle of the non-competitive connection holds imperial sway. At still another, perhaps, reciprocal trading for traffic may be paramount. And at a fourth the controlling line may exchange its loaded cars for an adequate supply of empty cars. In business life all these, as well as other minor factors, operate simultaneously and continuously. It is difficult, if not indeed impossible, to measure the exact influence of each force upon the volume of interchange.

Their exact working is not left to the chances of casual and extemporaneous trading. The "open route" in and of itself produces no machinery by which trading in interchange can develop its full business results. The "open route" is of importance to the shipper. He thereby obtains the privilege to route his freight over any line; even though, thereby, he short-hauls the original carrier; or obliges it to interchange with a competitor; or forces it to trade with a connection on a nonreciprocal basis. In actual practice these results rarely occur. The controlling line at the open gateway only infrequently trades against

TRAFFIC AND TRACKAGE AGREEMENTS

its own business interests. The connection which can least serve the vital needs of the initial line is thrown upon its own soliciting resources to get what little business it can.

The initial line in turn crystallizes its own business necessities in the form of definite understandings with that connection or those connections best calculated to promote its own traffic needs. These understandings—sometimes verbal and sometimes written—expressing the reciprocal traffic obligations and responsibilities of independent carriers are ordinarily known as traffic agreements.

Agreements of this character between particular carriers forming a through route set them off from others at an open gateway. They become the favored partners. The traffic controlling line selects one of the many connections to which it delivers traffic in interchange; and from which it expects corresponding reciprocity. The one line thus favored is the preferential connection; the other—the originating—line, solicits in its favor. Its entire organization: its solicitors, its car supply, its train schedules, its switching service, etc., is available to render this preference effective.

It is this preference which fattens up one connection and dries up another at the so-called open gateway. A physical connection between two major lines at a productive traffic center may create but little interchange. The Union Pacific terminates on the east at two gateways: at Kansas City on the south and at Omaha on the north. The Chicago, Milwaukee, St. Paul & Pacific connects with the Union Pacific at both gateways. This apparently successful setting for prolific interchange between the two carriers has led to authoritative suggestions for their consolidation. But the Kansas City connection yields little interchange of traffic; since according to Judge Robert S. Lovett, Chairman of the Union Pacific, "the traffic moves preferentially via Omaha and Council Bluffs." [9] The Union Pacific cannot reciprocate in the trading of traffic at the other gateway; it "has nothing or practically nothing to offer in exchange at Kansas City since, . . . it handles such business through Omaha and Council Bluffs." [10]

The extent to which a traffic agreement can tie up traffic for movement over a particular route is well indicated by the contract (the execution of which was made contingent upon its being entered by the Interstate Commerce Commission as a condition in its approval of the proposed Loree Southwestern Unification) of July 30, 1926, between the Southern Pacific Company and the St. Louis Southwestern Railway Company. The line of the latter between St. Louis and Memphis on the north and east, and northern Louisiana and eastern Texas on the south and west serves as a bridge for the carriage of Southern Pacific business to and from these points to destinations beyond. The parties agreed to maintain satisfactory rates; to coördinate their schedules to provide adequate competitive service; to provide a high-class freight service; to maintain through merchandise package cars. That is how the business is to move. But now to get the business: The St. Louis Southwestern agrees "actively and preferentially" to solicit traffic for the Southern Pacific. The latter agrees "to solicit without discrimination" against the routes formed by and with the St. Louis Southwestern.[11]

The disproportionate burden of soliciting responsi-

TRAFFIC AND TRACKAGE AGREEMENTS 237

bility assumed by the parties to the transaction is explained by their relative control over the traffic movements. The traffic moving over this route is largely controlled by the Southern Pacific. It can, if it finds it good business to do so, send the business over some line other than the St. Louis Southwestern. The latter controls some traffic moving over this route; particularly the cotton grown in its territory moving to Houston and Galveston for export. Compared to that controlled by the Southern Pacific, it is relatively small. The controlled business of the Southern Pacific capable of movement over the St. Louis Southwestern is large. It is vital to the latter's revenue interests. It is therefore willing, on all traffic that can be so routed, to prefer the Southern Pacific. The latter in turn, enjoying a strategic bargaining position, surrenders only the freedom to discriminate against the other party. It reserves the liberty to trade any part of its traffic with any of its other numerous connections when in its judgment it can promote its own welfare by doing so.

The mutuality of interests thus expressed through a traffic agreement creates a solid basis for an active efficient through route. Other routes exist at the open gateways of northern Texas and Louisiana. Competitors of the St. Louis Southwestern participate in the "open routes." The Missouri-Kansas-Texas, the St. Louis & San Francisco, and the Missouri Pacific are all there; ready and able to carry all business offered. But they get little. For the St. Louis Southwestern is the preferred connection. Business flows smoothly and efficiently over the joint route of the Southern Pacific–St. Louis Southwestern. The properties are independently owned and operated. This does not, however, impair the service rendered to the public. This existing "channel of trade and commerce" is indeed independent of the fortunes of consolidation; if, that is, consolidation can be expressed in terms of efficient service. Unity in ownership is not always necessary to excellency of service; and, if a basis of business reciprocity prevails between connections, then the resultant channel for the movement of traffic is as well assured as would be the case if the two lines were consolidated for ownership as well as for service.

A traffic agreement may under some conditions be an integral part of a program in creating a new through route. Construction of additional main line mileage, terminal or interchange facilities may be financially justified only by an assurance of an adequate volume of traffic. This may be secured by proper traffic arrangements with connections. A few years ago new interests acquired control of a small carrier in eastern Oklahoma. This road, the Kansas, Oklahoma & Gulf, was a typical weak short line of the type, the preservation of which, regardless of their financial stability, is in many quarters considered as one of the chief aims of a national program of consolidation. It had been incurring perennial deficits for many years. The property developed little traffic in its own territory. It was, nevertheless, strategically located for the carriage of through traffic between Missouri River points and points in north and central Texas. On the north its line terminated approximately fifteen miles from a connection with the Kansas City Southern. That line controlled a considerable southbound interchange tonnage, particularly that received from the Chicago, Burlington & Quincy and the Union Pacific. The Kansas City Southern over its own system mileage served only a small section in south-

TRAFFIC AND TRACKAGE AGREEMENTS 239

eastern Texas. The Kansas, Oklahoma & Gulf extended throughout the length of Oklahoma and connected with numerous lines at its southern terminus at Denison in north central Texas. The Southern Pacific, extending south therefrom, offered commodities brought by the Kansas, Oklahoma & Gulf and received by it from the Kansas City Southern an extensive market in Texas.

These considerations establishing a mutuality of traffic interest led to negotiations which resulted in the formation of a new "channel of trade and commerce." The fifteen-mile gap on the northern end of the Kansas, Oklahoma & Gulf was filled by construction of additional mileage by both that line and the Kansas City Southern. The two properties then concluded a traffic agreement by which each became a preferential connection of the other. Each party agreed "that in all lawful ways, it will support the interest of the other in all traffic movements which can be equitably and expeditiously done over the lines" of each other. Again in this agreement the obligations incurred were not proportionately reciprocal. The line controlling the major tonnage—the Kansas City Southern—qualifies its agreement to "use its best endeavors to solicit and route" via the other line on the basis of "revenue and service justifying." The Kansas, Oklahoma & Gulf, however, agrees to the same preferential routing and solicitation "on an equal basis of earnings in divisions."

This new traffic route for the movement of business between Kansas City and Missouri River points on one hand and Oklahoma and central Texas points on the other was opened on August 1, 1925. Its opening produced "a continually increasing interchange of traffic." By October of 1925 the interchange had amounted to 898 cars; and by October of 1926 to 1,687 cars.[12]

Upon occasion the traffic agreement has served as a medium by which the clash of rival corporate interests has been amicably resolved. The ambitious northwestwardly extension of the Chicago, Burlington & Quincy lines in the early nineties was halted by an agreement of this character. The continuous construction through western Nebraska and Wyoming pointed directly towards Northern Pacific territory. The latter had built itself into the great Northwest, in the states of Montana, Idaho, and Washington. It had, early in the nineties, encountered the competition of the recently constructed transcontinental line of the Great Northern. The prospective extension of the Chicago, Burlington & Quincy beyond Billings, Montana, threatened its traffic from another direction.

The Northern Pacific then, as now, extended from the Twin Cities on the east to the northern Pacific coast on the west. The preponderant trend of traffic then, as now, was eastbound. And the Northern Pacific carried its controlled business east to the Twin Cities for its long haul. The Chicago, Burlington & Quincy's line into southern Montana was not ill-fitted for the transportation of traffic to and from points in the central west, in the Missouri and Mississippi valley. It was peculiarly well-fitted financially to extend its lines directly into the heart of Northern Pacific territory north and west of the latter's terminus in southern Montana. And the Northern Pacific was proportionately ill-fitted to withstand such competition. The properties of the Northern Pacific had just been placed in the hands of a receiver; and business early in 1894 had turned for the worse.

TRAFFIC AND TRACKAGE AGREEMENTS

To avoid the seemingly disastrous character of the impending competition, by the Chicago, Burlington & Quincy, the Northern Pacific found it necessary to make far-reaching traffic concessions. At a meeting held in the spring of 1894 between the representatives of both properties, a settlement was reached as a result of which the Northern Pacific was saved from the direct competition of the Chicago, Burlington & Quincy in its own territory. A traffic agreement was concluded providing for the usual "open route" in the form of through rates and satisfactory divisions. In addition both parties expressly agreed to promote interchange to the largest practicable extent. And then—the heart of the arrangement—the Northern Pacific tied up its eastbound traffic destined to points on and south of a line drawn through Omaha, Nebraska and Burlington, Iowa and west of the Missouri River for delivery to the Chicago, Burlington & Quincy at Billings. Gradually in the operation of this contract the Northern Pacific's obligation extended to traffic west, but not east of the Mississippi River.[13]

The lumber and grain that had formerly moved east over the Northern Pacific lines in Montana, North Dakota, and Minnesota now moved over the more southerly lines of the Chicago, Burlington & Quincy through Wyoming, Nebraska and Iowa. The Northern Pacific had short-hauled itself on a large scale; it had agreed to deliver traffic to a line at Billings which it could have carried many miles to the east for interchange at the Twin Cities. The traffic agreement had created a new channel of trade and commerce; the importance and naturalness of which was emphasized by Professor Ripley in his report on the Tentative Plan to the Interstate Commerce Commission.

What vested rights this diversion of traffic affected does not appear. Some motive power and equipment, some terminal and interchange facilities, some additions and betterments had been provided to move Northern Pacific business over its line east of Billings. Some part of these facilities were rendered idle; and the spread of their capital charges over the remaining business did, perhaps, increase the unit cost of performing the transportation service.

Other than this, however, it is difficult to conceive any public interest in the traffic diversion and in the resultant formation of a new "channel of trade and commerce." The real measure of the public interest lies in the rendition of adequate service at reasonable rates. The route—the channel—over which the traffic moves would seem to be of little importance. The swift-moving and primary competitive forces may and do effect far-reaching changes in the movement of interchange traffic; but so long as costs are not substantially increased nor service seriously impaired, the public interest is not affected. And its guardians need not—or rather should not—be consulted.

The traffic diversion, which is necessarily implied from the designation of free trading at the interchange gateways, goes on unhindered by the existence of the "open routes." The traffic agreement at Omaha between two such independent properties as the Union Pacific and the Chicago & North Western need not, and does not, disturb through-rate arrangements of either carrier with any of the other connections. Neither need the community of financial interests at the Twin Cities between the Great Northern, the Northern Pacific and the Chicago, Burlington & Quincy affect the through routes and rates with

TRAFFIC AND TRACKAGE AGREEMENTS 243

the other carriers. "Open routes" prevail at both of these interchange gateways.

A considerable traffic exchange between other such carriers, as a matter of fact, occurs at both junctions. At the Twin Cities both the Great Northern and the Northern Pacific deliver a considerable tonnage to the Minneapolis & St. Louis, a competitor of the Chicago, Burlington & Quincy. Indeed, the deliveries of the two northern roads to that line rank in importance next to the Chicago, Burlington & Quincy. This interchange, however, is not due to the mere existence of an "open route." The interchange traffic received by the Minneapolis & St. Louis from the two northern lines is bought and paid for. That line penetrates a good grain country in Iowa, and reaches also the Peoria gateway. It delivers grain destined to Duluth to northern lines at the Twin Cities. This controlled traffic the Minneapolis & St. Louis could deliver to the Chicago, Milwaukee, St. Paul & Pacific for the Duluth haul. To obtain its tonnage the northern lines deliver some of their traffic to the Minneapolis & St. Louis.[14] Traffic reciprocity is good business.

Another competitor of the Chicago, Burlington & Quincy, the Chicago Milwaukee, St. Paul & Pacific, has little to reciprocate with the northern lines beyond the Twin Cities. It operates its own line into that territory. It therefore obtains almost no competitive traffic at the Twin Cities from the northern lines. Its interchange receipts from these carriers consists almost exclusively of local traffic.

Similarly at Omaha the competitors of the Chicago & Northwestern trade considerable tonnage with the Union Pacific. The Chicago, Burlington & Quincy short-hauls itself at Denver to get a share of the Union Pacific's eastbound business at Omaha. The Chicago, Milwaukee, St. Paul & Pacific interchanges considerably with the Union Pacific. How much of this traffic is local to wide-flung lines of both systems can be ascertained only after a laborious analysis of waybills.

The great preponderance of the tonnage interchanged at these gateways moves between the preferred carriers. Preferential solicitation moves the traffic over the established routes. The soliciting energy of the controlling line is concentrated on the routing over one particular line or lines, as against others. And this is the prime force in the formation of "Channels of trade and commerce." Nothing that was inserted in the consolidation section of the Act of 1920, nor anything done by the Interstate Commerce Commission under its provisions, has substantially modified its operation. Keeping the gateways open because of sound business judgment or Commission direction has not materially retarded the progress of preferential solicitation. The traffic agreement, either verbal or written, by providing for such preference has diverted the controlled traffic accordingly.

The traffic agreement or understanding, important as it is, is only one of the various devices whereby the flow of interchange traffic is fashioned into the existing channels. Many of the one-line routes rendering an efficient public service are not completely consolidated in ownership, as they are apparently in operation and in traffic unity. Tonnage is routed and moved over one line from point of origin to point of destination. The transporting carrier collects the freight rate and retains all of it for its own treasury; that is, it participates in no rate di-

TRAFFIC AND TRACKAGE AGREEMENTS 245

visions. Still it moves its freight over a line owned in whole or in part by another carrier. The form of use of the owning by the using line presents considerable complexities in business application. For present purposes, however, it is sufficient to consider only the trackage agreement.

This species of property rights is not mentioned in the existing law on consolidation; nor has its significance been given the attention it merits in the discussion on its proposed amendments. The law calls for "the consolidation of the railway properties"; and it is an open question whether that covers the many pieces of railroad property, both main lines and terminal facilities, that are jointly used. Some of the highly important traffic routes of the country carrying a substantial tonnage are based on trackage rights. The Wabash–Delaware, Lackawanna & Western route constitutes a short line between Detroit and New York. This route is made possible by an agreement in which the Grand Trunk gives the Wabash trackage rights from Detroit to Buffalo. Without this trackage the Wabash would have no noncompetitive connection to Buffalo. Not only that. It would be obliged to switch freight around the city, and increase the congestion of the already congested terminals.

Access of the St. Louis & Southwestern to Memphis is effected by a trackage arrangement held from the Chicago, Rock Island & Pacific; and access of the latter to Denver is accomplished through trackage over the Union Pacific. The highly important noncongested seven-line route for the carriage of bituminous coal from Baltimore & Ohio and Western Maryland territory to New England could not function without a bit of trackage over the Pennsylvania held by the Lehigh & Hudson Railroad.[15] Long stretches of main line are frequently used jointly: the Southern Railroad trackage over the Atlantic Coast Line, of 172 miles; the Great Northern over the Northern Pacific, of 173 miles; the Missouri Pacific over the Texas & Pacific, of 193 miles.[16]

Other important routes frequently consist of bits of trackage sandwiched in between pieces of owned lines. Thus, the New York Central Lines reach Cleveland from the Pittsburgh & Lake Erie at Youngstown over small owned tracks at both terminals and successive pieces of trackage over the Pennsylvania, the Baltimore & Ohio, and the Lake Erie & Pittsburgh Railway Company.[17] The plans of the New York Central for an alternative route from Chicago to New York over the Philadelphia & Reading and the Central Railroad of New Jersey rests in part upon several trackage rights. Its stub to Newberry Junction—the junction with the Philadelphia & Reading—consists in part of trackage rights over the Pennsylvania and the Buffalo, Rochester & Pittsburgh uniting the owned mileage on both sides. (See map on page 255.)[18] A profitable tonnage moves between Portland, Oregon and Tacoma, Washington between which the Great Northern, the Northern Pacific and the Union Pacific all use the same road.[19]

Trackage rights assume many different forms and respond to variable situations. A trackage agreement may be employed to facilitate the carriage of business through regions of light traffic density: the additional business may be insufficient to warrant the construction of a duplicate line. It may be used, on the other hand, to transport traffic through regions of heavy traffic density: the non-owning line may compel the owning line to permit track-

TRAFFIC AND TRACKAGE AGREEMENTS

age under the latter's threat of constructing a duplicate line. It is significant to observe, that with but few exceptions, the owning line surrenders nothing of its local traffic; the traffic the movement of which it controls. This tonnage the using line is expressly prohibited from soliciting. That is forbidden ground. Nothing in the trackage agreement, therefore, interferes with operation of those factors that enable the initial line to control the movement of originating business over lines and routes best calculated to serve its business needs.

From the standpoint of the fundamentals of traffic diversion—the control of the routing of the originated traffic—there is little difference between the traffic and the trackage agreement. Both leave undisturbed the preferential solicitation power of the initial carrier. There is, however, a fundamental distinction between the two. The traffic agreement obliges each road to stop short at its own boundary. Beyond that point its own operating organization dare not go. Its own engines and train crews cannot cross into foreign territory. There are, again, some qualifications to this generalization. A close community of traffic interest may lead to some pooling of traffic facilities even in the absence of any specific trackage arrangements. The exchange of motive power between the Wheeling & Lake Erie and the Pittsburgh & West Virginia, already discussed, may serve as one illustration. The operation of the trains of the Philadelphia & Reading beyond its terminus at Shippensburg, Pennsylvania, to Hagerstown, Maryland, in order to insure a high degree of service over the Shippensburg route, may serve as another.

These are, however, exceptions. In most instances the engines and crews of one carrier do not pass over on the tracks of the other. A carrier enjoying trackage rights does exercise that privilege. It retains control over its equipment and its personnel after they leave its own tracks. A road operating over an "open route" with or without preferential solicitation interchanges freight with connections in the usual way. The cars must be inspected, records must be made, deliveries on specific interchange tracks must be effected, trains must be arranged, new schedules coördinating those of the connecting lines must be observed, etc. A route based on trackage is exempt from most of these requirements with the attendant delay. The trains and crews of the using line move by its own motive power over the tracks of the owning road.

There is, moreover, a greater degree of permanence and stability attached to a trackage than to a traffic agreement. A trackage right ordinarily runs for a long period of time. During that time the using line establishes the route as a one-line route. It is advertised and solicited among the shippers as such. Its business details are not known to the owning line, since it is not obliged to transfer its waybills to the latter. The road forming a route in ordinary interchange solicits for a multi-line route, and its customers, furthermore, become well known to its connection. The using road to a trackage agreement cannot be disturbed during the term of its trackage; whereas the road, party to an "open route" even with a traffic agreement, has no assurance of the continuance of the traffic relationship.

This is not to gainsay the many vital problems involved in the practical operation and enforcement of trackage agreements. With hardly an exception, the train dispatchers are provided by the owner road. Even on the

TRAFFIC AND TRACKAGE AGREEMENTS

Northern Pacific line between Portland, Oregon and Seattle, Washington over which the Oregon Short Line and the Great Northern enjoy, according to Professor Ripley, "full trackage rights," [20] this is the case. The using road must, therefore, before conducting a switching or a train movement obtain the consent of the owner road. Frequently the trackage contract calls for an equivalence in treatment of the same class of trains of both carriers. This is difficult to enforce; the twilight zone is large; and if it is in the interest of the owner road to interpret practical situations narrowly, it usually does so.

The paramount status of the business of the owning road and the corresponding subordination of that of the using road is sometimes expressed in a different manner. A restriction of this character in a trackage arrangement with the Norfolk & Western justified in part the Chesapeake & Ohio in building a duplicate line. Both properties have within recent years enjoyed an increased westbound movement of bituminous coal. Part of this tonnage moves through Columbus, Ohio. The lines of the Chesapeake & Ohio extended only to a small point known as Waverly, a few miles south of Columbus, Ohio. From the latter point the Hocking Valley, an affiliated line of the Chesapeake & Ohio, extends northward to Toledo, and other trunk lines extend westward to Chicago & St Louis. This gap is filled by the Norfolk & Western. Over its line the Chesapeake & Ohio operated its trains on a trackage basis.

Its running rights were, however, hedged around with many limitations so as not to interfere with the traffic of the Norfolk & Western. The latter could limit the number of cars moved daily by the Chesapeake & Ohio to a minimum of 600 in each direction. It could, moreover, suspend the minimum proviso and embargo trains or cars of the Chesapeake & Ohio. The failure of the latter to remove its locomotives, trains, or cars from Norfolk & Western tracks immediately upon its arrival at the northern terminus of the tracks of the owning road would justify such action. A congestion of its facilities caused by engine or car failures of the Chesapeake & Ohio or a suspension of the movement of the trains of that road by reason of the operation of the law or for any other course, would permit the Norfolk & Western to institute a similar embargo.[21]

The very nature of the trackage device introduces considerations of equity as between the two lines involved. The owning road obliges the using road to pay a return, not only on the value of the initial plant dedicated for trackage, but also on all improvements subsequently made. The improvements may or may not be required to serve the business needs of the using line; but it ordinarily can exercise no voice in the determination of their necessity. Once they are installed the user must pay a return on the capital invested therein. Similarly as to maintenance, payments must be made on a wheelage basis. Payments vary with the number of cars and locomotives moved over the tracks. The owning road must maintain the physical property at a certain standard. It is easier to establish than to enforce such a requirement; and there is a wide difference between a defensive policy not to permit a standard to fall below a particular level, and an aggressive and progressive raising of that standard to insure the performance of a maximum grade of service. With inadequate improvements and inferior maintenance the using road could furnish only a poor service to

TRAFFIC AND TRACKAGE AGREEMENTS 251

its patrons. If the traffic of the owning road were light, the service given might be commensurate with the needs involved. The incurring of additional capital and operating expenses might from its point of view be unjustified. On the other hand, its traffic might be heavy; and that of the user road might be light. Then the owner might provide additions and betterments, raise the standards of maintenance, and assess part of the cost on the other carrier.

These considerations are merely suggestive of the possibilities of friction between the grantor and grantee. Yet there is the undeniable fact that one road owns a contractual right to operate its trains over the tracks of another. Whereas a road seeking to move its business over another line through the rules of ordinary interchange usually loses all control of the movement of its traffic the moment it leaves its tracks. The tense verbal battle waged by the New York Central and the Baltimore & Ohio over the control of the Philadelphia & Reading and the Central Railroad of New Jersey before the Interstate Commerce Commission in the Consolidation Proceedings—a battle presently to be renewed before that same body—exemplifies some of the practical aspects of that distinction.

Professor Ripley in his report had suggested the assignment of the two terminal properties to the Baltimore & Ohio. That system would thus have secured a direct entrance into New York City. The Baltimore & Ohio, as well as the New York Central, utilize these roads in the transportation of bituminous coal from Maryland and West Virginia and northwestern Pennsylvania respectively. Coal of the former line moving over interior Shippensburg route passes over the Reading from Shippensburg to Bethlehem; and a large proportion continues on over the Central of New Jersey from Bethlehem to Easton. The coal of the New York Central, originating in part on its own lines in Pennsylvania, and in part on the Buffalo, Rochester & Pittsburgh and on the Cambria & Indiana, flows eastward to Newberry Junction and interchanges with the Philadelphia & Reading. To some extent, the coal from the Pennsylvania and West Virginia fields carried over these rival lines competes in common markets. The route of the New York Central is shorter, at least to New York City, than is the composite route of the Baltimore & Ohio.[22]

On the basis largely of a car interchange study for October, 1920, Professor Ripley recommended the assignment of the lines to the Baltimore & Ohio. The study, while establishing "the substantial interest of the three great trunk lines" (the Pennsylvania being the third), "also makes [made] plain the predominant interest of the Baltimore & Ohio."[23] The recommendation was coupled with the necessity of the assurance of free utilization of both terminal carriers by the New York Central. This was to be effected by the grant of trackage rights by the proposed owner, the Baltimore & Ohio, to the proposed user, the New York Central.

The discussion of this recommendation before the Interstate Commerce Commission by representatives of the contending trunk lines brought out in bold relief the comparative, competitive status of "open routes" and trackage routes. The Baltimore & Ohio registered its satisfaction with the assignment of the properties in dispute to its system lines. It did not, however, perceive the necessity

TRAFFIC AND TRACKAGE AGREEMENTS

of granting the New York Central trackage over the carriers assigned it. The New York Central's Ashtabula-Newberry Junction stub was a single track road ascending an elevation of 1,767 feet. The tonnage flowing over it was insignificant as compared with that flowing over the main water-level line through Buffalo. The route through Pennsylvania may be 30 or 35 miles shorter; but, insisted Mr. Daniel Willard, president of the Baltimore & Ohio, "the difference in altitude which it has to overcome would much more than offset any economies because of the shorter distance." [24]

Further, the traffic over that route is not through business destined to New York City and beyond. Most of it is local to the lines of the Philadelphia & Reading and the Central Railroad of New Jersey. It seemed to Mr. Willard, in substance, "that the use which the New York Central will probably make in increasing the measure of that line, will be to pass such business into and out of that interior region as either originates there or is consumed there and in no sense would I [he] ever expect to see that made a part of the through line, handling New York Central business from Chicago to New York, because it would be uneconomical to do so." [25]

The Baltimore & Ohio would be glad to afford the New York Central the opportunity to send its business to points located on the Reading. It would be to the interest of that road, either as an independent company or as a part of the Baltimore & Ohio system, to develop the greatest possible volume of interchange. And that traffic would not compete with the Baltimore & Ohio "in any particular sense." The routes of course would have to be kept open. The traffic "would move in ordinary methods of interchange as the bulk of the business of the country is moved." [26] There was nothing to indicate that the business of the New York Central required any different operating methods.

This offer of the "open route" was declined by the New York Central. Mr. Willard "is human," said A. H. Smith, president of that line; and if you give the Baltimore & Ohio, the Central Railroad of New Jersey and the Philadelphia & Reading, you give it to a competitor for that traffic which moves from the coal mines of Pennsylvania eastward through Newberry Junction. And with Mr. Willard "as a competitor, I don't think I would get very much of a show on all that long-haul tonnage." [27]

Mr. Smith in turn suggested that the Central Railroad of New Jersey and the so-called Catawissa branch of the Philadelphia & Reading connecting the New York Central at Newberry Junction with the Central Railroad of New Jersey's line to Jersey City be assigned to the New York Central. That would insure the latter an alternative line to New York City. But it would place part of the access of the Baltimore & Ohio to New York City and to New England in the hands of a competitor. How would the Baltimore & Ohio reach New York? On what terms could it run over the Central Railroad of New Jersey tracks from Bound Brook to Jersey City? Would the New York Central insist upon subjecting the Baltimore & Ohio's traffic to the ordinary rules of interchange? No, it would not, said Mr. Smith. That traffic coming north from Philadelphia through Bound Brook to Jersey City "is the main business of the Baltimore & Ohio Railroad." He would be willing to grant it trackage over

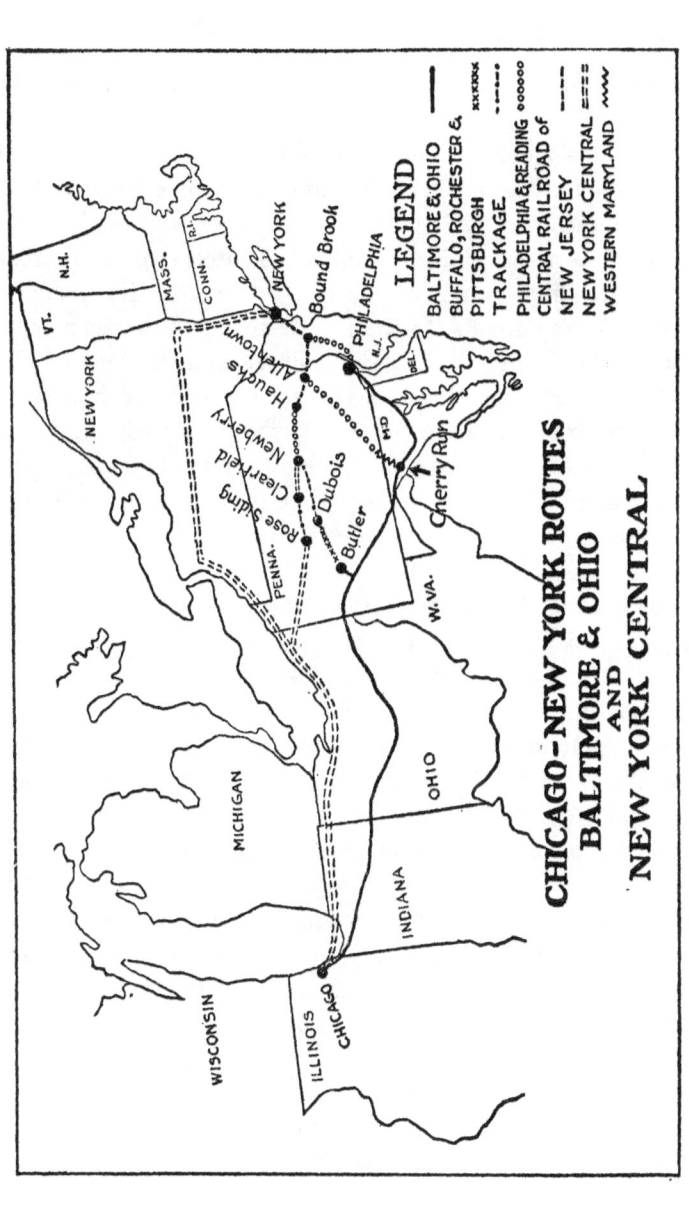

this line, "unlimited, unrestricted, for everything they got." [28]

And what arrangements would the New York Central make with the Baltimore & Ohio for business moving over the interior route? A large tonnage of soft coal moves over this route to New England. The coal received from the Reading moves east over the Central Railroad of New Jersey from Allentown to Easton; and then northeast over the Lehigh & Hudson and the system lines of the New York, New Haven & Hartford. Mr. Smith was willing to grant trackage for this traffic. But with regard to the handling of Baltimore & Ohio business beyond Easton to Bound Brook and Jersey City his views changed. He would grant no trackage over this mileage.

The Baltimore & Ohio wants to create a new through route from Chicago to New York, a shorter route, a more economical one. The proposed route will be 900 miles; the present route via Philadelphia is 983. Annual savings from its use are estimated to exceed $800,000.[29] Its line now operates east to Butler, Pennsylvania; the Allegheny & Western division of the Buffalo, Rochester & Pittsburgh would extend it to Dubois. Alternative plans are under consideration to fill the intervening gap to Newberry Junction. Its route, however, would be useless unless it could reach Jersey City. (See map on page 255.)

The New York Central indulges its own ambitions for an alternative route to New York through northern Pennsylvania. Its line to Newberry Junction is already in existence. It needs only the Catawissa branch of the Philadelphia & Reading and the line of the Central Railroad of New Jersey beyond to New York to complete this route. These properties, Mr. Smith suggested, should be assigned to the New York Central. Under this arrangement how could the Baltimore & Ohio, queried Mr. Julius Henry Cohen, Counsel for the Port of New York Authority, reach the port of New York from the west? It will get there the same way that the Western Maryland gets from Shippensburg to Allentown. "It is the same way railroads do business." Asked definitely what connection he would make over the Allentown-Bound Brook stretch for the Baltimore & Ohio, he replied: "Now, what will they [it] give me to get into Philadelphia? I can't make a trade one way here. You are standing there asking me what I will give when the other fellow doesn't give me anything. I have got $30,000,000 in this pot." [30]

The New York Central gladly offers its competitor an "open route" on competitive traffic; and the Baltimore & Ohio is happy to reciprocate with a similar offer. Trackage rights are banned. Owning lines are confident of protecting themselves against competitive traffic moving in ordinary interchange via "open routes." They are not so certain if the competitors render practically the same kind of service over the same trackage and the same terminal facilities.

Trackage is therefore not freely granted to competitors. An owning road devotes assiduous study to each proposal calculated to permit a competitor to use its tracks. An arrangement may be economically desirable; it may avoid useless duplication of physical transportation facilities. It may intensify the use to which the existing plant is subjected; and by reducing the per unit cost of production contribute to a possible reduction in the price of transportation service. Many trackage rights are indeed granted, and not infrequently to competitive lines.

It by no means follows that every trackage use is in the public interest. Professor Ripley's suggestion to grant the Northern Pacific trackage over the Great Northern from Billings, Montana, to Great Falls, Montana, in the event of consolidation of the latter line with the Chicago, Milwaukee, St. Paul & Pacific, was not kindly received by the president of the Great Northern. The merger of these two carriers, recommended by Professor Ripley, would supply the consolidated system with duplicate lines to Great Falls. Inasmuch as the Northern Pacific has no access to that community, it was logical to suggest the granting of trackage to that road. But, the Northern Pacific would carry no through business through that region; it would only compete with the existing line for the carriage of the local traffic available. This traffic is relatively limited in the sense that the construction of a duplicate line through the mountainous terrain would not be financially profitable to the Northern Pacific. Would it not be the height of bad business judgment for the Great Northern to surrender this profitable business? It is decidedly questionable whether the public interest would be served through any compulsory measures designed to oblige the Great Northern to share the local business with some other line.

It is, moreover, questionable whether the Interstate Commerce Commission can promote the use of trackage if such use is contrary to the business needs of the carriers concerned. The Commission has had some experience in promoting the two chief phases of the public interest in the use of the trackage device: in the formation of through routes, and in elimination of duplicate transportation facilities. A community of traffic interests led three small roads in Louisiana, Mississippi and Alabama to unite the

TRAFFIC AND TRACKAGE AGREEMENTS

operation of part of their lines for the purpose of transporting additional traffic over a proposed through route. Two of these lines—the Mississippi Central and the Louisiana & Arkansas—are small lumbering roads, extending from east to west in a direction contrary to the main trend of the north and southbound traffic. With the timber traffic on both roads declining steadily, it became imperative to develop new sources of traffic. These properties with the use of the Missouri Pacific ferry across the Mississippi between Vidalia and Natchez extended from Shreveport, Louisiana, on the west—an important traffic center—to Hattiesburg, Mississippi, a relatively unimportant point on the east. Ninety-five miles away, however, was Mobile, Alabama—a large community, a growing port for import and export and an important railroad center. Of the numerous roads serving Mobile, the Gulf, Mobile & Northern seemed best adapted to serve the purpose of the two small carriers operating west of Hattiesburg. The traffic destiny of the Gulf, Mobile & Northern lay in the carriage of traffic to and from the Ohio and the upper Mississippi Valley and the southeast. It did not compete with the small properties desiring access to Mobile. Moreover, it owned a branch line extending from a junction with the main line at Beaumont, Mississippi, to a connection with the Mississippi Central at Hattiesburg. Its own main line ran directly from Beaumont to Mobile.

Here, therefore, seemed to be the basis for a through route from Shreveport, Louisiana, to Mobile, Alabama; providing, that is, arrangements could be made with the Gulf, Mobile & Northern for entry into Mobile. The latter's branch line from Beaumont had not been operating at a profit; and the owner was willing to grant a long-term lease. The Mississippi Central demurred. It was not certain that the new route would attract much business. It was not willing, therefore, to assume a heavy overhead pending the development of a satisfactory gross revenue. A lease of the branch was therefore effected, terminable at the option of either party on one year's notice. Trackage on similar terms was then arranged over the Gulf, Mobile & Northern's main line from Beaumont to Mobile. A traffic arrangement, furthermore, was entered into between the Mississippi Central and the Louisiana & Arkansas by which each became a *preferential connection* of the other. Each solicited preferentially for the other.

The new through route thus formed did not reduce any rates. The same rates were open to the public before, but no material amount of traffic had moved. The new route —known as the Natchez route (see map on page 261)— was not the short route. It was, in fact, exceedingly circuitous. The short line between Shreveport and Mobile is the two-line route composed of the Vicksburg route and the Gulf, Mobile & Northern, 424 miles. This route was not practicable for freight traffic and was not used. Another route over the Vicksburg route and the Mobile & Ohio aggregated 448 miles. The distance via the new route equalled 547 miles. The undue circuity of the Natchez route was not balanced by any physical advantages.

Nevertheless the opening of the route was accompanied by a remarkable increase in traffic. A few figures may perhaps be in place. The through route was opened in 1921. Prior to that time the ton miles of revenue-freight of the Mississippi Central had never exceeded 25.8 millions. In 1921, 1922, and 1923 it increased respectively to 30, 54.7, and 87.2 millions. The Mississippi Central in

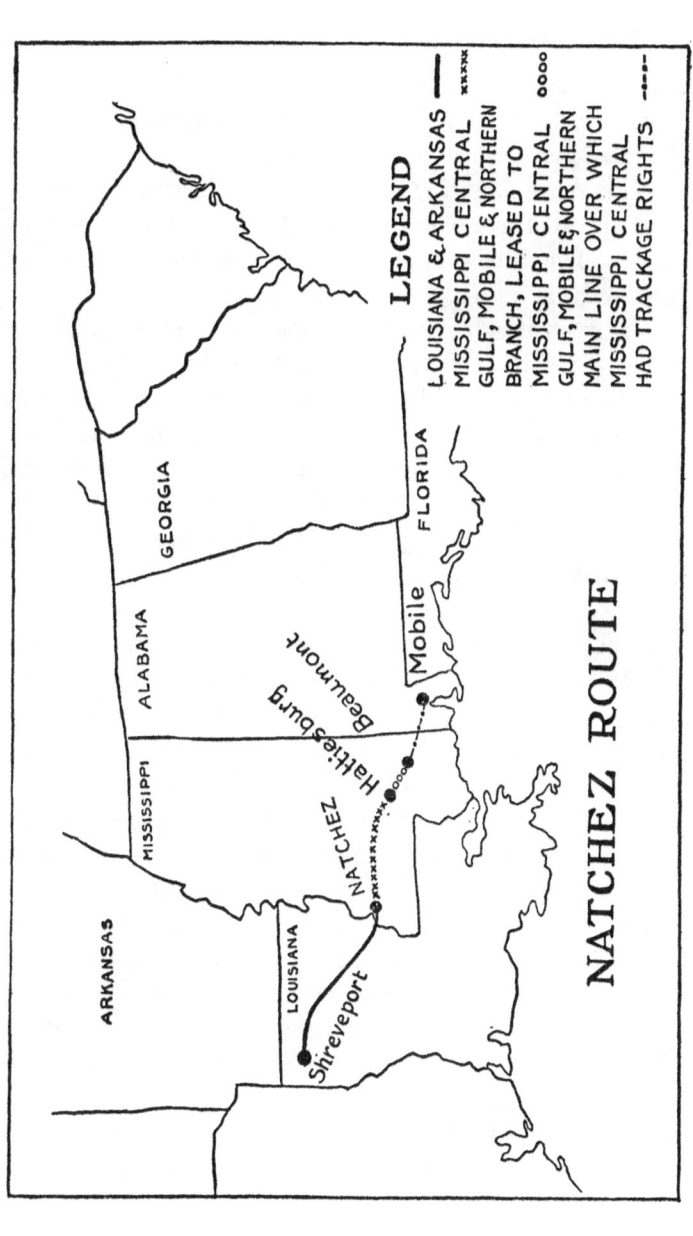

1923 handled 987,824 tons of revenue freight as compared with 605,073 tons, the maximum annual tonnage handled before the opening of the route.

This route composed of three lines independently owned and operated had carved out a channel of trade and commerce. The Interstate Commerce Commission had stated distinctly in two separate decisions that the preservation of the route was demanded by the public interest. Nevertheless, despite all the Commission could do to preserve it, the route was broken up within three years after its inception. From its own business standpoint the Gulf, Mobile & Northern found it advisable to sell its branch line to Hattiesburg. Its acquisition and operation by the purchaser required approval by the Commission. The Commission declined to extend its approval to the transaction except under condition of the maintenance of the Natchez route through the continuance of trackage agreements by the purchaser over the branch line and by the Gulf, Mobile & Northern over its main line. The Mississippi Central would thus be enabled to continue the operation of its trains directly into Mobile.

The interested parties could not agree upon mutually satisfactory terms for trackage rights. The case was again brought before the Commission; and after further hearing the Commission affirmed its previous decision. "It is conceded by all parties," stated the Commission, "that the continuance of the Natchez route will be in the public interest." It therefore for a second time conditioned its approval of the proposed sale of the branch line upon the granting to the Mississippi Central of trackage rights from Hattiesburg to Mobile. And "the through Natchez route [must] be maintained," reiterated the Commission.

TRAFFIC AND TRACKAGE AGREEMENTS 263

But the route was not maintained. It was completely destroyed. The original lease and trackage arrangements by which the Mississippi Central reached Mobile, and which contributed in part to the success of the Natchez route were cancelled to take effect on August 15, 1924. The purchaser of the branch line commenced operations on January 17, 1925. The roads had reached no agreement with respect to trackage; they had not arranged for dual operations; and the main line soon became blocked with trains headed in opposite directions. Two days later the Mississippi Central ceased operating any trains east of its terminus at Hattiesburg. The Natchez route was no more.[31]

Both the Mississippi Central and the Louisiana & Arkansas are weak, short lines. Their preservation as useful units in the public service is one of the chief aims of a national consolidation program. The Natchez route contained considerable possibilities of increasing the earning power of these two properties. The painful inability of the Commission to maintain the through route (based on trackage) points to the necessity of great caution in reaching conclusions of the extent to which trackage agreements can be used to carry out purposes that seem theoretically desirable in the public interest.

It is nevertheless abundantly clear that consolidation of the country's carriers into a limited number of systems will be accompanied by extensive resort to trackage. The consolidation plan of the Chesapeake & Ohio recently submitted to the Commission provides for a surprisingly large number of specific trackage arrangements. The spectacular struggle for the control of the Wheeling & Lake Erie seems destined to be decided via the trackage contract.

After a stock-market battle, reminiscent of the Hill-Harriman era, share control of that road found a resting place in the joint treasury of the Baltimore & Ohio, New York Central, and the New York, Chicago & St. Louis. Efforts of those carriers to secure directorates on the acquired carrier were blocked by Commission disapproval. Subsequently the Commission initiated proceedings under the Clayton Act to compel relinquishment of this control. The facts revealed that substantial competition existed between the acquired property and two of the acquiring carriers. The competition with the other owner—the New York, Chicago & St. Louis—was not as extensive.

The Chesapeake & Ohio, controlled by the same interests as is the New York, Chicago & St. Louis, now brings forth a plan providing for sole and exclusive ownership of the Wheeling & Lake Erie by a system of which the New York, Chicago & St. Louis is a part. The New York Central and the Baltimore & Ohio are to form part of other consolidated systems. Their share ownership in the Wheeling & Lake Erie is to be exchanged for trackage. Many additional trackage arrangements are suggested in both of the proposed consolidated systems in trunk line territory recently proposed.

Traffic and trackage agreements represent important property rights, and useful vehicles of performing transportation service. Consolidation of the carriers into a small number of systems will not obviate their continued use. Preferential solicitation will still lead to preferential interchange; and trackage rights will still be economically justified. Whether specific legislation and Commission supervision can regulate their use, or indeed, whether such regulation and supervision is necessary or desirable, is not

TRAFFIC AND TRACKAGE AGREEMENTS

so certain. The experience of the Interstate Commerce Commission since 1920 is demonstration of the futility of impeding the normal evolution of those forces which lead to voluntary traffic and operating coöperation of carriers based on a reciprocality of business needs.

NOTES TO CHAPTER IX

1. Unification of Southwestern Lines, Finance Docket 5679, exhibit no. 46.
2. Consolidation Proceedings, Docket 12964, Brief for Union Pacific, p. 27.
3. Acquisition of Ann Arbor, Finance Docket 4942, tr. p. 40.
4. Consolidation Proceedings, Docket 12964, Vol. XIX, p. 2889.
5. Construction by Virginian & Western Ry., Finance Docket 6067, tr. pp. 658-659.
6. Nickel Plate Unification, Finance Docket 4643, 4671, Brief for Applicant, Vol. II, p. 53.
7. Unification of Southwestern Lines, Finance Docket 5679, Brief for Applicant, Vol. II, pp. 42-43.
8. *Supra*, p. 42.
9. Consolidation Proceedings, Docket 12964, Brief for Great Northern in support of consolidation of Chicago, Burlington & Quincy, Great Northern, Northern Pacific and subsidiaries, p. 114.
10. *Supra*, Statement of Robert S. Lovett, April 2, 1923, p. 8.
11. Unification of Southwestern Lines, Finance Docket 5679, Brief for Applicant, Vol. II, p. 327.
12. *Supra*, Intervention of Kansas, Oklahoma & Gulf, pp. 4-5.
13. Consolidation Proceedings, Docket 12964, Vol. XI, pp. 1497-1502.
14. Great Northern-Northern Pacific merger, Finance Docket 6409, 6410, Brief for Applicants, Vol. II, p. 222; Brief for Minneapolis & St. Louis, pp. 10-11.
15. Lease of Lehigh & New England Railroad, Finance Docket 5639, Brief for Reading Co., p. 33.
16. Control of Buffalo, Rochester & Pittsburgh Railway, Finance Docket 5656, 6147, Brief for Baltimore & Ohio, p. 158.
17. Consolidation Proceedings, Docket 12964, Tabulated Statements, New York Central Lines, p. 4.
18. Proposed construction by New York, Pittsburgh & Chicago, Finance Docket 4741, Brief for Applicant, p. 42.
19. Consolidation Proceedings, Docket 12964, Brief for Great Northern in support of consolidation of Chicago, Burlington & Quincy, Great Northern, Northern Pacific and subsidiaries, p. 143.
20. Consolidation of Railroads, 63 I.C.C. 564.
21. Nickel Plate Unification Case, Finance Docket 4643, 4671, Brief for Applicant, Vol. II, pp. 10-11.
22. Consolidation Proceedings, Docket 12964, Statement of A. H. Smith, May 16, 1923, pp. 40-41.

266 RAILROAD CONSOLIDATION

23. Consolidation of Railroads, 63 I.C.C. 492.
24. Consolidation Proceedings, Docket 12964, Statement of Daniel Willard, May 19, 1923, p. 44.
25. *Supra*, p. 45.
26. *Supra*.
27. *Supra*, Brief for Reading Company, p. 15.
28. *Supra*, Brief for Port of New York Authority, p. 645.
29. Control of Buffalo, Rochester & Pittsburgh Ry., Finance Docket 5656, 6147, Brief for Baltimore & Ohio, p. 66.
30. Consolidation Proceedings, Docket 12964, Brief for Port of New York Authority, p. 381.
31. See Acquisition of Line by B. & H. S. R. R. Co.; 90 I.C.C. 448; 94 I.C.C. 358; also Cancellation of Rates and Routes via Mississippi Central, 100 I.C.C. 71.

CHAPTER X

CONSOLIDATION IN ACTION

The chief merits of consolidation of railroads into a limited number of corporate entities revolve around three considerations: the elimination of the so-called weak line problem, the introduction of operating economies, and the erection of systems of approximately equal competitive strength. The latter in turn will promote a more even-handed competition than can possibly prevail between properties of varying financial strength and credit standing, and will facilitate and simplify the problems of governmental regulation.

The vital necessity of the retention of the weak lines as a unit in the national transportation net has elicited a limitless volume of discussion. The late Senator Cummins presented consolidation as the only alternative to government ownership; as the necessary measure to save the weak lines, and to prevent their abandonment. It is only natural, of course, that the vice president and general counsel of the American Short Line Railroad Association should characterize the "whole plan and purpose of the transportation act as a ghastly failure . . . if the 22,000 miles of short-line railroads, fully as much as the 30,000 miles of permanently weak lines, such as the Minneapolis & St. Louis, the Kansas City, Mexico & Orient, the Missouri & North Arkansas, and others are not to be preserved, fostered and made more efficient through consolidation." [1]

Senator Cummins was forcibly impressed by the considerable number of the Class I railroads of subnormal earning power. In one of his last appearances before the Senate Interstate Commerce Committee he presented a list of such properties with average net railway operating income of less than 3 per cent on investment in road and equipment (book value) during the years 1922, 1923 and 1924.[2] These carriers—many of considerable size and decidedly poor earning power—the possible abandonment of which had presented serious problems to the communities directly affected, have in part been absorbed by stronger carriers through the process of voluntary unification.

These include such weak lines as the Ann Arbor, the Atlanta, Birmingham & Atlantic, the Cincinnati, Indianapolis & Western, the Kansas City, Mexico & Orient, the San Antonio & Aransas Pass, the San Antonio, Uvalde & Gulf. Other roads included in the list now enjoy a satisfactory credit standing: the Buffalo, Rochester & Pittsburgh, the Boston & Maine, the Colorado & Southern, the Erie, the Lehigh Valley, the Missouri Pacific, the Pittsburgh & West Virginia, the Western Maryland, the Western Pacific, and the Wheeling & Lake Erie. Many of these are on a dividend basis, and the others are exhibiting reasonably satisfactory earnings on their outstanding stock issues.

So important are some from the business standpoint that their competitive acquisition by rival lines has furnished the basis of many vigorous and dramatic contests before the Interstate Commerce Commission. The lease of the Buffalo, Rochester & Pittsburgh to the Delaware & Hudson met with Commission rejection; it was then bought up by the Van Sweringen Brothers, sold by them

CONSOLIDATION IN ACTION 269

to the Allegheny Corporation, and then resold to the New York Central and the Baltimore & Ohio. The three major eastern trunk lines and the Pittsburgh & West Virginia have since January, 1927, engaged in a continuous contest for the control of the Wheeling & Lake Erie. One of them—the Baltimore & Ohio—and the Pittsburgh & West Virginia are disputing the control of the Western Maryland. The control of another line, the Lehigh Valley, is securely held by the Pennsylvania. The latter (acquiring line), which competes in interstate commerce with the acquired line, not only has declined to secure official Commission sanction of the transaction; it has taken positive measures to place it beyond the pale of regulatory jurisdiction.

Numerous other carriers embraced in the list prepared by Senator Cummins are integral and essential portions of important systems: the Chicago & Erie, the Fort Worth & Rio Grande, the Houston East & West Texas, the Los Angeles & Salt Lake, the Morgan's Louisiana & Texas Railroad & Steamship Co., the Oregon-Washington Railroad & Navigation Co., the St. Louis, San Francisco & Texas, the St. Louis Southwestern of Texas, the Spokane, Portland & Seattle, the Texas & New Orleans.

Another line—the Northwestern Pacific—is sufficiently important to have justified the Southern Pacific in making a substantial investment in purchasing a 50 per cent stock interest from the Atchison, Topeka & Santa Fe.[3] The Southern Pacific now owns 100 per cent of that carrier, and operates it as a part of its system.

Of the remaining Class I properties listed, only a very few present any serious problems. The Chicago, Peoria & St. Louis, the abandonment of which was authorized by the Commission, was not abandoned. Its tracks were bought by various corporate entities; and common carrier service has been preserved for the community.[4]

Included in Senator Cummins' list are several subsidiaries of the Canadian Pacific. It is improbable that that carrier would abandon any of its share-controlled lines in this country. In the absence of accurate data on divisions between the parent and subsidiary lines, no conclusion can be reached on the real earning power of the latter. The payment by the Canadian Pacific of interest and principal on the bonds of the Central Vermont in receivership may not, perhaps, constitute the basis of a stable policy to be applied to all of its American-owned subsidiaries. It does indicate, nevertheless, that the Canadian Pacific is not ready to abandon its properties to the mercy of their bondholders.

Of the properties in receiver's hands, the Minneapolis & St. Louis and the Missouri & North Arkansas present major problems. Even including a few other cancers in the railroad net—such as the Ulster & Delaware, the Columbus & Greenville, the Pittsburgh & Shawmut—the 56,464.13 miles of Class I roads listed by Senator Cummins drop down to a relatively minor factor.

The Class I carriers have not, however, borne the brunt of discussion over the fate of the weak lines. In no unification case presented before the Commission have any of them appeared to support the necessity of their existence. None (except, perhaps, the Minneapolis & St. Louis in the pending unification of the Hill lines; and the Missouri & North Arkansas in the Southwestern Unification case) have asked the regulatory body to oblige any other carrier to acquire them. They appear well satisfied with

CONSOLIDATION IN ACTION 271

their present status and future prospects. It is the smaller roads—the Class II and Class III lines—that have served to focus public attention upon the weak line problem. The representatives of the American Short Line Association, of which a majority of these lines are members, have appeared before legislative committees and regulatory bodies to discuss the problem. And it was largely due to its representations that the Interstate Commerce Commission handed down its famous weak line dictum in the first Nickel Plate Unification case.

The normal and stable development of the country's resources and the accompanying improvement and extension of its railroad net have resulted in the absorption of many of the short lines into the systems of the larger carriers. The Southwestern-Gulf region, which was featured in 1921, according to Professor Ripley's report, by an excess of roads which could "be supported by the available traffic," and by the presence of "more railways in fact than the country can [could] probably support for many years ahead," [5] has been characterized by the acquisition of large numbers of weak lines by the leading systems. Particularly in the state of Texas a substantial part of the mileage of the weak lines has been taken over as part of the expansion programs of such lines as the Southern Pacific, the members of the Missouri Pacific family, the Atchison, Topeka & Santa Fe, and the St. Louis & San Francisco.

Of particular significance in the determination of the public interest is the circumstance that many of these short lines are well satisfied with their status. They represent successful units of transportation service; they earn a reasonable return on their investment, and do not care to merge their corporate interests with the larger trunk lines. Their extent and importance may be, perhaps, gleaned from the situation in the New York Central Unification Case. This case was featured by elaborate consideration of the connecting short lines. An examiner of the Commission recommended denial of the proposal of the New York Central to lease its system lines unless adequate disposition be made of the weak and short lines. Despite this official invitation for short-line intervention only 9 out of 71 connecting lines requested the Commission to include their properties in the New York Central system.[6] Many of the short lines are exceptionally prosperous, some of them coming within the purview of the recapture clause.

These factors lead to the question whether the problem is one of major national importance. That some lines ought to be, and will be, abandoned, and that many have been abandoned is no doubt conceded by all. How many of the remaining lines, the preservation of which is necessary to the welfare of many persons resident on their lines, can be kept in operation without their consolidation with trunk-line connections, cannot be definitely ascertained. There is ample reason for the opinion that their mileage is not sufficiently large to make their disposition a critical problem requiring the use of heroic measures, such as a nation-wide program of consolidation.[7]

The promotion of economies is the second important purpose to be achieved through a well-conceived program of consolidation. This subject has already been touched upon in other connections. The costs of doing business—and economies of course are reflected in lower costs—are difficult to measure. They represent a complex of many factors: movements of commodity prices, changing standards of living requiring adjustments of wages, increasing or decreasing volume of business, and sheer elimination of waste. A consolidation of a strong with a weak line may increase the wage bill of the latter line and so lead to increased rather than decreased expenses. On the other hand, the elimination of duplicate reports, shop facilities, etc., may be productive of economies. If, however, as is often the case, the property of the acquired line must be reconstructed to enable it to carry heavy traffic, or to render the higher standard of service demanded from trunk lines that is not demanded from local lines, the additional operating or capital costs may go far to offset other savings.

Added service may in itself be considered a virtue of consolidation. The rendition of additional service of the same standard or even of a higher standard may not necessarily stamp a particular unification of properties with the impress of the public interest. The acquisition of the Cincinnati, Indianapolis & Western—a typical weak line, poorly maintained—by the Baltimore & Ohio was followed by requests for the establishment of through service from Springfield, Illinois, to Washington. To give that service the Baltimore & Ohio spent $600,000 in maintenance in one year; and for that year it did not earn interest on its investment. That road, however, happens to lie in the direction of an important trend of freight traffic. And the Baltimore & Ohio expects to establish a competitive line that will carry a sufficient business to give it a return on its investment.[8]

That acquisition may therefore prove to be in the public interest. The added business to be moved over the acquired line will also make the transaction in the private interest of the acquiring line. Suppose, however, that the acquired line is not so located as to admit of its carriage of a heavier volume of traffic. Most of the short and weak lines are strictly local carriers; their tonnage cannot be increased. That is why, generally, the trunk lines do not want to buy them. There is nevertheless no reasonable doubt that their acquisitions will be followed by demands for better service, at least for the same brand of service afforded by trunk lines on their other branches. The establishment of this service could be obtained only at increased expense. How establish the real standard of the public interest in this conflict between better service and lower expenses?

Indeed the entire concept that lower expenses will follow in the wake of railroad consolidation is gradually being abandoned. Alfred P. Thom, General Counsel of the Association of Railway Executives, whose intimate contact with experienced railroad men may be assumed, appearing before one of the Congressional Committees considering amendatory consolidation legislation, referred to "the opinion generally of railroad men . . . that it [consolidation] cannot affect that branch of it [referring to wages] very much." [9] Daniel Willard, the President of the Baltimore & Ohio, whose unusual clarity of thought has shed so much light on the subject, told the Senate Interstate Commerce Committee that he had "never been able to see how there could be so very much economy in the terminal situation in large centers because all the cars get there." [10] He laid particular stress upon the difficulty of "making any direct definite estimates of savings to be had by consolidation of considerable sized systems when the lines

CONSOLIDATION IN ACTION 275

are now independent." [11] The officials of neither road have knowledge of the operating practices of the other.

The validity of Mr. Willard's views is reënforced by the difficulty experienced by the New York Central in computing the savings actually realized by a major consolidation—perhaps the largest unification in actual fee ownership effected during the past two decades. The consolidation of the old Lake Shore & Michigan Southern with the New York Central & Hudson River into the present New York Central was effected in 1914. In advance of that consolidation the officials prepared careful estimates of possible savings. In 1926 the vice president of the New York Central inquired of the comptroller of the extent to which the forecasted savings had been realized. "As might have been expected," the vice president informed a Congressional Committee, "he could not tell; that undoubtedly savings had been realized, but changes came so rapidly in prices of labor, the volume of business and the expenses and what not, that it was not possible to go back and verify a particular prophecy as to a certain amount of savings." [12]

There are, of course, numerous economies which consolidation may bring about. But they are minor; and railway representatives have been careful to explain that they will not be substantial enough to warrant any reduction in rates. The trend of thought has therefore been gradually veering towards the idea of improved service, rather than lower expenses, as the probable result of consolidation.

It is a wide-open question, moreover, whether many of the improvements in service cannot be realized without consolidation. It is a matter of common knowledge that the past few years have witnessed a great increase in operating efficiency, and a corresponding increase in the standard of railroad service. This improved service has been widespread; it has been nation-wide. It has characterized unified, as well as independent, properties. The united Missouri Pacific system in the Southwest has increased its standard of shipping service; but so has the competitive route of the Southern Pacific–St. Louis Southwestern. In the east a combination of five independent lines has been able to match and even to better the service accorded by the consolidated systems on freight movements from Pittsburgh to St. Louis. And farther east no criticism has been made of the service given on the carriage of bituminous coal from West Virginia to New England over a seven-line route. The preservation of this interior patched-up route is indeed necessary in the public interest; since, despite its circuity, it goes around congested New York Harbor, rather than through it.

The continuous pressure of competitive transportation agencies—the gas engine, the airplane, the steamboat—is driving the steam carriers into an ever increasing degree of coöperation. The coördination of the nation's car supply through the coöperative efforts between the Car Service Division of the American Railway Association and the Interstate Commerce Commission; the gradual replacement of the previous methods of interchange by direct yard to yard transfers; the reciprocal use of switching, engine, yard facilities, etc., indicate the necessity of a careful examination into the comparative service improvements capable of being rendered by coöperation between independent lines on one hand, and by corporate consolidation on the other.

The third major purpose of a national program of consolidation is the substitution of competition between a host of roads of varying physical traffic and financial strength by a more nearly equal and forceful competition between a limited number of systems which in the language of the statute "shall be so arranged that the cost of transportation as between competitive systems and as related to the values of the properties through which the service is rendered shall be the same, so far as practicable, so that these systems can employ uniform rates in the movement of competitive traffic and under efficient management earn substantially the same rate of return upon the value of their respective railway properties."

The genesis of this idea lies in the troubles encountered by the Interstate Commerce Commission in its rate-regulating activities. Under present competitive conditions a rate schedule approved by the Commission produces varying financial results upon different railway properties. A rate capable of yielding a fair return for a financially strong carrier is incapable of yielding such a return for a financially weak one. And a rate high enough to sustain the latter yields to the former more than a fair return. Under the régime of a limited number of consolidated railway properties, each property will enjoy uniform production costs, and under efficient management will be able to earn similar rates of return under any particular rate structure.

If consolidation can thus accomplish in the railway business what has never been accomplished in any other business, it will have amply realized a full measure of success. The Commission, in order to set up consolidated properties of approximately uniform financial strength, must furnish each one with many business necessities. The vital need of many of these factors together with their corresponding effect on earning power can be judged with some degree of reliability. The accessibility to fuel supply, the use of adequate terminal facilities, the control of important sources of traffic, the enjoyment of a broad base of traffic diversity, are elements the extent of whose contribution to financial strength can be predicated upon the basis of known definite and tangible factors. Add to the system's earning power the profits due to realized economies and deduct the losses which may be incurred through the acquisition of financially weak lines; and a new earning power, deduced from the earnings of the component lines as a base, is established.

This analysis in most cases is likely to lead to inaccurate conclusions. It assumes that the gross revenue of the consolidated system will equal the combined gross of the constituent properties. It ignores the principles of traffic diversion, and of the formation of railway routes. Any consolidation is certain to upset the flow of traffic which has produced the gross earnings of the properties consolidated. The exact scope of the diversion cannot be accurately estimated; it depends upon a considerable number of complicated factors. Some are purely personal in character; and others, discussed in preceding chapters, are based directly on the broad foundation of mutual business interest. The possible manifestations of the latter vary greatly in number and in form; and they may represent the result of transient expediency or of permanent self-interest. Neither can a governmental agency in most cases appraise the extent to which these forces may reflect themselves in increased or decreased gross earnings to a particular system.

CONSOLIDATION IN ACTION 279

It is possible, nevertheless, within limited bounds to classify the forms which these traffic diversions assume; and reach some conclusion with respect to their bearing on the public interest involved in the problem of railroad consolidation. The simplest and most common case is the diversion of traffic originated by the acquired road from a particular connecting line to the acquiring line. The mechanism operates with particular directness in the acquisition of the strictly local short line. It is there complicated by no counter considerations of business policy. Usually no situations compelling short-hauling by the acquiring carrier exist; nor, as a rule, do any problems of trading in traffic with other connections arise. The argument of the weak lines in the two large eastern trunk line unification proposals for absorption of their properties in the connecting major systems is, for example, supported in part by the demonstration of the ease and certainty with which the suggested acquiring line would obtain the traffic of suggested lines to be acquired—traffic that now moves over other lines.[13]

In another case the Seaboard Air Line was anxious to buy control of a line under conditions which in the language of an Interstate Commerce Commission examiner would have resulted in "no substantial saving in general or traffic expenses."[14] However, "it is [was] obvious that the Seaboard Management in control of the South Georgia could and would [have] route[d] the traffic now originating on that line and delivered to the Georgia Southern & Florida and the Georgia & Florida via its own rails."[15]

The business justification of the acquisition of local feeders through the resultant diversion of traffic is well exemplified by the expansion program of the St. Louis & San Francisco in the St. Francis Valley in southeastern Missouri and northeastern Arkansas. Between 1900 and 1904 that system acquired about 350 miles of tap lines. These lines fed into the St. Louis Southwestern at numerous connections; and it handled the equipment and furnished most of the business. By 1904 the short lines had been acquired by the St. Louis & San Francisco. The latter cancelled the rates, and closed the routes; and the effect of this policy, according to the traffic manager of the St. Louis Southwestern, "was a very severe loss in the total traffic of the Cotton Belt (St. Louis Southwestern) and that traffic went to the Frisco." [16] (St. Louis & San Francisco).

The operation of the principles of traffic diversion under a system of national control of these acquisitions, as exemplified by the purchase by the same acquiring line of further feeders in the same general region, was not substantially different from the condition that prevailed a quarter of a century earlier in an era of free and unrestricted business negotiation and contract. In 1925 the St. Louis & San Francisco with the consent of the Interstate Commerce Commission acquired control of the Jonesboro Lake City & Eastern—a line situated in the southern part of the St. Francis Valley. The acquiring line again cancelled rates and closed routes, and eliminated the interchange of the acquired line with the St. Louis & Southwestern. Upon the basis of 1924 data that procedure cost the latter road 40,701 tons of interchange and $100,923 in revenue per annum.

In 1927 the same acquiring line purchased control of two more lines in the same general territories: the Butler

CONSOLIDATION IN ACTION 281

County and the St. Louis, Kennett & Southeastern. The St. Louis Southwestern furnished an unusually high-grade service with the latter line on business to and from St. Louis. But the St. Louis & San Francisco could also provide a service to that point. So after its acquisition of the short lines it cancelled rates and closed routes with the St. Louis Southwestern, "thus diverting that business from the Cotton Belt to the Frisco." In 1925 the acquired lines delivered to the St. Louis Southwestern 37,791 tons upon which the latter received a revenue of $106,282.[17]

If the acquired line is more than a local feeder, if it is a road with well-developed interchange relationships with its neighbors, the acquiring line usually refrains from closing routes and cancelling rates. Danger may lurk in such a policy. The acquired line may receive certain traffic from those connections which compete with the acquiring line. That interchange traffic may be valuable, and the acquiring line may not want to endanger that business by a course, which although probably within its legal rights, may invite reprisals from a competitor.

It remains true nevertheless, that the controlled traffic, the traffic initiated by the acquired road—even though that road be one of considerable magnitude—is eventually diverted to the acquiring line. The very first major unification approved by the Interstate Commerce Commission clearly illustrated the usual kind of diversion. Late in 1924 the Commission approved the acquisition through majority share control of the Gulf Coast Lines by the Missouri Pacific. The acquired line loaded in its own territory considerable tonnages of fruit and vegetables destined to territory beyond St. Louis and Memphis. This was long-haul business, and therefore profitable. For a number of years this traffic moved via Houston, thence over the International Great Northern, Texas & Pacific, and Missouri Pacific and its connections to destination.

In 1921 the business interests of the Gulf Coast Lines and the Missouri Pacific clashed. The latter reduced the divisions accorded the former, and it also did not give the Gulf Coast Lines satisfactory equipment service. The latter complained "that the American Refrigerator Transit Co. (a subsidiary of the Missouri Pacific) exacted excessive charges for equipment, and that relations with this company were otherwise unsatisfactory." [18]

From Houston, the Gulf Coast Lines operated a line 278 miles eastward to Baton Rouge, Louisiana. There it connected with the Illinois Central. (See map on page 283.) In 1921 these two lines entered into a preferential agreement; and to move satisfactorily the traffic to be received from the Gulf Coast Lines, the Illinois Central purchased 1,000 refrigerator cars.

In December, 1924, the Interstate Commerce Commission approved the acquisition of control by the Missouri Pacific of the Gulf Coast Lines. In the spring of 1925 Charles H. Markham, the then president of the Illinois Central, testified that his road had already lost the great bulk of that business, "amounting to several thousand cars a year." [19] Within six months after Commission action, the business that three years before had moved over the Missouri Pacific, and had then been diverted over the Illinois Central, had three years later been rediverted over the Missouri Pacific.

The real public interest in these diversions is difficult to measure. The service rendered to shippers in originating territory was probably as good over the Illinois Central

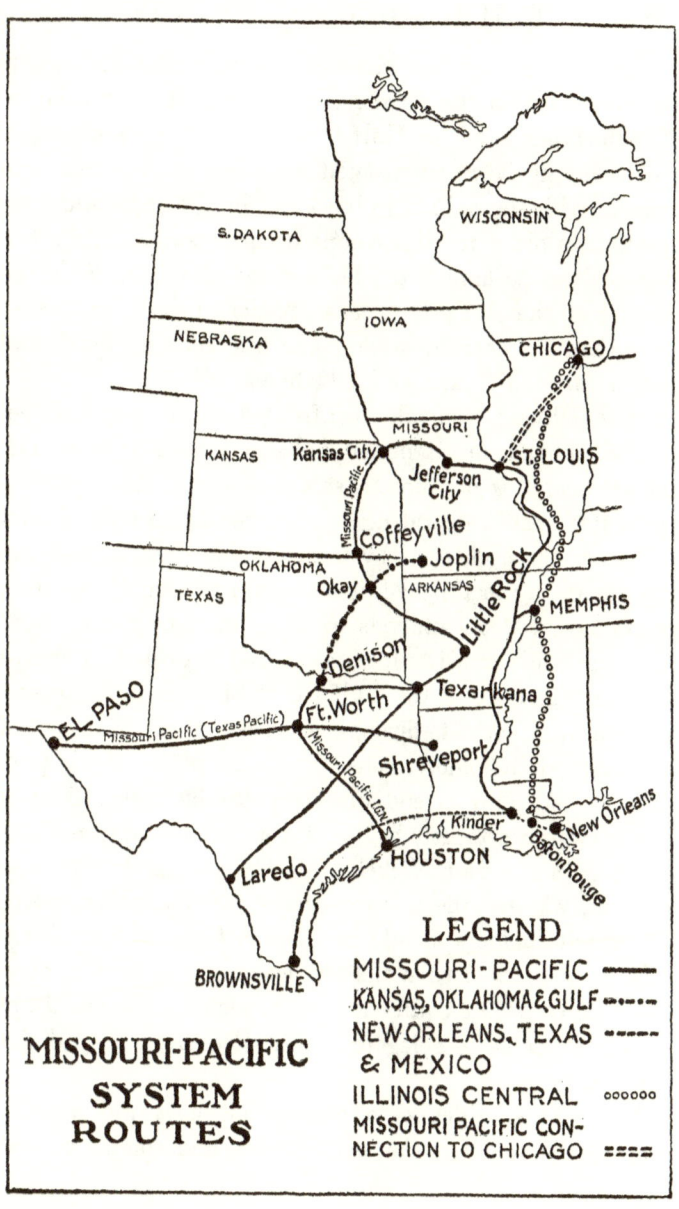

as it now is over the Missouri Pacific. The distance to destinations via the former is greater than via the latter. On the other hand the Gulf Coast Lines, "by reason of its lines having been constructed with low grades and light curves with the primary object in view of economical operation in order to meet competition by water, is in a better position to handle the bulk of the all-rail traffic originating on the carrier's (a small feeder in southern Texas) line than the carriers with grade line running north and south through Texas and Oklahoma." [20]

The Illinois Central, "confronted by no physical obstacles of grade or alignment," [21] surely can transport traffic as cheaply if not more cheaply, than the lines with considerable grades operating west of the Mississippi River. Whether the high costs by the west-side lines is made up by the saving in mileage, is an open problem. Its solution must be based on analysis by those operating and traffic experts familiar with local railroad conditions. Perhaps the short-hauling of the Gulf Coast Lines in order to suit system needs might, through its effect on the fortunes of minority shareholders, constitute some phase of the public interest. This is a distinctly debatable issue. Despite the views entertained by the Interstate Commerce Commission in the first Nickel Plate Case, it is clearly questionable whether the private interests of conflicting groups of security-holders should be aired before an administrative body charged with the promotion of the public interest. The courts of equity are still open; and it would appear reasonable to relegate such controversies to judicial forums.

What is significant to observe is the rapidity with which an important channel of trade and commerce was formed between two properties that had recently been at loggerheads. The Gulf Coast Lines (the acquired carrier) and the Missouri Pacific (the acquiring carrier) had disagreed over divisions and over car service. Within a few months after a majority share interest was acquired, the combined system properties succeeded in diverting a substantial tonnage over system lines. Thus, the chief business purpose of consolidation was realized: to get more traffic.

This almost immediate shifting of business, and the resultant formation of railway routes or channels of trade and commerce as they are sometimes designated, is characteristic of changes in corporate control or community of interest. Not in all cases are data available to study the changes in detail. Information frequently becomes public property not through governmental action; nor through voluntary publication by the acquiring or the acquired carriers. Third parties, connecting with either of the latter, who appear in unification cases before the Commission, may present the published material. The competitive situation in the Sacramento Valley in California, to which the Western Pacific with its recent expansion program has contributed an additional flavor of vim and vigor, is an excellent illustration in point. A local feeder, the Sacramento Northern, which under independent operation interchanged considerable long-haul transcontinental business with the Southern Pacific and the Western Pacific, was acquired in 1921 through majority share ownership by the Western Pacific. To what extent this transaction was a success to the acquiring carrier, that is, to what extent it had succeeded in diverting the feeder's traffic to its long haul that had formely moved over the lines of another transcontinental carrier, was not known for some years.

And it might, perhaps, not even be publicly known at present had not the Southern Pacific essayed in 1925 to purchase control of another feeder immediately to the south of the Sacramento Northern. The lines of the Central California Traction Company and the Southern Pacific parallel each other from Sacramento to Stockton; and at the latter point the Atchison, Topeka & Santa Fe makes direct connection with the feeder the Southern Pacific proposed to acquire, i.e., the Central California Traction. The latter originated a considerable transcontinental deciduous fruit traffic aggregating, from 1920 to 1924 inclusive, almost 17,000 cars. Of this tonnage the Southern Pacific handled only a little over 20 per cent, and the Santa Fe about 43 per cent.[22]

The proposal of the Southern Pacific to acquire control of this little property was opposed by the Santa Fe. Apparently there were no economies involved. The Southern Pacific's view that its acquisition of the local line would relieve it of the necessity of double-tracking its own line was met by an analysis of an engineer of the Santa Fe which showed an annual saving to the Southern Pacific of $132,000 by double-tracking as against the purchase of the feeder.[23] The Santa Fe declared that the diversion of the transcontinental haul from its lines to the lines of the Southern Pacific was the prime objective of the proposed acquisition. It feared that traffic now moving over its lines to a destination would after acquisition move over those of the Southern Pacific.

To indicate that this eventuality was not a mere academic possibility, the Santa Fe pointed to the results that

CONSOLIDATION IN ACTION 287

actually flowed from the Western Pacific's acquisition of the Sacramento Northern four years previously. It checked up on its own traffic records; and found that, whereas in 1920 (the last year in which the short line was independently operated) it received 204 cars of transcontinental business from the Sacramento Northern, in 1921 it received only 41 cars; in 1923, 25 cars; and in 1924, 29 cars. Some part of this drastic decrease was due to increasingly severe Panama Canal competition. Nevertheless, the celerity with which traffic delivered to the Santa Fe dropped after acquisition may be accepted as a probable indicator of a corresponding increase of traffic delivered to the acquiring line—the Western Pacific.[24]

In a similar manner in Texas did some of the results of the operation of the principles of traffic diversion develop. In the southeastern section of that state the San Antonio & Aransas Pass originated a considerable tonnage which it transferred to its various connections. At Waco it connects with the Missouri-Kansas-Texas, a keen competitor of the Southern Pacific.

In 1924 the latter acquired the San Antonio & Aransas Pass; and one would expect a diversion of interchange away from the Missouri-Kansas-Texas to the acquiring carrier. And one is not disappointed.

No data, however, were available until two years later the Missouri-Kansas-Texas laid its program for the acquisition of the St. Louis Southwestern before the Interstate Commerce Commission. It endeavored to justify the necessity of its acquisition plans in part in order to counteract the effects of the steps taken by its neighbors to execute their unification programs. Among various instances mentioned was the absorption into the Southern

Pacific system of the lines of the San Antonio & Aransas Pass. Comparing the first six months of 1924, 1925 and 1926, its receipts of vegetables and fruits from the latter carrier, declared the Missouri-Kansas-Texas, amounted respectively to 675, 268 and 129 cars. A similar comparison for livestock for the same period revealed receipts of 1370, 460, and no cars.[25]

Traffic diversion, as an incident to railroad unification, thus assumes its most characteristic form in changing the flow of traffic originating on an acquired line. The latter, in control of routing, shifts business from present routes to new routes formed by and with the acquiring line. It frequently happens, however, that lines are purchased which originate a small tonnage. They contribute, apparently, but little business to system lines. Their acquisition, even if their earning power be low, may be justified, however, by another form of traffic diversion. An important terminal line may have two or more gateways through which it receives traffic destined to its territory. One gateway may be relatively congested. Via the other gateway the terminal line can carry a large tonnage at low cost and with as high a brand of service as that afforded over its relatively busy gateway.

Leading from the noncongested point is a short line which connects with many of the trunk lines carrying goods destined to the terminal line. The trunk lines do not interchange with this short line; they prefer to haul their shipments a few miles farther to a direct connection with the terminal line. In this way they receive a longer haul and a larger division of the rate. The terminal line then buys the short line. It then makes direct connection with the trunk lines via both gateways. It cancels through

CONSOLIDATION IN ACTION

rates with some of the trunk lines via the busy gateway and the latter are therefore obliged, against their own best business interests, to route their traffic accordingly. This policy increases the traffic and, hence, the revenue of the acquired line.

A diversion of this character was successfully carried out by the New York, New Haven & Hartford in connection with its acquisition in 1904 of share control of the Central New England. This line originates little tonnage —less than 3 per cent of its total in 1924. It connects the main line of the acquiring carrier with numerous trunk lines. The interior route thus formed by the Central New England acting as an intermediate link between the trunk lines on the west and the acquiring line on the east as an ordinary "open route" would have carried little business. The acquiring line, however, closed its route via New York Harbor to numerous carriers connecting with its acquired line: the Erie, the Delaware, Lackawanna & Western, the Central Railroad of New Jersey (which make connection through the Lehigh & Hudson or the Lehigh & New England).

The effect of this move upon the acquired line is well stated by the Public Service Commission of Massachusetts:

"In the hands of the New Haven Company the position of the Central New England became greatly changed. The New Haven being a great reservoir of traffic was in a position to divert, and did divert, a very large tonnage to the Poughkeepsie Bridge route." [26]

As a result the tonnage of the Central New England —the acquired line—in the score of years following its acquisition by the New Haven increased 700 per cent. Its originated tonnage actually declined.[27] The increased tonnage consisted of overhead business passing to and from the New Haven and connecting trunk lines.

Traffic diversion thus manifests itself in a different form: the acquiring line under certain conditions induces other—and independent—carriers to feed its acquired line with additional business. In this way the acquiring line realizes a return on its investment in the acquired carrier.

Perhaps more usual is the acquisition of a line with little traffic, which the acquiring line feeds directly with its *own* tonnage. The Cincinnati Southern, for example, operated now for almost a half century by the Cincinnati, New Orleans & Texas Pacific, has never developed sufficient local traffic to support the successful operation of a first-class road. Its high standard of service and its financial strength have been due entirely to the through traffic contributed by the parent road—the Southern Railway. More than 50 per cent of the through traffic of the acquired line is received from the affiliated lines of the Southern Railway system.[28]

Illustrative of the control over routing enjoyed by the line of origin is the shifting of deliveries to the same railroad from one junction to another. Observe its working in the Missouri Pacific system. The Missouri Pacific is the parent of the system established in 1924 with Commission sanction. The parent line was wont to deliver some southbound traffic to the Kansas City Southern at Texarkana. That was—prior to the formation of the system—the long-haul junction of the former. Among other lines acquired was the Gulf Coast Lines. That carrier connected with the Kansas City Southern at a small point—De

CONSOLIDATION IN ACTION 291

Quincy, Louisiana—many miles to the south of Texarkana, the point, be it noted, at which the Missouri Pacific made delivery. When the Kansas City Southern applied to the Commission for authority to establish a new southwestern system it produced data tending to "indicate that the traffic which the Kansas City Company had been receiving at Texarkana had been influenced for the long haul to the Missouri Pacific lines and delivered to the Kansas City Company at De Quincy." [29]

In somewhat similar fashion the St. Louis Southwestern lost a haul. It formerly received traffic at Memphis from the Illinois Central destined to Texas points. The latter's acquisition of the Alabama & Vicksburg and the Vicksburg & Shreveport & Pacific gave it a system line to Shreveport. The Illinois Central now carries its traffic from Memphis to Shreveport, and there delivers traffic to the St. Louis Southwestern. The latter loses a haul from Memphis to Shreveport.[30]

Here there is no loss in interchange tonnage. The volume remains the same. But the distance the volume travels is less. Ton miles, not tonnage, is diverted.

Traffic diversion from the acquiring to the acquired line generally results from the possession by the acquired carrier of a strategic line between important traffic centers. The Cincinnati Southern fills in the last gap of the through route of the Southern Railway system from New Orleans to Cincinnati and the Ohio Valley. This route also affords the Southern direct physical connection with the New York Central system lines.

The competitive rivalry between the Pennsylvania and the Reading for the acquisition of the Lehigh & New England is based on the control by the latter of a short and noncongested line to New England. The proposed lease of this carrier by the Reading was justified in part by a description of additional routes to enable it to forward additional through business over the acquired line. The Pennsylvania also has given serious consideration to the advisability of acquiring this line, as a short and noncongested route to New England. And it successfully opposed before the Commission its projected absorption by the Reading.

Beyond the direct diversions to and from acquired and acquiring lines are the comparatively indirect diversions to and from connecting lines. To the carrier soliciting for a share of this business, it is usually (though not always) overhead traffic: shipments received from one connection and delivered to another for further movement to destination. This is business, the routing of which is not controlled by the constituent lines of a particular unification. Members of the new consolidated group may, as independent lines, have competed against each other; and each and all of them in turn may have competed with other lines for the privilege of performing the same transportation service.

The exact nature and scope of this competition is unusually difficult to appraise. What proportion of the traffic interchanged by the constituent lines with connections is sufficiently competitive to permit of successful traffic diversions depends in part upon the destination of many individual shipments. An acquired line may have been interchanging with a competitor of the acquiring line; and as a part of the latter's system it would be disinclined to continue the exchange. Obviously, that part of the business destined to local points on the competitor's

CONSOLIDATION IN ACTION

line would still be forwarded and received. Some traffic, however, may be carried by the competitive connection to points reached by other lines; and some to other connections for carriage to destinations reached by neither the competitive connection of the acquired line nor by the acquiring line.

Many of these complicated phases of traffic diversion developed in connection with the lease of the so-called Vicksburg route (consisting of the Vicksburg, Shreveport & Pacific, and the Alabama & Vicksburg) by the Illinois Central. The competitive background here was unusually keen. The acquired lines developed a substantial tonnage destined chiefly to points in the upper Mississippi Valley. The Illinois Central together with many of its competitors reached these common markets either directly over its own lines or via connections. The Vicksburg route in fact crossed nineteen roads. Direct competition for traffic to and from the Vicksburg territory existed with such systems as the Missouri Pacific, the Chicago, Rock Island & Pacific, the St. Louis Southwestern, and the Kansas City Southern.

Of the traffic of the Vicksburg destined to Illinois Central territory, only a small part was handled by the latter road. Elaborate calculations based on the period from January 1 to March 31, 1924, were prepared. A few figures may typify the situation. Out of 29,373 tons of lumber originating on the Vicksburg, Shreveport & Pacific moving to states served by the Illinois Central, only 5,000 were delivered to the Illinois Central system; and of the 13,254 tons of the same commodity delivered in the state of Illinois, only 2,132 moved by the Illinois Central.

Of the total tonnage originated by the Alabama & Vicksburg and shipped to points on other carriers only about 33 per cent was forwarded via the Illinois Central.

The Vicksburg route not only was an important originating carrier; it was also a highly useful bridge carrier. It was a central link in the short route between the southeast and the southwest. Cotton, grain, lumber, and oil moved east over its lines bound for southern and eastern destinations, while manufactured products moved west through Shreveport.

Again, though a substantial proportion of this business moved to Illinois Central territory, only a small tonnage moved via that line. Of the overhead lumber traffic of the Vicksburg, Shreveport & Pacific, for example, 50 per cent moved to states served by the Illinois Central or its proximate connections. Only 4 per cent, however, was carried by that line. The Alabama & Vicksburg traffic was somewhat similar: of its overhead tonnage of lumber, piling, and shingles, 64 per cent moved to Illinois Central territory; but less than 4 per cent moved over the Illinois Central.

The Illinois Central, furthermore, through its western extension to Council Bluffs introduced another uncertain factor. From grain states thus reached by the Illinois Central, the Vicksburg territory received considerable grain. This flowed mostly over other lines, particularly the Kansas City Southern.

In this case the traffic motives behind consolidation were unusually clear, divorced as they were from forced claims of operating and capital savings on one hand, and from undue solicitude for the welfare of the weak lines on the other. Both the president and the general freight agent of the Illinois Central clearly stated the purpose of the

CONSOLIDATION IN ACTION 295

lease of the Vicksburg. "To the greatest extent possible," stated the former, "in the interest of the long haul of the Illinois Central, in the interest of the Vicksburg, Shreveport & Pacific and of the Alabama & Vicksburg, we want to encourage the movement of all the business that we can force over the line of the Illinois Central, giving it its long-haul in connection with the Alabama & Vicksburg and Vicksburg, Shreveport & Pacific." [31]

The general freight agent put the situation even more clearly. The Vicksburg route handled only a small proportion of what it ought to handle between the southeast and the southwest; and he believed a strong system like the Illinois Central could increase the volume moved over the route.

He also expected the Illinois Central "to give a great deal of business to the Vicksburg, Shreveport & Pacific or Alabama & Vicksburg that now moves over other connections." [32]

That is, the acquiring line would give the acquired line more traffic. He was equally clear in his belief that the acquired line would give the acquiring line more, as well. Witness this:

Q. "You will gain the advantage of hauling over your own lines out of competitive territory cargoes that are now being hauled by connecting carriers of the Vicksburg route, with the Vicksburg route. Is that one of the anticipated benefits to the Illinois Central?"

A. "I think so." [33]

And as a result, he states in another connection, the Illinois Central will "get 100 per cent of the revenue, where we [Illinois Central] now get 50 per cent or more as the case may be." [34]

This anticipation of traffic diversions called forth definite statements of traffic and revenue losses expected to be suffered by some of the carriers affected. The Kansas City Southern trading with the Vicksburg route at Shreveport, the latter's western gateway, estimated that the proposed lease of the Vicksburg route with the Illinois Central would entail a loss to it of 57.7 per cent of the average earnings received on tonnage interchanged at that point. This estimate of probable loss on interchange, as detailed as it was, still was incomplete. The data were insufficient to enable one to reach a sound conclusion. It was assumed that all cotton, oil and lumber originating on the Vicksburg and hitherto delivered to the Kansas City Southern would now be lost to that carrier. Perhaps so. That could not be safely asserted, nevertheless, until the destinations of that traffic were known. That part destined to strictly local points must still have moved over the Kansas City Southern. But it might have moved over it in part only. It may have been possible for the originating line to route the business so as to permit the Illinois Central to secure a part of the haul instead of no haul at all.

Another proportion may have been destined to points located on connections of the Kansas City Southern. That business might have moved east instead of west to the Illinois Central for routing over its connections. Or perhaps the routing via the Kansas City Southern and its connections might have given the Vicksburg shippers a service superior to that afforded by any other possible route. If that were so, then this interchange might have been relatively safe from diversion. The Kansas City Southern produced no data to permit consideration of these items.

CONSOLIDATION IN ACTION

The Texas & Pacific, also interchanging with the Vicksburg route at Shreveport, had a traffic and revenue interest at stake. For 1923 it received a revenue of approximately $605,000 from this interchange; and its traffic executive was confident that "the volume of tonnage now being delivered and received at Shreveport will be materially decreased if the Vicksburg, Shreveport & Pacific and Alabama & Vicksburg should pass to the exclusive control of the Illinois Central system." [35]

This road, however, was not fearful (as was the Kansas City Southern) of the loss of tonnage originating or terminating on the Vicksburg route and delivered to and received from the Texas & Pacific. This traffic (if moving eastward) was partly controlled by the Texas & Pacific as the initial carrier; and (if moving westward) flowed mostly in a direction contrary to the general trend of the Illinois Central. That part which moved northward into competitive territory, into territory reached by the Illinois Central and its long-haul connections, the Texas & Pacific believed it could control by effective solicitation and a high standard of service.

The fears of this road lay in another direction. It stressed the probable loss of business which was overhead to the Vicksburg route. This was traffic moving between the southeast and Texas-Louisiana and California, and which used the Vicksburg as a link in the route. It was long-haul traffic to the Vicksburg, received by it on the east at Meridian, Mississippi (primarily from the Southern Railway), and carried for its full length to Shreveport on the west. There is no reason apparently why the acquiring line—the Illinois Central—should not continue, indeed encourage, this business over the Vicksburg.

But there might be a reason why the Southern—the controlling line—would decline to continue it. It happens that the Southern and the Illinois Central are competitors, and in accordance with well-established principles, the former might refuse to trade freely with a competitor. The Southern has other gateways for the carriage of this traffic: Memphis to the north and New Orleans to the south. Should the Southern divert the traffic, both the acquired line and one of its friendly connections would lose. The volume of affected tonnage is apparently substantial since the traffic authority of the Texas & Pacific states, "that the great bulk of the traffic moving in either direction is overhead traffic, coming from beyond Meridian to us [Texas & Pacific] or going from us to beyond Meridian." [36]

Whether in practice the Southern would actually divert traffic from the Meridian to some other gateway cannot be definitely affirmed. That it has the power to do so is evident; that it will exercise that power is not so evident. The Southern and the Illinois Central are large systems. They have many interchange points. They may work out a trade. The Illinois Central at some competitive junction point or points may divert some tonnage to the Southern that now goes to other lines; and in return the Southern many continue the Meridian interchange. There are other business possibilities. The actual results cannot be foretold or foreseen by any except those intimately associated with the management of the property.

These traffic diversions which thus accompany rearrangements of corporate ownership represent the major problem in the national program of railroad consolidation. The establishment of a limited number of financial

CONSOLIDATION IN ACTION

equals capable of competing as equals is the ultimate ideal. To achieve this aim, each carrier must have access to traffic-producing territory; it must have adequate terminals; it must have its share of short and direct lines between important areas of production and consumption. It must enjoy the opportunity to share in those limited economies that flow from consolidation; and what is more significant, it must have the management, which can realize not only these economies but the much greater ones that result from the wise application of large capital investments.

Within wide limits these fundamentals can be provided for, and their possible effects on earning power and competitive ability estimated. It is far more difficult, however, to provide for an apportionment of competitive interchange among the various claimants. It may be possible to give each carrier in trunk line territory its share of originated iron and steel traffic, to give each one access to the lower Lake Erie ports, and to give each one access to the major oceanic ports. With all this provided for, the equivalence of earning power among all systems would not be established. No system can live unto itself: it cannot exist without an adequate share of interchange traffic. What this share is, each system probably cannot estimate itself. Neither can any governmental body estimate it with any degree of accuracy.

Yet the solution of this problem is vital to the successful establishment of railroad carriers of competitive and financial equivalence. It is a problem which cannot be solved by rules of administrative bodies, nor by legislative fiat. Its elements must be carefully assayed in the crucible of careful and well-informed judgment. In one case it may require a minimum of governmental interference;

and in another such grave possibilities of unwise traffic diversion may be suggested as to necessitate governmental interdiction.

In the final analysis, however, it still remains true that the carriers affected—directly or indirectly, favorably or adversely—are best equipped to appraise the situation. And if, in any particular unification proposal none of the competitive carriers interposes any objection, it may be safely assumed that none requires any protection against any possible loss of competitive interchange. In the proposed unification of the Southwestern Lines, the only possibility of traffic diversion raised by the carriers was privately settled. No interchange problem whatsoever was raised in the Nickel Plate Unification case; and the presumption, despite partial Commission disapproval, rests in favor of the proposal. To the pending unification of the Hill lines in the northwest, the Chicago, Milwaukee, St. Paul & Pacific has raised serious objections on the score of the competitive disability to which it might be subjected as a result of its consummation. This presents a case of necessary governmental action: of thorough and exhaustive analysis of the possible and probable diversions of traffic away from one road and to the lines of the others —parties to the unification. Here is a case, it would seem, requiring intensive research to appraise the probable effect of a proposed unification upon the fortunes of a trunk line competitor. Regardless of its merits, the proposed system seemingly could not be considered desirable if it brought in its wake as one of its consequences any decided weakening of its neighbor. Whether that is likely to ensue is clearly a problem deserving of careful study, and the exercise of a well-balanced and impartial judgment.

CONSOLIDATION IN ACTION

NOTES TO CHAPTER X

1. Hearings before the House Committee on Interstate Commerce, 69th Congress, 1st session, on H.R. 11212, Part VI, p. 184.
2. Hearings before the Senate Committee on Interstate Commerce, 69th Congress, 1st session, on S. 1870, pp. 39-40.
3. Control of Northwestern Pacific R. R., 150 I.C.C. 119.
4. Abandonment of Chicago, Peoria & St. Louis R. R., 76 I.C.C. 801; Acquisition and Operation of Line by A. & E. R. R., 94 I.C.C. 571; Acquisition and Operation of Line by J. & H. R. R. Co., 105 I.C.C. 243; Acquisition and Operation of Jacksonville & H. R. R. Co., 150 I.C.C. 551.
5. Consolidation of Railroads, 63 I.C.C. 616.
6. New York Central Unification, 150 I.C.C. 294.
7. The author has in preparation a treatise on the relation of the weak lines to railroad consolidation.
8. Hearings before the Senate Committee on Interstate Commerce, 70th Congress, 1st session on S. 1175, Part I, p. 167.
9. *Supra*, Hearings, etc., on S. 2224, p. 71.
10. *Supra*, Hearings, etc., on S. 1175, Part I, p. 183.
11. *Supra*, p. 170.
12. *Supra*, Hearings, etc., on S. 1870, Part II, p. 244.
13. Control of Erie R. R. and Pere Marquette Ry., Finance Docket 6113, 6114, Brief for Short Line Interveners, pp. 35, 83; New York Central Unification, Finance Docket 5688, 5690, Brief for Chicago, Attica & Southern, and Southern New York Ry., p. 38.
14. Acquisition of Southern Georgia Ry., Finance Docket 6580, Report of Examiner, Sheet 4.
15. *Supra*, Exceptions for Seaboard Air Line, p. 5.
16. Construction of Lines by St. Louis Southwestern Railway Co., Finance Docket 7031, 7032, Abstract of Testimony and Exhibits, p. 26.
17. *Supra*, p. 27.
18. Fruits and Vegetables from Texas Points, 74 I.C.C. 577.
19. Lease of A. & V. and V. S. & P., Finance Docket 4775, Brief for the Illinois Central, p. 216; *supra*, Brief for Interveners, pp. 128-129.
20. Control of Houston & Brazos Valley, 86 I.C.C. 595.
21. Consolidation of Railroads, 63 I.C.C. 548.
22. Acquisition of Central California Traction Co., Finance Docket 5008, Brief for the Atchison, Topeka & Santa Fe, pp. 5-6.
23. *Supra*, p. 25.
24. *Supra*, tr. pp. 141-142; Brief for Applicant, p. 30; exhibit nos. 13, 31.
25. Unification of Southwestern Lines, Finance Docket 5679, 5680, Brief for Applicants, Vol. II, p. 28.
26. Central Railroad of New Jersey *vs.* New York, New Haven & Hartford, Docket 16721, Brief for Central Railroad of New Jersey, p. 140.
27. *Supra*, p. 141.

28. Lease of Cincinnati Southern Ry., 138 I.C.C. 749.
29. Unification of Southwestern Lines, Finance Docket 5679, 5680, Brief for Applicants, Vol. II, p. 27.
30. *Supra*, pp. 27-28.
31. Lease of A. & V. and V. S. & P., Finance Docket 4775, Brief for Jackson Traffic Bureau, Intervener, p. 72.
32. *Supra*, tr. p. 1096.
33. *Supra*, tr. p. 1097.
34. *Supra*, Brief for R. E. Kenington, *et al*, Interveners, p. 16.
35. *Supra*, Brief for Jackson Traffic Bureau, Intervener, p. 83.
36. *Supra*, Brief for Illinois Central, p. 202.

CHAPTER XI

LEGISLATIVE PRINCIPLES

The chief aim of consolidation from the standpoint of the carriers—of those parties, that is, who must propose and execute the plans—is to increase the gross volume of business moved over system lines. An increase in tonnage over one line means some corresponding—though not exactly proportionate—decrease on another. The latter may be a financially strong carrier; and a small loss in traffic may not seriously impair its ability to serve the public. A much larger loss may, however, reduce its strength and its public usefulness. If the road which loses the traffic is a financially weak one, the effect may even be more serious.

It is accordingly necessary to set limits, if possible, to the scope of this traffic diversion. Consolidation should not permit the strong to grow stronger at the expense of the weak; nor the weak to grow excessively strong at the expense of the strong. Legislative authority should provide for the constitution of systems of substantially equal financial strength; and in order to effect this, each system must receive its due share of the available traffic. To appraise the nature of the legislation required to accomplish this purpose, it is necessary first to consider the stages through which corporate consolidation passes, and the extent to which traffic diversion occurs in each stage.

The consolidation of roads—of properties completely unified in fee ownership—from roads independently owned is usually achieved by a series of steps. One road may acquire a controlling share interest in another; and this does not necessarily mean the ownership of a majority of the stock outstanding. Various species of control can be exercised through a substantial minority shareholding.

Or, as is more usually the case, the owning line may acquire a majority share control. This species of ownership may last for many years. During that time the owning line quietly and unostentatiously accumulates additional stock owned by minority interests. Its management may, and occasionally does, facilitate additional accumulations by preventing a too rapid increase in the earning power of the controlled line. It may surcharge the maintenance account by extensive retirement or rehabilitation programs; it may short-haul the controlled carrier, and change the apportionment of the through rate between the two lines.

If a large majority of stock has been acquired, the owning line then leases the other. The lease may be effected within a few years after acquisition of share control; or it may be delayed for many years. Both possibilities are well illustrated by the pending application before the Interstate Commerce Commission by the Missouri Pacific for authority to lease part of its system lines. In 1924 that road enjoyed a majority share control of both the Gulf Coast Lines and the Texas & Pacific. By 1929 it had substantially increased its holdings in the former—owning almost 90 per cent of its stock. Despite the prosperity of the latter and the accompanying increase in the value of the stock, only a relatively small increase in its holdings has been acquired by the Missouri Pacific. The minority holdings in the Texas & Pacific are apparently not for sale. The Missouri Pacific therefore proposes to lease the Gulf Coast Lines, but not the Texas & Pacific.

Minority share interests, small in number or influence as they may be, effectively preclude the consummation of a consolidation. The dissolution of a corporation and the conveyance in fee title of its property to another corporation require the consent of all the shareholders. This can only rarely be secured. Sometimes, as in the organization of the present New York, Chicago & St. Louis in 1922, the shares of the dissenting shareholders are purchased for cash. In many cases small stock holdings are held by parties with exalted ideas of the real value of their properties—ideas that differ radically from those held by the management of the controlling carrier. The latter may believe that the consolidation made possible through the ownership of all of the stock of the leased or share controlled line would produce benefits incommensurate with the financial burdens incident to the purchase of the minority stock. Railroad systems thus consist in large part of properties controlled by lease and by majority share interest.

The major purposes of consolidation are realized in varying degrees by rearrangements of corporate unifications in their various stages. Considerable operating economies and higher standards of railroad service have followed the acquisitions of share control in one road by another. The minority interest of the Baltimore & Ohio by the Western Maryland has produced a substantial operating saving through the elimination of interchange at a small point in West Virginia,[1] and has made possible a one-morning-earlier delivery from Baltimore to Cleveland, Chicago and St. Louis.[2] The public interest in the minority share holdings in the St. Louis Southwestern by the Chicago, Rock Island & Pacific was demonstrated by detailed operating savings realized within sixty days after the purchase of the stock, and by further savings expected to be worked out gradually.[3] The proposed unifications through majority share control of the Kansas City Southern–Missouri-Kansas-Texas–St. Louis Southwestern system, and the Chesapeake & Ohio–Erie–Pere Marquette system promised (through reciprocal trackage arrangements, pooling of car supply and shop facilities, joint use of terminal facilities, etc.) to achieve some savings.

The extent of the savings possible through lease, that are not possible through majority share holdings, are indefinite and uncertain. Certain accounting savings can be realized. One carrier which controls another through majority stock ownership incurs considerable responsibility to minority interests of the controlled line. Compensation must be paid to each other for the use of each other's property. Some of the resultant accounting expenditures can be saved, if the road is leased. With this exception, most of the major economies, for example, which were to have followed the first Nickel Plate Unification through lease, were (according to its proponents) also to have followed from the second unification through majority stock ownership. Perhaps additional minor savings arising from the greater freedom in routing freight over system lines due to the absence of minority interests may be realized through lease. In view of the speed with which traffic diversion from one route to another accompanies changes in share ownership, the scope for further diversions that await the execution of a corporate lease seems to be limited. The leasing of the share controlled New York Central system lines promised "a potential aggregate saving of 11,796,789 car-miles per year through direct routing." [4] Some of the direct routes are not used because of the possible detriment to minority shareholders; but others cannot be used without physical improvement. What part of the savings from lessened car-mile costs will be absorbed by increased capital and maintenance costs resulting from the use of the short routes cannot be deduced from available data. The volume of uneconomical traffic routings due to the necessity of protecting minority interests in a share controlled system, is dependent in part upon the aggressiveness, the watchfulness, and the degree of concentration in the minority holdings. With the necessity of considering the welfare of these parties removed by a lease, traffic can be moved irrespective of the effect upon the earnings of any road within the system.

Those further traffic diversions and economies that are realizable only through complete consolidation in fee ownership are small indeed. They fall into two main groups. A slight saving in capital costs results from a consolidated system. Many investors prefer bonds secured by a mortgage on property owned in fee to one secured by share or bond collateral, or by a leasehold. This preference, which is reflected in state laws regulating the investments of savings banks and trust funds, produces a higher market price and lower capital cost for those companies with properties owned in fee than for those with properties otherwise owned or controlled. Savings in accounting costs are also effected: tax reports and reports submitted to state and federal authorities are reduced in number; intercorporate accounting is eliminated, etc.

Some economies, some changes in traffic routings, therefore, arise from leases and from complete fee consolidations that do not characterize unifications effected through stock control. But these advantages are relatively minor in the appraisal of the extent to which a new corporate alignment contributes to the fulfillment of the major purpose of consolidation. Consolidation of railroads is justified as a national policy by the erection of a limited number of properties of approximately equal financial strength and earning power capable of competing as equals in the rendition of a high standard of service at reasonable rates. To bring this about each system must be provided with a fair share of terminal facilities, access to important markets of production and consumption over reasonably direct routes, as well as its due proportion of interchange traffic. These factors and forces in their major aspects are worked out in the initial control stage. Subject to the exceptions already indicated—arising primarily from the necessity of protecting the vested rights of the minority shareholders—a carrier controlling another through stockholdings enjoys free use of the latter's facilities and traffic advantages. It moves its traffic over those routes and lines that give the system the greatest profit; and it realizes also a large proportion of the relatively small savings that flow from the establishment of systems unified in ownership.

Control through share holdings (and occasionally through lease or operating contract) is not only the first, it is the most significant and vital step in the promotion of systems of substantially uniform competitive strength and earning power. This first step realizes most of the advantages that flow from consolidation: it effects most of the savings, and diverts most of the interchange traffic available for diversion. And, if and when necessary, necessitous and necessary lines are taken over.

It is this first control stage in the steps leading to ultimate consolidation that must therefore be regulated in the public interest. What status the new corporate unification will ultimately occupy in the scheme of completely consolidated properties—what its competitive position will be, its traffic diversity, its command of markets, its access to lucrative sources of traffic origin, in fine its eventual financial strength and earning power—is largely determined in this inital stage. If, for example, trunk line control of the Wheeling & Lake Erie or the Western Maryland is likely to restrain substantially existing competition between the acquiring and the acquired lines, then most of the important consequences likely to ensue therefrom will manifest themselves through a relationship of share control.

It is, furthermore, significant to observe that the current consolidation deadlock in trunk line territory is based on situations developing from share ownership. The minority share ownership by the Pennsylvania in the Wabash and the Lehigh Valley nullifies the possibility of carrying out any alternative grouping of these properties that may be deemed advisable by Commission judgment. The rapid transfer of the share control of the Buffalo, Rochester & Pittsburgh and the Wheeling & Lake Erie to and from a number of trunk lines and a private non-carrier holding company represents different phases of a concerted effort to gain working control. Thereafter it may prove advisable to lease the roads—particularly if a watchful, well-informed, and belligerent minority insists upon obliging the controlling road to distribute a fair share of the earnings of the controlled road to all the shareholders. A lease may limit the dilution of the financial strength of the latter carrier through the provision of a fixed rental. The remaining earnings over and above the rental may not, necessarily, constitute a fund for the improvement of its property. There are many ways in which the earnings of a controlled line may be siphoned to the other. If the shareholders of the controlled line get less in dividends, those of the controlling line get more. The lease—as well as the technical consolidation involving a unity of fee ownership—thus adds relatively little to the vital public interests involved in consolidation.

To grant plenary powers over corporate unification in its first control stage requires the consideration of a number of nice problems of jurisdictional significance. Should the law embrace in its plenitude control over non-carrier parties? There may be weighty factors against this proposal; but if they be permitted to preponderate, then a full measure of regulation over the forces underlying consolidation can never be achieved. The evasion of the prohibition of carrier activities—not only in consolidation, but in many other fields of action—by the interposition of fully controlled companies is a device that dates back to the early years of railroading. To deny the Pennsylvania Railroad the legal opportunity to own the shares of particular carriers, but to grant that opportunity to a company controlled by it, or by a number of its officials or former officials, is a tragic confusion of shadow and substance.

Is it wise to grant a governmental body complete power to pass upon the public interest involved in every transfer of a large block of railroad stock? For this is what the proposal amounts to. What proportion of voting control is needed to dominate the management of a property depends upon circumstances. If the non-controlled stock is widely held by scattered parties incapable of organizing to express—if not to protect—their vested interests, then perhaps the ownership of 30 per cent is sufficient to insure working control. If these holdings are more concentrated, then an actual majority of stock may be necessary. But, whether this stock rests in the hands of a holding company, an investment company, a voting trust, or a person in his own name would appear to be of slight importance. The really significant question is: to the benefit of what carrier or carriers does the control made possible by the share holdings redound? It is a decidedly open question whether any administrative or judicial body can effectively regulate the use of the multifarious instruments of corporate finance. Nevertheless, it would seem imperative, if a positive policy of regulation of consolidations is considered essential, at least to clothe the government with the powers needed to supervise the transfer of share control of railroads.

Having done this, the legislators are confronted with another problem requiring for its solution the exercise of sound judgment. The control of corporate properties cannot always be effected by private direct negotiation with the dominant shareholders. It may be necessary to buy shares on the organized stock exchanges of the land. To purchase many shares in that manner requires considerable secrecy, since otherwise many holders might demand a hold-up value; and groups of wealthy and well-informed speculators might purchase large blocks of stocks for resale to the acquiring carrier at advancing prices. The purchases must, furthermore, be made patiently and over an extended period of time. A sudden demand in the market for large amounts of stock might produce a substantial rise in price; and at the advanced values, the acquisition of share control might not be considered wise by the acquiring carrier. Under these circumstances is it good judgment legally to require the carriers to obtain consent of a particular unification before purchasing any stock to make that consent financially practicable? This is the provision in the pending House bill on consolidation. Or should stock accumulation be allowed to proceed in the ordinary manner, the program of projected control then laid before the supervisory body, and the latter either approve or reject the program?

The Fess bill pending in the Senate in a compromise effort to solve the problem distinguishes between an acquisition "not sufficient to constitute control" and a unification. Shares to effect the former may be freely bought subject to the ordinary provisions of law, both state or federal; but the acquired shares may not be voted on a unification proposal without consent of the Interstate Commerce Commission. What constitutes "control" is not clearly defined; and indeed it cannot be defined. Control may be realized through the ownership of varying percentages of stock—and in many cases less than majority. Sufficient economies and traffic diversions may be effected through the ownership of a substantial minority, even though no formal unification program may be presented for Commission approval.

Thus to legalize substantial shareholdings seems to overlook the primary forces underlying consolidation. It places the emphasis upon the latter—the less important—steps

LEGISLATIVE PRINCIPLES 313

in the various stages leading to complete consolidation. This provision, if enacted into law, will probably prove a great deterrent to its successful administration. A carrier with a concentrated stock holding in another may not ask Commission approval of "unification"; the Commission with no opportunity presented to it to consider the public aspects of control may not be able to decide the proper place the road should occupy in a national program of consolidation. If, furthermore, the Commission should disapprove a proposed unification, the carrier against which the order of disapproval is directed cannot be required to sell that part of its stock holdings "in an amount not sufficient to constitute control." [5] The Commission would again be precluded from considering the assignment of the road to some other grouping.

The law having made adequate provision for the regulation of share acquisitions, the remaining steps leading to fee ownership can satisfactorily be provided for. If the initial stage has been approved by public authority, the latter thereby assumes the responsibility of facilitating the accomplishment of the full consolidation. If the advantages of the first step redound to the public benefit, so will the succeeding steps (in lesser degree, however) similarly be expressive of the public weal. The problems that arise in these final stages have been repeatedly discussed and sifted in exhaustive detail before Congressional Committees in the last six years. They include the establishment of a legal machinery of providing for public hearings, of defining the nature and scope of the right of intervention, of the form of the order for approval, of the establishment of the consent of the carriers, of the clothing of the resulting consolidated corporations with the powers necessary to discharge their responsibilities and enjoy their privileges, of the equitable rights of dissenting shareholders, of the condemnation of those shareholdings that obstruct the completion of the last step in a consolidation approved as in the public interest, etc. The bills pending in the House and Senate make provision for all these; and in view of the high calibre of legal talent participating in their draftsmanship there is no reason to doubt of their sufficiency.

The very multiplicity of detail in the proposed law, however, will probably provide grounds for varying interpretations. That the invitation to such legal contests with the accompanying expense and delay is necessary, is not at all evident. The Interstate Commerce Commission has enjoyed the exercise of full power over leases. The federal law permitting, it has also gone the full length in sanctioning the establishment of complete fee consolidations. The first Nickel Plate system involving 1,695 miles of line and operating through the heart of eastern trunk-line territory from St. Louis through Chicago and the lower Lake ports to Buffalo was organized under state laws. The Commission granted the state corporation a certificate of convenience and necessity to acquire the consolidated properties.[6] Consolidation of parent companies with 100 per cent stock-owned subsidiaries has also met with Commission approval.[7]

Two sections of the law on consolidation preclude the Commission from doing anything further. It may not approve a plan for complete consolidation, presented squarely to it for its consideration, unless the proposal is in harmony with a general plan which the Commission itself must first prepare. Nor may it extend its approval unless the capitalization does not exceed the property valuation.

Negatively, therefore, it is believed that these two provisions in the present law should be repealed. It is highly questionable whether the Interstate Commerce Commission, or any other single body, can prepare a satisfactory plan for the allocation of all common carrier properties to particular railroad systems. The subject is too complex. The country is too large. The local conditions bearing on transportation service are too many and too complicated to permit any group of men to master them, and what is even more significant, to appraise their relationship to the economics of railroad consolidation. The experience of the last nine years has supplied ample data to demonstrate the justification for relying upon the development of private initiative to serve public purposes; and for affording considerable scope for the play of private interest, subject to governmental control, without the restrictions inherent in the existence of a preconceived plan.

The form and direction which private initiative spurred on by private profit takes, and which frequently leads to public benefits, defies any classification. Equally does it defy the well-laid plans of governmental and of nongovernmental bodies. The manifold ways in which small and weak carriers have been absorbed into the national transportation system bear no relation to any of the proposals or prophecies with respect to them made only a few years previous. Sometimes the initial propulsion is supplied by a carrier lacking preferential connections to supply itself with overhead traffic, for the transportation of which it is well suited. Observe the Gulf, Mobile & Northern, a road with a substandard earning power, and one formerly supported by lumber traffic, which is now steadily decreasing. Aside from the carriage of its originated business, its traffic destinies seem to point toward Mobile. That is the only port it reaches over its own rails. To the north it reaches Jackson, Tennessee. By the use of the Illinois Central rails north of this point, it has been able to solicit for traffic to and from the middle west and points in its own territory. The Illinois Central and the Gulf, Mobile & Northern compete for this business, so the latter cannot expect any unusual coöperation from the former. Any of this business that the Gulf, Mobile & Northern carries it must solicit with its own salesmen.

The Gulf, Mobile & Northern is also in direct competition with the Mobile and Ohio—a Southern Railway property. By a process of elimination it is logical to conclude —as the Interstate Commerce Commission did in 1921— that this property should be placed with the Louisville & Nashville. The latter did not, however, display any interest in the Commission's suggestion.

Acting in response to its business needs, the Gulf, Mobile & Northern has carved out for itself a status which neither the Commission nor any other party, including officers and owners of the road itself, even remotely suggested. Approximately 145 miles from its northern terminus is the Chicago, Burlington & Quincy—a competitor of the Illinois Central. That road reaches the Mississippi River at Paducah, Kentucky. Connecting these two lines—the Chicago, Burlington & Quincy on the north, and the Gulf, Mobile & Northern on the south—is the Nashville, Chattanooga & St. Louis. Over its lines the latter secured access to the lines of the Burlington via the trackage agreement. This enabled the latter to interchange

LEGISLATIVE PRINCIPLES 317

directly with the Gulf, Mobile & Northern. The two lines then negotiated a reciprocal traffic agreement, providing for preferential solicitation.

The big traffic prize in the lower Mississippi Valley is not Mobile. It is New Orleans. The Gulf, Mobile & Northern always did some little business with New Orleans via the New Orleans, Great Northern to Jackson, Mississippi and the Alabama & Vicksburg eastward to Meridian, Mississippi. The latter was acquired by the Illinois Central in 1925; and, while this route was not to be closed as a result, it was certain that the Gulf, Mobile & Northern could not expect a competitor to coöperate with it in a business move calculated to take business away from it.

Extending from the line of the Gulf, Mobile & Northern in eastern Mississippi south and southwest in the general direction toward New Orleans was an isolated carrier. The Jackson & Eastern—a short and financially sick Class II carrier—connected with its line at Union, Mississippi, and continued westward for a few miles. This carrier had, in 1921, obtained permission from the Interstate Commerce Commission to build to Jackson, Mississippi; in 1926 the line had not yet been completed. The Gulf, Mobile & Northern acquired control of this carrier, and extended it to Jackson.

At that point it met the New Orleans, Great Northern which, in order to connect directly with the Gulf, Mobile & Northern, had abandoned a trackage agreement with the Illinois Central, and built six and one-half miles of new line. The New Orleans, Great Northern also built a terminal at Jackson to be jointly operated with the Gulf, Mobile & Northern.

There was thus created a new through route from

Chicago to New Orleans. Its circuity, as compared with the direct line of the Illinois Central, will not prevent the movement of a substantial tonnage preferentially solicited by parties to the route.

Because of these operations, conducted under the stimulus of private gain, the continued operation of an important but weak stub line carrier has been assured. Also, the financial status and the standard of service furnished to the community by two Class I carriers have been increased. To what extent these beneficial results might have been prevented by the existence of a Commission's final plan providing for the allocation of the Gulf, Mobile & Northern to the Louisville & Nashville, it is idle to speculate.[8]

Other local considerations have produced beneficial rearrangements of corporate ownership of a character that perhaps no governmental plan could have carried out. In the fertile St. Francis Valley in northeastern Arkansas and southeastern Missouri were a number of short lines earning little and generally providing a poor service. In 1926 the president of the St. Louis Southwestern, in reviewing their status, described one as serving "no town of any importance not served by either the Frisco [St. Louis & San Francisco] or the Cotton Belt [St. Louis Southwestern], and its future is [was] largely that as a part of the logging operations of the lumber company."[9]

Referring to another one, he stated, "I do not believe that it should be considered as a permanent line."[10]

Two years later in pursuance of business moves, initiated apparently by the traffic diversion policies of the St. Louis & San Francisco, both lines were acquired and absorbed into the St. Louis Southwestern system.[11]

LEGISLATIVE PRINCIPLES 319

They have become an integral part of a proposed comparatively direct main line from St. Louis to Memphis.

The Commission's assignment of these properties to the St. Louis Southwestern prior to 1926 would have met with no favor by that line. It required certain competitive business developments to justify it in assuming the financial burdens of weak lines. The absence of a final plan served the public interest; its presence might have had the contrary effect.

Other instances might be mentioned—the organization of the Illinois Terminal system under the guidance of the Illinois Power and Light interests, the Atlantic Coast Line's absorption of the Atlanta, Birmingham & Atlantic, etc. Enough has been said, it is believed, to indicate the unwisdom of repressing private initiative by the relatively rigid allocations of a preconceived plan. Making the plan subject to change might slightly reduce, but not substantially so, the inherent dangers involved. Despite all its grave abuses, private initiative acting under the stimulus of private profit, is still too important a feature of economic life to risk its serious impairment, except to purchase some public good otherwise unobtainable.

The limitation of the par value of the outstanding securities of the consolidated corporation to the value of its properties is also unsound. It leads to effective objection by shareholders. And their consent must be had in any voluntary consolidation program. Physical valuation rarely represents exchange value. Commission valuation assessed the common stock of the Kansas City Southern and of the St. Louis Southwestern at a minus quantity; while it assessed the stock of the bankrupt Atlanta, Birmingham & Atlantic, completely wiped out in its last reorganization prior to the sale of the company's property to the Atlantic Coast Line, at a substantial figure. To base consolidation on valuation would repel, rather than invite, shareholders' coöperation and acquiescence.

On the positive side, the legislative desiderata are: (1) that the Commission be empowered to approve or disapprove any changes in ownership of the shares of any common carrier that might give the new owner sufficient control to divert traffic from some other road to its own lines; (2) that the Commission's jurisdiction over changes in control be unrestricted as to the means by which such changes are effected; (3) and that the subsequent steps leading to complete fee consolidation be subjected to Commission discretion, that body acting under the guiding star of the "public interest," and to be given power as in the present law to approve and disapprove in whole or in part "under such rules and regulations and for such consideration and on such terms and conditions as shall be found by the Commission to be just and reasonable in the premises."

The first two points here suggested are fundamental to any effective system of public regulation. Together they give the Commission power to regulate in the public interest the first stage in the process of consolidation—the stage in which the large stakes are won or lost. In this control stage the controlling carrier realizes the major proportion of the increase in gross revenues, and of the decrease in expenses that characterize a successful consolidation. Here in substance occur the greater part of those developments that are expected to produce a limited number of financially and competitively equal railroad systems.

LEGISLATIVE PRINCIPLES

Public regulation of these changes cannot be complete and effective, furthermore, unless the Commission's authority embraces each and every transfer of control. The purchase and sale of stock and the vesting of title therein can be accomplished in many ways. The Van Sweringens use a holding company; the Pennsylvania may use a voting trust; the controlling shareholder in the Western Pacific bought stock control of other lines in his own name, as indeed did the Van Sweringens; and Loree and his associates sold a block of Missouri-Kansas-Texas stock held by the Kansas City Southern to shareholders of the latter road. Control may be acquired and maintained in these and other ways; but the control is eventually used for the same purpose. And to enable the Commission properly to supervise the evolution of consolidated systems it must be enabled to regulate all phases of the control stage.

Against this proposal to grant the federal Commission full supervision over the transfer of voting securities in the way indicated above, there is the thought that the open market accumulation of stock necessary to the development of some unification programs might be rendered impossible. It has been suggested that if the Commission passes upon, approves in advance, any particular unification or control, then the price of the voting securities will be so advanced as to make it unprofitable for the carriers to consummate the proposal. This result need not necessarily follow. The carriers may acquire the stock in the usual manner. They may be prohibited from voting the stock on any question, however, pending Commission approval (and herein is this proposal distinguished from that in the Fess bill which interdicts the voting of the stock only on a unification program). In the event of a favorable decision, the carriers acquire full title. If unfavorable, the stock may be disposed of in various ways: the Commission may trustee it, pending its assignment, to serve some other purpose more suited to carry out some phase of the public interest deemed important by it; the Commission may order the stock sold to some other carrier, etc. Regardless of what the law may provide, or the Commission do, litigation will probably follow.

The preliminary stages of acquiring the degree of control necessary to compete effectively—that is, to divert traffic successfully—having been effected, the resulting system must be further developed. All separate corporations must be eliminated; and the title to all the property deeded to one corporation. Only in this way, it is urged, will all the possible economies expected to flow from consolidation be realized; and many complex legal tangles eliminated.

It is decisively questionable, however, whether the public interest requires in all cases the establishment of corporations completely unified in direct ownership as well as in operation. Certainly this ideal, written into the present law, does not accord with railroad practice. Certainly it is not necessary to the successful operation of such American railroad systems as the Pennsylvania, the Baltimore & Ohio, the New York Central, the Southern, the Atlantic Coast Line, the Louisville & Nashville, the Atchison, Topeka & Santa Fe, etc. The existence of individual corporations, united by lease, common share ownership, operating contract, etc., within the limits of a single system does not substantially reduce its financial nor its competitive strength. The Pennsylvania cannot be

LEGISLATIVE PRINCIPLES 323

said to be a weaker unit of the country's transportation machine than the Chicago, Milwaukee, St. Paul & Pacific, merely because it owns in fee a smaller proportion of its mileage. And surely the suggestion cannot be seriously advanced that the Baltimore & Ohio suffers a competitive disability against the New York, Chicago & St. Louis because the latter operates over a line almost completely unified in ownership, while the former pulls its trains over tracks owned by the parent corporation through varying legal titles.

Yet there is an undeniable advantage in the formation of a completely unified railroad system. Accounting, administrative and legal expenses are somewhat reduced. Against that advantage are many patent disadvantages. There is the practical fact that essential parts of American railway routes are made up (in part or in whole) of trackage rights, leased lines, bridge agreements, jointly owned lines, terminals, and terminal approaches, etc. The disturbance of these contractual arrangements would create uncertainty and confusion and produce economic losses that would assuredly outweigh the relatively small benefits that would be realized from the operation of each system by a single corporation owning all of the system property.

There are many other problems: Can a corporation, organized under the laws of a state which provides for shareholders' and directors' meetings and for other details of corporate machinery, merge other carriers into itself, become a consolidated corporation, and then use its corporate machinery—state machinery—to carry out a purpose that may be illegal under state laws? Can the federal government confer added powers upon a state corporation in order to enable it to carry out the intent of Congress with respect to interstate commerce—an intent which in its exercise violates the law of the state—without having the state corporation forfeit its charter? If this constitutional complexity makes federal incorporation imperative, will not the almost certain opposition of state commissioners and other state authorities lead to jurisdictional clashes, which in the interest of wise administration, had rather be avoided?

And then there is the perplexing puzzle of obtaining unanimous consent of all shareholders—a condition necessarily precedent to a corporate dissolution and the association of that company with others to form a technically complete consolidation. There is an almost universal belief, particularly among the representatives of the railways, in the unwisdom of compulsory consolidation. It is therefore all the more curious to observe the decided assurance with which statutory provisions are being planned and discussed to compel unwilling minority shareholders to dispose of their holdings to majority shareholders. It is unwise and perhaps unconstitutional to oblige a prospective buyer to buy, but it is considered wise and perhaps even constitutional to oblige a seller to sell. To form any particular consolidation will require in most cases the consent of shareholders not desirous of selling their property. The proposal to use the right of eminent domain to force the seller to sell his personal property may be constitutional, but assuredly this will not be decided except after protracted litigation.

These constitute only some of the problems involved in consolidating American railway properties in such a way that each system will own all it operates, and operate

LEGISLATIVE PRINCIPLES 325

all it owns. Is it worth while? What are the benefits realizable from a complete, and not from an incomplete, consolidation? First, the internal legal relations of a system will be simplified, since there will be one instead of numerous corporate entities to be dealt with. Second, there will be certain savings in accounting and administration, of a relatively small extent. Third, there will be a slight saving in the cost of obtaining new capital. Many conservative investors prefer bonds secured by a mortgage on property owned in fee to those secured even in part collaterally or by leaseholds. The former can therefore be sold at a slightly higher price.

Is it worth the price to purchase these advantages? Merely in order to achieve these purposes is it necessary to "hot-house" complete consolidations? For the primary objectives of consolidation are not involved. The preservation of necessary weak and short lines, the rendition of good service, the preservation of channels of trade and commerce, the constitution of systems competitively and financially equivalent can be effected almost as well with incomplete as with complete consolidation.

It is therefore better to permit, and encourage, the development of acquisitions and unifications along sound business lines; so long, that is, as they do no harm to what is considered the "public interest." If an opportunity to divert traffic appears, a unification will be arranged. If, as a result, another road is not vitally injured, and the shipping public is not deprived of access to established markets, then the proposal is in the public interest. If the unification, sound in itself, seems to carry with it possibilities detrimental to the public interest, the Commission has shown itself capable of inserting conditions calculated to meet the situation. It may, if deemed necessary, oblige the petitioning carrier to assume the burden of acquiring weak but necessary short-line carriers; it may require it to keep open line routes or terminals; it may provide for joint ownership of particular properties, etc. The Commission's views on these matters, developed as a result of several years of experience, are well known to interested carriers.

Remove the requirement for a plan of consolidation, and the restriction of outstanding capitalization to the property valuation; remove also the insistence upon the immediate consummation of complete consolidation; and the elaborate framework of legislation pending in Congress resolves itself primarily into the erection of a statutory machinery to effect unification to replace the one built up by the Commission. Detailed rules and regulations established by Commission discretion are to be preferred to those provided by statute. The latter possess no flexibility. They cannot be adapted to the constantly changing conditions of modern business life.

What is vitally needed, however, is a further grant of authority to enable the Commission to supervise every change in common carrier control which carries with it the possibility of diverting traffic. For this is the chief means whereby consolidation affects the earning power of railroads. With this added power and its present twofold restriction upon its existing power removed, the Commission will be adequately equipped to control the unification process. To go further, and lay down detailed rules for the machinery of proposing and completing unifications, is merely substituting Congressional for Commission judgment.

LEGISLATIVE PRINCIPLES

The evolution of complete consolidation will not be completely held up. Some have been effected under existing statutory authority. With the removal of the mandate for the plan and of the valuation provision, others will be effected. Those unifications opposed by dissenting shareholders will not graduate into the class of complete consolidations. The resultant public loss will not be great; and their consummation may well await the evolution of the major unifications. These will indicate the approximate extent to which an inter-system competitive and financial equilibrium will have been attained. And this result is, in the last analysis, the primary aim of consolidation.

NOTES TO CHAPTER XI

1. Hearings before the Senate Committee on Interstate Commerce, 70th Congress, 1st session, on S. 1175, Part I, p. 165.
2. Proposed Construction by Pittsburgh & West Virginia Railway, Finance Docket 6229, Brief for New York, Chicago & St. Louis, Intervener, p. 12.
3. Proposed acquisition by the Chicago, Rock Island & Pacific of the St. Louis Southwestern, Brief for the Chicago, Rock Island & Pacific, Finance Docket 4809, pp. 35-48.
4. New York Central Unification, 150 I.C.C. 292.
5. Report No. 1884. Calendar No. 1925, 70th Congress, 2nd session, Report to accompany S. 5817, p. 8.
6. Acquisition and Stock Issue by New York, Chicago & St. Louis Railroad, 79 I.C.C. 581.
7. Acquisition by Pittsburgh & West Virginia Railway Co., 150 I.C.C. 84.
8. Public Convenience Certificate to Jackson & Eastern Railway, 70 I.C.C. 110; Operation of Line by G. M. & N. R. R. Co., 111 I.C.C. 583; Control of Jackson & Eastern, 111 I.C.C. 587; Construction by New Orleans Great Northern R. R., 111 I.C.C. 739.
9. Unification of Southwestern Lines, Finance Docket 5679, tr. p. 1300.
10. *Supra*, p. 1304.
11. Construction of Lines by St. Louis Southwestern Ry., 150 I.C.C. 685.

INDEX TO ROADS

Alabama & Vicksburg, 16, 45, 174, 222, 291, 293, 294, 295, 297, 317

Allegheny Corporation, 36, 269

Ann Arbor, 5, 16, 155, 185, 186, 187, 268

Atchison, Topeka & Santa Fe, 25, 26, 30, 77, 82, 83, 84, 86, 87, 110, 111, 130, 131, 134, 137, 154, 164, 166, 167, 269, 271, 286, 322

Atlanta, Birmingham & Atlantic, 18, 205, 268, 319

Atlantic Coast Line, 18, 30, 71, 80, 81, 109, 173, 205, 221, 246, 319, 322

Baltimore & Ohio, 1, 9, 12, 15, 32, 33, 36, 42, 43, 57, 58, 61, 62, 89, 90, 92, 93, 102, 103, 106, 109, 118, 121, 125, 126, 131, 145, 146, 150, 155, 157, 168, 173, 185, 193, 196, 200, 204, 207, 213, 214, 217, 219, 245, 246, 251, 252, 253, 254, 256, 257, 264, 269, 273, 274, 305, 322, 323

Boston & Albany, 111, 112, 168, 170, 184, 192

Boston & Maine, 4, 32, 40, 49, 78, 170, 184, 192, 207, 228, 268

Boyne City, Gaylord & Alpena, 18

Buffalo, Rochester & Pittsburgh, 9, 17, 147, 222, 246, 252, 256, 268, 309

Butler County, 163, 280

Cambria & Indiana, 252

Canadian Pacific, 270

Carolina, Clinchfield & Ohio, 71, 81, 173, 174, 221

Casey & Kansas, 19

Central California Traction, 286

Central New England, 79, 102, 103, 104, 289

Central Railroad of New Jersey, 1, 32, 33, 36, 42, 43, 44, 55, 56, 62, 65, 91, 102, 103, 106, 108, 131, 145, 146, 155, 156, 169, 170, 196, 213, 214, 246, 251, 252, 253, 254, 256, 289

Central Vermont, 229, 270

Chesapeake & Ohio, 9, 14, 43, 66, 67, 68, 71, 81, 135, 168, 185, 201, 216, 217, 218, 219, 220, 224, 233, 249, 250, 263-64, 306

Chicago & Alton, 84, 137, 165, 167, 233

Chicago & Eastern Illinois, 84, 165, 232, 233

Chicago & Erie, 269

Chicago & North Western, 12, 54, 85, 94, 130, 137, 187, 203, 205, 208, 223, 231, 242

Chicago, Attica & Southern, 18

Chicago, Burlington & Quincy, 26, 29, 62, 77, 84, 85, 94, 129, 130, 137, 151, 164, 165, 166, 168, 169, 179, 199, 200, 208, 210, 211, 212, 223, 230, 233, 238, 240, 241, 242, 243, 316

Chicago Great Western, 48, 49, 72, 73, 84, 85, 137, 165, 166, 187, 188, 231, 233

INDEX TO ROADS

Chicago, Indianapolis & Louisville, 54, 55
Chicago Junction, 173
Chicago, Milwaukee & Gary, 151, 155
Chicago, Milwaukee, St. Paul & Pacific, 6, 12, 25, 30, 54, 59, 77, 84, 85, 129, 130, 136, 151, 152, 153, 155, 161, 162, 166, 168, 169, 179, 187, 196, 197, 199, 200, 203, 205, 208, 223, 233, 235, 243, 244, 258, 300, 323
Chicago, Peoria & St. Louis, 269
Chicago River & Indiana, 173
Chicago, Rock Island & Pacific, 5, 9, 10, 40, 45, 46, 70, 71, 72, 73, 81, 83, 84, 86, 107, 110, 137, 139, 140, 142, 143, 145, 165, 203, 230, 245, 293, 306
Chicago, Terre Haute & Southeastern, 151
Cincinnati, Hamilton & Dayton, 185, 186, 187
Cincinnati, Indianapolis & Western, 268, 273
Cincinnati, New Orleans & Texas Pacific, 290
Cincinnati Northern, 216
Cincinnati Southern, 290, 291
Cleveland, Cincinnati, Chicago & St. Louis, 70, 110, 216, 217
Colorado & Southern, 130, 131, 268
Columbus & Greenville, 270

Delaware & Hudson, 9, 17, 40, 78, 137, 147, 170, 192, 207, 222, 268
Delaware & Northern, 18
Delaware, Lackawanna & Western, 65, 104, 106, 147, 168, 179, 180, 229, 245, 289
Denver & Rio Grande Western, 94, 164, 166, 221

El Paso & Southwestern, 15
Erie, 14, 32, 65, 71, 103, 106, 135, 168, 173, 201, 216, 217, 218, 220, 224, 229, 233, 268, 289, 306

Federal Valley, 19
Fonda, Johnstown & Gloversville, 19
Fort Worth & Denver City, 59
Fort Worth & Rio Grande, 269

Georgia & Florida, 188, 279
Georgia Southern & Florida, 279
Grand Rapids & Indiana, 7
Grand Trunk, 229, 245
Great Northern, 58, 64, 106, 129, 130, 151, 161, 168, 169, 179, 197, 199, 200, 208, 210, 211, 212, 223, 240, 242, 243, 246, 249, 258
Gulf Coast Lines, 70, 98, 100, 144, 281, 282, 284, 285, 290, 304, 305
Gulf, Mobile & Northern, 33, 188, 259, 260, 262, 315, 316, 317, 318

Hocking Valley, 14, 185, 186, 201, 216, 217, 233, 249
Houston East & West Texas, 269

Illinois Central, 16, 26, 40, 45, 70, 143, 174, 175, 222, 282, 284, 291, 293, 294, 295, 296, 297, 298, 316, 317, 318
Illinois Terminal, 319
Indiana Harbor Belt, 54, 55
International & Great Northern, 6, 45, 99, 100, 145, 171, 215, 282

Jackson & Eastern, 317
Jonesboro, Lake City & Eastern, 163, 280

Kanawha & Michigan, 7
Kansas City, Mexico & Orient, 40, 86, 267, 268

INDEX TO ROADS 331

Kansas City Southern, 10, 15, 58, 68, 69, 70, 71, 81, 82, 83, 84, 94, 98, 99, 100, 101, 135, 142, 145, 166, 167, 222, 233, 238, 239, 290, 291, 293, 294, 296, 297, 306, 319, 321

Kansas, Oklahoma & Gulf, 38, 40, 86, 238, 239

Lake Erie & Pittsburgh, 246

Lake Shore & Michigan Southern, 14, 79, 167, 168, 179, 180, 275

Lehigh & Hudson River, 38, 40, 42, 43, 102, 108, 155, 213, 246, 256, 289

Lehigh & New England, 38, 40, 42, 43, 65, 102, 108, 155, 156, 196, 213, 289, 291

Lehigh Valley, 32, 55, 56, 65, 103, 106, 147, 150, 168, 229, 268, 269, 309

Long Island, 108

Los Angeles & Salt Lake, 269

Louisiana & Arkansas, 259, 260, 263

Louisville & Nashville, 29, 30, 71, 80, 174, 221, 233, 318, 322

Maine Central, 4

Michigan Central, 14, 54, 79, 167, 168, 216

Minneapolis & St. Louis, 243, 267, 270

Mississippi Central, 259, 260, 262, 263

Missouri & North Arkansas, 267, 270

Missouri-Kansas-Texas, 6, 15, 25, 58, 59, 60, 61, 81, 82, 83, 84, 94, 95, 96, 97, 98, 99, 100, 101, 107, 111, 131, 135, 166, 222, 233, 237, 287, 288, 306, 321

Missouri Pacific, 6, 7, 16, 25, 38, 45, 61, 70, 71, 81, 83, 84, 107, 110, 115, 135, 144, 145, 151, 164, 165, 166, 167, 189, 215, 219, 221, 231, 237, 246, 259, 268, 271, 276, 281, 282, 285, 290, 291, 293, 304, 305

Morgan's Louisiana & Texas Railroad & Steamship 269

Nashville, Chattanooga & St. Louis, 233, 234, 316

New Orleans Great Northern, 317

New Orleans, Texas & Mexico, 5, 6, 7

New York Central, 1, 7, 8, 9, 18, 19, 26, 32, 33, 54, 55, 57, 58, 62, 63, 65, 79, 88, 89, 90, 91, 93, 108, 110, 112, 116, 118, 119, 120, 131, 145, 146, 162, 167, 168, 170, 173, 179, 180, 182, 184, 186, 192, 193, 195, 196, 207, 213, 214, 216, 217, 219, 229, 246, 251, 252, 253, 254, 256, 257, 264, 269, 272, 275, 307, 322

New York Central & Hudson River, 167, 275

New York, Chicago & St. Louis, 4, 6, 9, 14, 34, 58, 89, 90, 117, 180, 181, 182, 183, 193, 216, 229, 233, 264, 305, 323

New York Connecting Railroad, 56

New York, New Haven & Hartford, 4, 32, 33, 40, 44, 55, 56, 78, 79, 102, 103, 106, 121, 137, 155, 156, 169, 192, 207, 229, 256, 289, 290

Nickel Plate, 135, 200, 220, 224, 284, 314

Norfolk & Western, 17, 43, 66, 67, 81, 172, 201, 249, 250

Northern Ohio, 34, 117

Northern Pacific, 58, 64, 106, 129, 130, 151, 152, 153, 161, 168, 169, 179, 196, 197, 208, 210,

332 INDEX TO ROADS

211, 212, 223, 240, 241, 242, 243, 246, 249, 258
Northwestern Pacific, 269

Oregon Short Line, 249
Oregon-Washington Railroad and Navigation, 153, 269

Pennsylvania, 1, 7, 26, 33, 40, 43, 56, 58, 77, 78, 79, 103, 106, 108, 109, 110, 118, 119, 120, 137, 147, 150, 156, 162, 164, 168, 173, 192, 195, 196, 201, 207, 217, 219, 229, 245, 246, 252, 269, 291, 292, 309, 310, 321, 322
Pere Marquette, 4, 14, 71, 89, 201, 216, 217, 218, 224, 233, 306
Philadelphia & Reading, 9, 32, 36, 40, 42, 43, 91, 102, 103, 108, 110, 121, 126, 145, 156, 157, 170, 207, 213, 214, 246, 247, 251, 252, 253, 254, 256, 291, 292
Pittsburgh & Lake Erie, 34, 91, 116, 117, 118, 119, 120, 121, 126, 162, 200, 246
Pittsburgh & Shawmut, 270
Pittsburgh & West Virginia, 5, 33, 34, 36, 90, 91, 92, 93, 115, 116, 117, 118, 119, 120, 121, 123, 125, 126, 162, 200, 247, 268, 269
Pittsburgh, Cincinnati, Chicago & St. Louis, 7
Pittsburgh Terminals, 164

Sacramento Northern, 285, 286, 287
St. Louis, Kennet & Southeastern, 163, 176, 281
St. Louis-San Francisco, 5, 25, 40, 46, 61, 71, 72, 73, 83, 84, 85, 86, 111, 137, 142, 143, 162, 163, 164, 166, 167, 171, 175, 176, 204, 215, 232, 237, 271, 280, 281, 318

St. Louis, San Francisco & Texas, 269
St. Louis Southwestern, 9, 10, 15, 38, 40, 44, 45, 46, 68, 82, 83, 85, 86, 94, 95, 96, 97, 98, 100, 107, 110, 124, 131, 135, 139, 140, 142, 143, 145, 163, 165, 175, 176, 203, 205, 222, 233, 236, 237, 245, 276, 280, 281, 287, 291, 293, 306, 318, 319
St. Louis Southwestern of Texas, 269
San Antonio & Aransas Pass, 205, 268, 287, 288
San Antonio, Uvalde & Gulf, 268
Seaboard Air Line, 5, 30, 50, 80, 81, 109, 174, 205, 279
South Georgia, 279
Southern, 5, 30, 81, 112, 221, 233, 234, 246, 290, 291, 297, 298, 322
Southern New York, 18
Southern Pacific, 15, 16, 18, 25, 30, 37, 40, 45, 59, 60, 68, 85, 86, 87, 94, 95, 96, 97, 101, 107, 123, 124, 131, 144, 165, 202, 203, 205, 236, 237, 239, 269, 276, 285, 286, 287
Spokane, Portland & Seattle, 64, 269

Texas & New Orleans, 269
Texas & Pacific, 5, 40, 45, 80, 104, 215, 246, 282, 297, 298, 304, 305
Texas Midland, 205
Toledo & Ohio Central, 7, 168, 185, 186
Trinity & Brazos Valley, 140

Ulster & Delaware, 270
Union Pacific, 17, 18, 30, 49, 64, 65, 85, 86, 94, 106, 123, 130, 161, 165, 166, 187, 203, 205, 208, 223, 230, 231, 235, 236, 238, 242, 243, 244, 245, 246

INDEX TO ROADS

Vicksburg, Shreveport & Pacific, 16, 45, 174, 222, 291, 293, 294, 295, 297

Virginian, 17, 66, 67, 171, 201, 232

Wabash, 4, 16, 84, 91, 107, 115, 117, 137, 155, 164, 185, 189, 193, 208, 229, 231, 233, 245, 309

Waco, Beaumont, Trinity & Sabine River, 98, 101, 309

Western Maryland, 5, 15, 32, 36, 42, 43, 61, 91, 102, 103, 115, 118, 119, 120, 121, 126, 155, 157, 162, 196, 200, 214, 245, 257, 268, 269, 305, 309

Western Pacific, 86, 87, 166, 268, 285, 287, 321

Wheeling & Lake Erie, 1, 5, 9, 33, 34, 36, 57, 58, 88, 89, 90, 91, 92, 93, 115, 116, 117, 118, 119, 120, 123, 125, 126, 180, 181, 182, 183, 200, 247, 263, 264, 268, 269, 309

(1)

www.ingramcontent.com/pod-product-compliance
Lightning Source LLC
Chambersburg PA
CBHW020636230426
43665CB00008B/195